Human Resources or Human Capital?

Human Resources or Human Capital?

Managing People as Assets

ANDREW MAYO

Routledge
Taylor & Francis Group

LONDON AND NEW YORK

First published 2012 by Gower Publishing

2 Park Square, Milton Park, Abingdon, Oxon OX14 4RN
711 Third Avenue, New York, NY 10017, USA

Routledge is an imprint of the Taylor & Francis Group, an informa business

First issued in paperback 2016

British Library Cataloguing in Publication Data
Mayo, Andrew.
  Human resources or human capital? : managing people as
assets.
  1. Personnel management. 2. Human capital. 3. Employees--
Rating of. 4. Organizational effectiveness.
  I. Title
  658.3-dc22

Library of Congress Cataloging-in-Publication Data
Mayo, Andrew.
  Human resources or human capital? : managing people as assets / by Andrew Mayo.
    p. cm.
  Includes bibliographical references and index.
  ISBN 978-1-4094-2285-3 (hardback)
  1. Human capital. 2. Management. 3. Intellectual capital. I.
Title.
  HD4904.7.M377 2012
  658.3--dc23

                                                                    2011031300

ISBN 978-1-4094-2285-3 (hbk)
ISBN 978-1-138-25354-4 (pbk)

Contents

List of Figures

List of Tables

Acknowledgements

This book has been a relatively long time in preparation, as I have absorbed more and more learning about the practical application of 'human capital management'. I acknowledge the major contribution from clients and colleagues in my consultancy and business school work over the years.

The UK Chartered Institute of Personnel and Development (CIPD) have been assiduous over the last ten years in their studies and reports in this area, and I am indebted to Angela Baron there for leading this work and for her constant encouragement.

My colleague Fiona McDonnell has once again helped me greatly with the final touches of respecting copyrights and indexing, and this has been invaluable support.

Finally, I am indebted to Jonathan Norman, Fiona Martin and Kevin Selmes at Gower Publishing for their belief in this project and for all their professionalism in bringing it to publication.

Reviews for
Human Resources or Human Capital?

Andrew Mayo has unique, integrated, and insightful observations on human capital (people) and human resources (the department). His recent book is a marvelous summary and extension of latest thinking about defining, measuring, and improving both human capital and human resources. It offers business leaders perspectives and visions for HR investments and it offers HR professionals tools and actions to make wise HR investments.

Dave Ulrich, Ross School of Business,
University of Michigan, USA and Partner, The RBL Group

This book is the most comprehensive and practical guide to date to creating organisational value through people. Andrew takes us on a well structured, systematic journey from different approaches to measuring human capital. This provides an excellent foundation for targeted and relevant people strategy development through to the critical roles and skills required for HR professionals to add real value effectively. A real contribution to HR professional development.

Dr Tim Miller, Director, Property, Research & Assurance

Introduction:
The Essential Need for Human Capital Management

Nothing is achieved in organisations without people. This truism is frequently acknowledged in the clichéd 'people are our most important assets'. Yet what most employees experience in their organisations is that they are expendable 'costs walking on legs', mere 'human resources'. How do we explain this dichotomy between theory and practice?

There is no doubt that the dominance of financial management in both private and public organisations has a lot to do with it. Financial systems typically see people as 'headcount' and make no distinctions between their role as 'costs of production' and 'investments in our future'. People are, almost universally today, the major source of expenditure in an organisation. The two lenses of people as both a cost and a value creating asset are rarely balanced.

'Human capital management' is a term that recognises that it is the intangible assets in an organisation that are the powerhouse of creating value (whether financial or non-financial). Furthermore, value is only maintained and increased by people, both as individual contributors and working together in teams. Not all the people employed are part of this – it is essentially the talented and mission-critical: and some, indeed, may be deemed 'liabilities', that is, they subtract value from stakeholders.

For all intangibles we have to ask two questions. The first is 'How do we understand the human value they have, in order to manage it effectively?' We do not want to lose it, and at the same time we want to grow it. The second is 'How do we manage the link between that value and its deployment in creating value for the organisation and its stakeholders?' We can ask these questions about our brand, our customer relationships, our unique knowledge and systems, and our people. The latter is what human capital management is about.

To many HR professionals, the term immediately implies 'measurement'. Rightly so, as what gets measured gets managed and gets attention. The information managers receive about their people is usually far less systematic and helpful than what they receive about their money. It is more difficult to provide, and often more difficult to interpret, and is at least equally important. But it is more than measurement – it is a whole way of managing.

Part One of this book addresses this task. We start with a review of how value is created in organisations and then look at the part people play, and how people related measurement frameworks can be, and have been, created.

The diagram below outlines the structure of this book. The numbers in circles refer to the chapters.

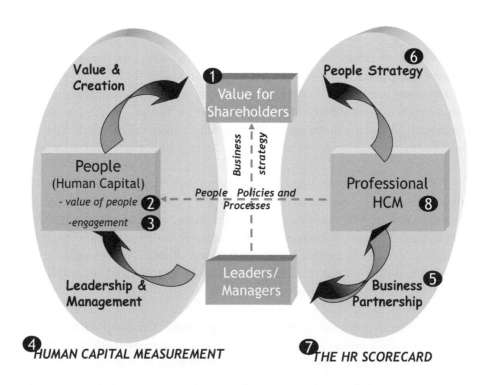

There is a vital role for 'people professionals' to play in human capital management, and this is the subject for Part Two. Mostly known as 'Human Resources' (HR) functions, they have often struggled to create the balance referred to above.

There are organisations who are successful without HR functions, and others who see their contribution as so fundamental that the Human Resources Director is on the Board. All support functions, even finance, agonise about how seriously they are taken, about their representation in top level decision making, and their ability to contribute strategically. None gaze at their navel in this kind of agony more than HR, or Personnel as it was known - and still is in many places around the world. This was probably started by Robert Townsend in 1977 who upset Personnel people mightily in his *Up the Organisation*, a book of sound bites based on his experience of running Avis, with his exhortation '*Fire the Personnel Department*'. And in January 1996, Tom Stewart wrote in *Fortune*:

> *Nestling warm and sleepy in your company, like the asp in Cleopatra's bosom, is a department whose employees spend 80 per cent of their time on routine administrative tasks. Nearly every function of this department can be performed more expertly for less by others. Chances are its leaders are unable to describe their contribution to value-added except in trendy, unquantifiable, and wannabe terms - yet, like a serpent unaffected by its own venom, the department frequently dispenses to others advice on how to eliminate work that does not add value.*

Ten years later I asked Tom how he saw things today. 'Actually' he said, 'back in 1996 I was trying to wake up people to the potential of HR's contribution. There has been a lot of change, but the question remains – can you prove that the company would not be better off without you?' In other words, is the function adding more value to the stakeholders of the organisation than it costs?

If we adopted Robert Townsend's exhortation to fire (or outsource) the department, what would we miss? We would save its costs, but what else would we lose? Would it be merely the loss of a group of well meaning but bureaucratic and policing people who delight in stopping us doing what we want to do, and who create complex processes which absorb more of our time than the end result justifies? A group of idealists constantly telling us what is wrong with the way we manage? Or would our loss be of wise, sensitive, supportive, creative people who help us maximise value creation through people, and achieve our objectives in better ways than we could do on our own?

Professor Dave Ulrich of the University of Michigan has done more than any contributor in current times to help HR functions understand how to deliver value for their organisations. His work, together with the development of new technological tools, has stimulated a new and widespread confidence in the potential importance of the function. Through restructuring, 'transformation', and renaming of departments and roles, the appellation 'business partner' is now ubiquitous. And yet it often seems that this announcement of partnership has been somewhat unilateral, and that new wine has been poured into old skins.

Part Two discusses the role for people professionals in a value adding partnership with operational managers, how to create effective people strategies and to measure and monitor functional effectiveness. It concludes with studying the knowledge and skills needed for playing a full part in human capital management.

Mervyn Davies, previous CEO of Standard Chartered Bank, was one of the great champions of the importance of people and his legacy lives on in the Bank. In an interview with *Personnel Today* in February 2006, he said:

> There are two types of HR people – there are robots – who believe in processes and that's all. Then there are those with a real passion for people and are willing to take the risks.

At the end of each chapter are 'Challenges for Action', and if this book provides encouragement and help to managers and HR professionals alike in furthering human capital management, then it will have served its purpose.

This book is intended to be a follow up to my 2001 book *The Human Value of the Enterprise.* The present book covers what has been learnt and developed over the subsequent years. The earlier work is referred to from time to time, but interested readers may find it helpful as a 'prequel'.

A Letter to Chief Executives of all Kinds of Organisations

Dear CEO

Maybe you have been heard to say that your people are your most important assets. You know in reality that it is most people who are – not everybody on the payroll, but those who are especially valuable because of their knowledge and skills, or particularly talented as individuals and leaders. Unfortunately, the administrative systems of organisations know their costs, include them in headcount, but rarely have any systematic and quantitative understanding of their value, either as individuals or teams.

Research shows that performance – adding value to stakeholders – is a function of the value of people (in terms of their competence and capability) and their engagement, their commitment to the organisation's goals. This book argues the case for having as systematic an approach to people measurement, reporting and intervention, as you have for finance. Assets need managing, and managing requires measures to set targets and track progress.

I'd like to encourage you to demand this from your HR people. Not masses of statistics and data for their own sake, but relevant, focused, useful indicators that will help you and your managers manage more successfully. After all, nothing can be achieved without people.

Today's HR professionals are keen to be involved with the business and its strategies. They can provide further valuable contributions in creating people strategies and initiatives that will benefit the business. This book is aimed at helping them do just that.

May your expectations be set high!

Andrew Mayo
Professor of Human Capital Management

PART 1

People and Value Creation

1

How Organisations Create Value Through People

'Maximising shareholder value' as the raison d'être *of a commercial organisation slips easily off the tongue, and yet it is an outcome that is the result of a complex process. No outcome is successfully achieved without an understanding of the chain of cause and effect that lies behind it. This chapter leads us through a holistic analysis of how value is created, and uses an approach that is equally valid for both commercial and non-profit organisations. The different kinds of value that are the desired outcomes are discussed, and the 'value creating process' that leads to them is introduced. The success of this process depends on two key factors – the value of the resources an organisation has at its disposal, and its efficacy in harnessing them.*

1.1 The Creation of Value – What Organisations are For

All organisations only exist to create value, or worthwhile *benefits*, for their stakeholders. The concept of 'value' is not as simple as being purely economic. Just as we all mourn the loss of sentimental items in a burglary much more than replaceable, more expensive goods, so much of the value created by organisations is qualitative. The stakeholder map for many, especially in the public sector, is complex. Usually there is one *prime* stakeholder group, but the satisfaction of others is essential to the long-term interest of that group. In the case of purely commercial organisations, the ultimate stakeholders are the owners or shareholders, and the prime created value is financial. The pursuit of 'shareholder value' has been the mantra of American capitalism – albeit under question and scrutiny more recently - with or without the word 'sustainable' added to it. Success, however, is dependent on loyal, profitable customers and loyal, productive employees.

Not-for-profit organisations create different kinds of value/benefits for their stakeholders. A charity primarily serves its beneficiaries – providing value in the form of healthcare, education, economic support and so on. Government organisations are the most complex of all. In a democracy they primarily exist to serve the public (though this is not always obvious); in a totalitarian state they serve the interests of the rulers.

There is both a tension and interdependency between stakeholders. What is in the interest of one may not be seen as beneficial to the other – for example, providing excellent customer service costs money and this comes out of potential profits. On the other hand – as my one time business partner said to me – 'Remember, my friend, if you don't have a customer you don't have a business'. Without customers wanting to buy, there won't be any profits. In more socially minded countries, the interest of the community in having local jobs and the close connections between politicians and business, may lead to decisions that are not ideal for shareholders. I recall an acquisition in Germany of a company called Mannesmann-Kienzle that one of my employers, ICL Computers, was planning back in the 1990s. Our financial analysis indicated we would need to close a rural factory. As soon as the Mannesmann group heard of this, they secretly did another deal with Digital Equipment who promised no closure. That company bitterly regretted the acquisition in years to come, and itself was soon taken over by Compaq.

Figure 1.1   The stakeholder map in a commercial organisation

Some stakeholders have more power than others. Institutional shareholders have increasing power over commercial companies, as a counter to the excesses of managers. Monopolies have power over their customers who have no choice. When excessive power exists, it will (normally) be used to the disadvantage of other stakeholders and a disproportionate amount of value extracted. The hierarchy of power of stakeholders, and the dependencies between them, needs to be well understood. A common example of how this can be *mis*understood is when in the case of an acquisition, in the interest of 'synergy' (that is, profits and perceived shareholder value), sales resource is 'rationalised', and suddenly the company finds the customer base (for which they paid a premium) is falling away. Key customer relationships are destroyed. Exit revenues, and as soon as this is realised in the market, down goes the share price and up go the statistics of the percentage of mergers and acquisitions which lose shareholder value.

THE 'EXCHANGE OF VALUE'

In a steady state of interdependency between an organisation and a stakeholder group, there is equilibrium between what a stakeholder offers an organisation and what it receives. Illustrated in Figure 1.2, the 'Stakeholder equilibrium' is about the exchange of value that takes place between an organisation and its stakeholders. Where the expectation of value delivered on either side is perceived as inadequate, the party will seek to redress the balance, and if unsuccessful will think about working with an alternative. The value that is exchanged may be either financial or non-financial or a combination of both. The principle works provided the stakeholder has choice – in the case of beneficiaries from a charity, or the public dealing with a government department, this may not be so. Choice, however, is a fundamental platform of western capitalism, and over recent years it has extended into many public services also.

Not everyone exercises their choice, even under provocation. Customers of banks are traditionally reluctant to change even though they may be frequently angry with their bank of many years. Employees may put up with a lot because of resistance to change or a lack of confidence in their ability to get another job. I think of a certain airport car park which simultaneously put the daily price up *and* cut the service from six buses an hour to four. That's a good recipe to send your customers looking for a better choice. But sadly in this airport, choices are limited. Organisations themselves put up with poor performance of employees due to *inertia* in tackling the issues; they continue with loss-making customers because they cannot contemplate telling anyone they do not want their custom.

'The Principle of Stakeholder Equilibrium'

Stakeholders in an organisation, and the organisation itself, have a relationship because they add value to each other. Either party will only continue the relationship for as long as it believes it is receiving a satisfactory return of both financial and non financial benefits, which when combined are sufficient to balance the value provided by the other party. This equilibrium is not static; it is in the interest of both parties that the overall sum of value exchanged is constantly increasing.

THE STAKEHOLDER ⇐ (£ ADDED VALUE) +
OFFER   ⇒ (non £ ADDED VALUE)

Figure 1.2   Stakeholder equilibrium

The 'healthy value creating' organisation, however, encourages this equilibrium to be alive and sustained by dialogue. For good reason – this is an equilibrium that is 'upwardly mobile' as each party seeks *more* value over time – to deliver the same, year in and year out, is inconsistent with the modern concept of progress. We are all on an escalator of ever improving performance. Most stakeholders expect more as time progresses from their relationship with an organisation. As the value given on one side increases, so the expectation of value received increases too.

The way this works can be illustrated as follows; the organisation offers new services to customers, not directly for extra revenues, but to retain loyalty – and is rewarded by a higher spend. However, the level of expectations has been reset on both sides; it is hard to go back, so the overall level of value exchanged has increased. Or an employee provides excellent performance and is promoted; what is expected of the employee in the new position is increased and naturally a commensurate reward is expected in return. The value exchange 'equilibrium' for that employee has increased to a new level.

When an organisation is bought or sold the price is typically well in excess of the balance sheet net assets – the 'tangible assets'. A large premium is paid for the 'intangible assets' which represent the underlying strength of the organisation and its future. Combining Figures 1.1 and 1.2 expresses this in another way - it could be said that the total value of the organisation is, at any given time, the sum of all these 'stakeholder *equilibria*' value exchanges.

'ADDING' VALUE

This is a loosely used term. Organisations exist to create and *provide* value. The larger part of an organisation is concerned with 'servicing the current value expectations' that the organisation is engaged with. The daily operations carry on; building products, servicing the public, purchasing materials, paying employees and so on. However, there are other activities aimed at a different future – innovating in order to change the levels of value exchange. In very small organisations it may be only the boss who is thinking about this; but larger organisations have executives, strategy managers, systems improvement people, marketing, trainers, management and organisation development, and maybe research for new products – all of whom are engaged in changing the levels of value exchange. These activities are one meaning of the term 'adding value'.

THE NATURE AND COMPONENTS OF VALUE

The concept of equilibrium immediately raises questions of understanding and measuring the value that is being exchanged. A clear *description* of the value that is expected by each party needs to be explicit and mutually understood. Many an organisation has been surprised when it tested what value meant to its customers, only to find that it was quite different to what they had been thinking. So we often hear the phrase 'When we asked our customers, what we found was …' It is a constant battle to maintain stakeholder focus as organisations have a natural tendency to be absorbed with themselves, and – constantly stimulated by the finance function – achieving their budgets and targets.

It is vital to remind ourselves that 'value' is in the eye of the beholder, and that it can be both financial and non-financial. What matters for a stakeholder is the combination of these two categories that together make the sum 'sufficient' for our expectations. Even shareholders look at a combination: just because the return from a company has dropped does not mean they will automatically sell their holdings – they will take into account future prospects based on the strength of 'intangibles'. All stakeholders have a ranking of the components of the overall value they receive. At the top of the ranking are the few critical 'drop dead' factors – which if they fall below a certain threshold will cause them to break the relationship. With many customers, for example, price is not the determining factor. How many accounts have been lost because customers could not take the complicated and impersonal automated call centres imposed on them any longer? How many employees have tolerated a below-market salary increase because of other benefits they valued greatly from their organisation? How many suppliers have tolerated price deductions because of the prestige of working with a well-known company and the reputation it brings?

If we really want to understand the various *equilibria* with key stakeholder groups we must:

- break down the components of value that matter to each, and understand their relative importance;

- ensure we have measures of the non-financial components as well as the financial – measures which enable dialogue, target setting and management.

When it comes to having a comprehensive 'scorecard' of value added to stakeholders, organisations are generally weak. The problem is that there are relatively few measures that have real meaning at the level of the organisation as a whole – or the 'enterprise' level. Of course we can measure overall shareholder returns at the very top level but when it comes to other stakeholders, they are in groups which do not have exactly the same interests. Senior managers have a different 'value exchange profile' to front-line employees. Different types of customers look for different things. Consolidated figures are needed for discussion with shareholders and governments, but are the enemy of usefulness in managing other stakeholder relationships. So, just as budget management has to be distributed across and down the organisation to work effectively, so there is a pattern of stakeholder value 'chains' which, in an organisation that is functioning well, is integrated and synergistic, making up a map of co-ordinated value provision.

Having discussed the question of value generically so far, henceforth our focus will be on the people in an organisation.

1.2 People Related Measures – the Measurement Process

Accountants have life relatively easy as they only have one basic currency, namely money. There are a range of difficulties with quantifying areas which are people related. Far fewer things can be 'counted' – we are often dealing with judgements and perceptions. Everything can be measured – and this is an important start point. We have to be skilled at choosing and managing a variety of measurement indicators. Sometimes, but not always, we can make logical and credible links to financial benefit. Table 1.1 gives us a checklist of the qualities of a good measure.

Table 1.1   A checklist of good measures

Good measures:
• are simple to understand
• are clearly defined so people interpret them in the same way
• do not require an amount of data collection that is disproportional to the resulting usefulness of the measure
• are made in a consistent way and are seen to be reliable
• are not the result of one person's judgement
• do not have built-in biases, such as 'leading' or 'loaded' questions in a survey
• are credible as 'roughly right, not precisely wrong'
• are consistent with other measures in the same area
• are at the right level of detail to enable appropriate action to be taken
• can be used for tracking change
• are taken at the right frequency and chosen to provide useful trends and comparisons
• have clear ownership by an individual or team

'Counting' things is at one extreme of objectivity. For example, there are or are not five people with PhDs in a particular department. Calculating the cost of a particular recruitment is somewhat less precise, since different people may make different assumptions – but we can standardise formulae for calculating such costs and then use them consistently.

At the other end of the scale, in understanding both customer and employee value, we need to utilise *perceptions*. Multiple subjective perceptions verge on objectivity, but there will always be questions of design and interpretation. How biased were the questions? What did the extremities of the scales really mean? How were the results analysed and presented?

We will need different kinds of measures for whatever measurement framework we choose to work with, and also in setting objectives for programmes and initiatives.

Table 1.2 lists the types of measures that are people related.

Table 1.2   Types of measures needed in people management

Type of measure	Usefulness and areas to watch
• Existence or non-existence – policies, processes	• Used sometimes in creating 'human capital indices' – but the *quality* of what exists is the issue. To say 'we have a performance management system' says nothing about what it achieves
• Association – events *due to …*	• This is very useful in aligning cause and effect. Thus, we may set a target that we will have 'no losses *due to* dissatisfaction with development prospects,' or 'no accidents will result from employees having inadequate protective clothing'
• Costs/financial savings	• Should be evaluated wherever possible but needs care and 'reality' checks. Note that accounting systems do not normally pick up such things as the costs of non-added value work, losses of productivity, reduced work quality, and so on.
• Statistics – such as proportions, percentages, ratios	• Will be used a lot. There may be issues of reliability of the original data and this needs care. In comparing figures watch for the true comparability of the bases of measurement. Productivity is a key measure here
• Collated perceptions – potential, behaviours, cultural characteristics, service delivered, satisfaction, motivation	• A critical measure for assessing stakeholder value. Care in questionnaire design and question wording is critical, avoiding biased 'leading' questions. Sample size is significant in drawing conclusions
• Capability – knowledge, skills, experience, contacts, behaviours, qualities	• Essential in defining objectives and evaluation of learning programmes. A complex area, but essential for understanding the value of individuals and teams – what we might call 'human capital value' (as discussed in Chapter 3)
• League tables - for checking external perceptions, benchmarking, and so on.	• Often produced by subjective judgements and differentials between places on the table can be small. Nevertheless, those who will be influenced by them may not 'look at the small print'
• Trends – to determine the direction of an indicator	• Often more useful than absolute measures – to assess the *direction* of change. The measures used must be made on a consistent basis over time
• Indices – weighted or non-weighted summaries of selected indicators	• Often useful in balanced scorecard indicators, for example, so long as we do not lose sight of the detail behind them. Example: 'team effectiveness index'; 'employee motivation index' – made up of several weighted contributory factors

Each of these deserves expansion but we will particularly mention the area described as 'collated perceptions'. This will include:

- assessing the capability of an individual, particularly skills and behaviours;

- measuring progress against cultural goals;

- tracking employee satisfaction, motivation and engagement;

- assessing how employees value or react to an initiative and how they see the value provided to them.

The wording and design of surveys is a specialised activity and professional help is advisable. We have several different types of questions that can be asked:

- open-ended – seeking a written, qualitative answer, often the most powerful although hard to sum up in analysis;

- a checklist – what has happened and what not?

- binary question – yes/no;

- multiple choice;

- scale completion – very positive, through neutral to very negative;

- ranking of items.

Today's technology enables surveys to be done quickly and anonymously online, together with analysis and reports.

Once we have a measure we need to decide whether it is on the positive or the negative side. That can rarely be done by looking at a figure in isolation. It must be compared with something – a previous figure, a benchmark or a target.

DANGERS IN DATA COLLECTION

Even finance people have to cope with the difficulties of apparently sound data not being quite what it appears. This is particularly true of estimates and forecasts where people play political games, providing the information that they believe is wanted. We have seen many scandals in recent years where financial data has been misrepresented, even though founded in some kind of truth. There is a distinction between data that is indisputable, and that which is open to interpretation. Whatever data framework we have it is important to understand into which category each set of numbers fits.

Data that is based on the management information system may be assumed to be factual, provided the input was correct. Any data that relies on questions and perceptions is subject to a number of biases. The wording of questions is very influential. Professional questionnaire designers ask questions in different ways in order to attempt to confirm answers. The politics of the question can make a difference. If I know my manager will or will not get a bonus based on what I say, this could influence me one way or another. If I am asked my reason for leaving, or being absent, I may provide an answer which will be more acceptable than the true reason.

1.3 The Value Creating Process

In the literature about strategy the term 'value chain' is used to describe how economic value is distributed between suppliers, producers and customers. Our interest here is the process of value creation by an organisation or a part of one; inputs which are processed by the organisation to produce outputs.

This is shown in Figure 1.3. Although applying to an organisation as a whole, it can also apply to a team or part of an organisation. Indeed it is using it in this way which makes it a practical tool for connecting measures of *value input, value conversion* and *value output*.

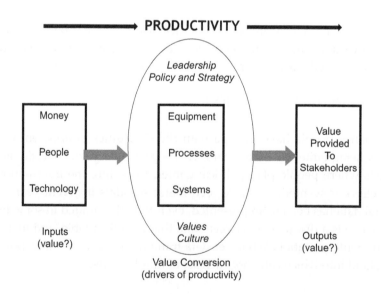

Figure 1.3   The value creating process

By value input, we mean the resources available to the organisation. We have identified three (though we could add raw materials for basic industries) – namely money, people and technology or knowledge. These are not just costs but have value associated with them. The organisation – with all its own characteristics, strengths and weaknesses – harnesses the value they offer to generate the desired outcomes for stakeholders; or does not, as the case may be, as we saw classically in the worst of the dot com companies in the late 1990s, in some financial institutions in 2007/8 and certainly in some parts of the public sector.

A commercial organisation may see this process simplistically as: the organisation takes in costs and converts them to revenues, and in so doing generates a surplus called profits for the owners. But the approach can be applied to all kinds of organisations, whether financial revenues are, or are not, the direct output. This applies not only to all of the non-profit sector, but also many *parts* of commercial companies. It may be more challenging to measure the value being added as an outcome, but the effectiveness of 'conversion' of inputs to outputs is of essential interest.

Organisations have discrete populations to which this analysis can be applied; sharing two things in common:

- the qualities of the people and the type of technology used are similar;

- common outputs to stakeholders.

Examples of what is meant here would be a retail branch, a factory team, a support function, a call centre, a doctors' practice, or the teachers in a school. There will be one primary stakeholder but there may be a secondary one too. For example, in a call centre the primary would be customers – but 'shareholders' have an interest in the costs also. It is a good example of where maximising the value for one may mitigate doing the same for another.

Three sets of measures are needed:

- the value of the resources which we start with;

- indicators of the effectiveness of the organisation and its processes in value conversion;

- the value of the output(s).

Unfortunately we can not measure all of these in the same currency, which has undoubtedly been a barrier to adopting this more holistic and ultimately more useful approach to performance management.

We shall look at these three components in turn, starting with the outputs.

1.4 The Output Measures

In 2004 Sir Tony Atkinson, a UK Professor of Public Policy, was asked by the government to chair a review of public sector productivity, which culminated in his report *Measurement of Government Output and Productivity* for the National Accounts. In it he quotes the Eurostat Handbook as follows:

> *The Eurostat Handbook distinguishes between activities, outputs, and outcomes. These are described in more detail below:*
>
> *a) Activity is, 'for example, the number of operations in hospitals or number of patrols carried out by the police. Such data can often be found. Activity indicators reflect what the non-market units are actually doing with their inputs and are therefore closer to the output. However, suppose for example that new improved forms of medical treatments reduce the number of operations necessary. Taking the number of operations, as an indicator would imply a decrease of output and productivity, which does not seem appropriate in this case. Using activity indicators often does not lead to reasonable productivity numbers. However, for some collective services, activity indicators may be the only indicators that can be found.'*
>
> *b) Output 'is the preferred approach. However, it is not always easy to define exactly what the unit of output is. For individual goods and services it is in principle possible to define the output, since an actual delivery of that output takes place from the producer to the consumer(s) … For example, for education, the output is the amount of teaching consumed by a pupil. For hospital services, the output is the amount of care received by a patient. For cultural services, the output is the amount of theatre plays consumed. For collective services, however, there is no transaction between producer and consumer since these are*

provided simultaneously to the society as a whole. It becomes therefore very difficult to define the output. It is very difficult to say for example what the unit of output is of defence or police services.'

c) Outcomes are 'for example indicators of the level of education of the population, life expectancy, or level of crime. Such indicators might be influenced by factors that are unrelated to the activity, and therefore are generally not representative of the output. In some cases, however, outcome indicators can be used as indicators for the quality of the output'

(Reproduced under the terms of the Click-Use Licence)

My local community proudly announced in a news sheet that it had delivered £50m worth of improvements to the county's highways in the last year. For 'improvements' read 'spending'. Many of their projects were notoriously overspent and a flood of letters to the newspapers questioned their usefulness. This is a typical example of the confusion between activity and outcomes.

One might think that one thing organisations should be good at is measuring their outcomes – which we argue is the provision of value to stakeholders. Surely this is what 'performance' is about. Sadly, this is not the case. Finance functions (frequently, not always) hijack the attention of the organisation to their own agenda. In the private sector this demands rigid attention to budgets and profits – even though the logic of sticking to rigid budgets set months before in a turbulent world is very questionable. Likewise, today's public sector organisations are more likely to be focused on controlling their budget (the money *input*), than any stakeholder benefit measures.

FINANCIAL OUTCOMES

Financial outcomes are relatively easy to measure. For typical stakeholders they might include:

Table 1.3   Financial outcomes

Stakeholder	Value measure(s)
Shareholders/owners	• capital value increase • share yield • retained earnings • increase in returns
Parent Companies	• budgeted revenues and profits
Customers	• special discounts • price reductions • 'value for money'
Employees	• salary and benefits • deferred benefits
Suppliers	• sustained revenues • acceptable price margins
The Public	• reduced taxes • cheaper services • 'value for money'
Government	• revenues from services • increased budgets/grants and so on
Community	• donations and grants

MEASURES OF NON-FINANCIAL VALUE

When we come to non-financial value (which still can be measured) we need some care. Sheer volume of output does not indicate that the output is the *right* output, and in defining it we may need to specify both volume and quality. We experience daily the dangers of volume targets which have been assigned to public servants, and often not providing any value at all to many of those affected by them.

The 2005 *Atkinson Report*, mentioned above, is a magnificent study of the measurement of outcomes from Government activity. It starts with stating the convention that the value of outputs equals the value of inputs:

> *The inputs taken into account in recent years in the United Kingdom are the compensation of employees, the procurement cost of goods and services, and a charge for the consumption of fixed capital.*

> *(Reproduced under the terms of the Click-Use Licence)*

This convention has always been questionable, implying a 100 per cent productivity ratio, and is now replaced in national accounts by an EC ruling that states that direct measures of output must be used. The Report discusses such measures in the areas of Health, Education, Public Safety, and Social Protection.

The Appendix (page 327) lists, in tabular form, types of non-financial added value to individual stakeholder groups and is adapted from *The Human Value of the Enterprise* (Mayo 2001).

For an enterprise as a whole, to take all possible measures for all stakeholders would require a considerable number of measures and targets. A performance management system needs to be devised which *starts with each stakeholder* and identifies the critical areas of value delivered to them. This can be cascaded down through the organisation to pick relevant measures for each employee group. Unless an organisation has only one product or service it is in reality a set of interacting 'value creating processes'.

Alternately, we can start with each process; define for them the prime, and maybe secondary, stakeholder who is the beneficiary of their efforts. We then choose not more than three or four key aspects of the value provided which we will measure and target in such a way that the stakeholder will be satisfied – and want to continue the relationship. This 'bottom-up' approach can then be matched with the 'top-down' cascaded approach.

INTEGRATING FINANCIAL AND NON-FINANCIAL OUTPUTS INTO A PERFORMANCE MANAGEMENT SYSTEM

The balanced scorecard is a performance measurement framework that added strategic, non-financial performance measures to traditional, financial metrics to give managers and executives a more 'balanced' view of organisational performance. The balanced scorecard has evolved from its early use as a simple performance measurement framework to a full strategic planning and management system. Kaplan and Norton (1996) describe the innovation of the balanced scorecard as follows:

> *The balanced scorecard retains traditional financial measures. But financial measures tell the story of past events, an adequate story for industrial age companies for which investments in long-term capabilities and customer relationships were not critical for success.*

These financial measures are inadequate, however, for guiding and evaluating the journey that information age companies must make to create future value through investment in customers, suppliers, employees, processes, technology, and innovation.

Not every work group and individual (and contingent contributors) in the organisation is able to relate what they do to adding value for stakeholders. Some are employed in maintenance and administrative roles. Indeed, an important ratio is that of value adding people to non-value adding – similar to 'indirect: direct' ratios in traditional manufacturing. But for those who are in value adding roles (whether current or future):

- Each job profile should specify the stakeholders that the role is supporting, and the measures applicable.

- Measures are used in target setting, and therefore, bonus schemes.

- Each individual or team is reviewed on their progress against those targets as a regular part of performance management.

1.5 The Value of Resource Inputs

The three key types of input suggested in Figure 1.3 – money, people and technology – all have a value that needs to be assessed. Even money itself is not straightforward – depending on where it comes from, it may have different costs attached to it and conditions regarding its availability. People and technology also vary in value, though are more difficult to assess. We devote the whole of the next chapter to the question of valuing people.

We all know cases of where money is fed into organisations and nothing worthwhile emerges – 'feeding a black hole'. In general, when money is spent in an organisation it should be possible to link it with one (or more) of the measures of value for stakeholders. It is not always the case. All organisations have to absorb part of the input they receive in looking after themselves. Indeed this is a key measure for charities – how much of raised funds are used up in administration. We have to spend money in maintenance, in housekeeping and in compliance – costs that do not specifically add value in themselves but are aimed at safeguarding the interests of stakeholders. If we do not keep accurate accounts and records, or ensure employees are trained in health and safety – to name but two of the many and increasing such activities that the modern organisation has to do - we run the risk of *subtracting* value from either stakeholders or the organisation itself.

What is important is that we know what any specific expenditure is *aimed* at – and this is often sadly confused in many areas. In summary there are four kinds of spend (Table 1.4).

Table 1.4   Four kinds of spend

Spending on instruments of production	Labour or machines needed for value creation
Spending for 'organisational maintenance'	Avoiding value subtraction
Spending on knowledge and capability which *provides and maintains* an agreed level of value	Keeping the value equilibrium
Investing in knowledge and capability which *increases* the level of value that can be offered in the future	Upgrading the value equilibrium

It is rare for accounting systems, or even simple headcount systems, to classify jobs or people according to the extent to which they are primarily costs or investments. The first three categories above are essentially costs; the latter is an investment.

We suggest that this is a better way to distinguish how money is spent than the increasingly blurred distinction between 'capital' and 'expenses', which is the basis of the 'old' business model that assumes all capital is physical, and therefore depreciable, or financial.

When costs need to be reduced, management should seek out first those that are not value creators. However, they rarely have the information that enables them to do this, and hence value adding assets can be lost. It is afterwards that the loss is discovered. The response of senior management to 'bottom line' performance problems is usually to cut – cut projects, cut staff, amalgamate, centralise, streamline, outsource, and so on. They give insufficient thought to the parallel loss of current and future value creating sources, lacking the value measures which balance the costs saved.

1.6 Productivity as the Measure of the Success of the Organisation's Value Conversion

We are not only interested in measuring the outputs to stakeholders to compare with our targets. We need to know whether the process of conversion was efficient, given the level and quality of resource we used as input. Did we get 'value for money'?

Two types of measure will help us monitor and manage this process; the first is those which tell us how efficient it actually *is*; the second is about the 'drivers' of efficiency, that is, the influences on the first set. This is the all important principle of measuring both 'cause' and 'effect' and understanding the strengths of the links between them.

PRODUCTIVITY

The classic efficiency measure is *productivity* – defined as the ratio of an output to the level of relevant input. Total productivity is about the way we utilise all the resource inputs of money, people and technology; they are interrelated. It is people who decide how money should be spent and technology utilised. Nevertheless, it is helpful to look at them separately. Financial productivity will be taken care of by ratios of the cost of producing the desired outcome. People productivity is more complex.

It is common practice to use 'FTEs' ('Full Time Equivalents') as the denominator in people productivity. There are problems with this; such ratios can lead to lazy productivity improvement programmes through just cutting the number of 'heads' (what Hamel and Prahalad called 'denominator management') – giving an apparent improvement when the value added has not improved at all. Also, the fact is that FTEs have different costs – not only within a national organisation but significantly between countries.

The denominators of a productivity ratio should be the *cost* and/or the *time* spent in human effort. The latter is a cost too, of course, but by looking at both we get two different dimensions. The OECD (Organisation for Economic Co-operation and Development) Productivity Manual – aimed at governments concerned with national productivity - recommends that labour inputs be described as 'hours worked by workers at different skill levels, weighted together using expenditure on each of these categories'.

Furthermore, in today's organisations, 'fully contracted employees', whether full time or part time, may be only a proportion of the human effort used to produce value to stakeholders. Every manager knows headcount can be reduced by exchanging employees for (usually) more expensive contractors – and productivity could actually reduce. It may be that 'per head' is needed for easy comparison purposes, but it is more logical to use as the denominator, 'total people compensation costs – FTEs + subcontractors + consultants'.

COMMERCIAL SECTOR FINANCIAL PRODUCTIVITY RATIOS

Where we have bottom line numbers for an enterprise or part of one, we can look at financial outcomes and utilise some financial ratios. *Financial Value Added (FVA)* is a standard term which is defined as follows:

> *The wealth created through the efforts of the enterprise and its people*
>
> *Wealth is not the same as profit. Employees create wealth which is distributed to various stakeholders, and some is retained in the business and used for further investment.*

FVA is simply calculated as the difference between the revenue accruing from goods and services and the costs of bought in materials and services. Two variations are in use, depending on whether *depreciation* is subtracted from the resulting figure – if so it is called the *gross value added*. If not, and depreciation is seen as part of the distribution of the wealth, then the amount is the *net value added*.

Value added is used to pay employees (the greatest percentage of the total distribution); to pay taxes, bank interest, and shareholder dividends. What is left is retained and available for future use.

In today's world it is an interesting question as to whether 'bought in goods and services' should include temporary and consultant staff. It depends on whether they are 'value adding' in themselves and we return to this in the next section.

FVA should be calculated as far down the organisation as revenue breakdown figures permit, enabling us to assess the added value from *teams* within the organisation. In some cases, such as salespeople and consultants, it can even be calculated at the level of the individual employee.

Statutory and conventional reporting in most countries does not include value added statements, and consequently says little about the productivity and contribution of the human resource. As far back as 1977 the UK Government recommended that companies should produce such statements (at that time there was a movement to use it as a source of profit sharing) but this has not materialised. It is, however, often found in Scandinavia.

EFFICIENCY RATIOS BASED ON VALUE ADDED

The absolute amount of value added can be divided by the number of people, to give a ratio 'per FTE', but as discussed above this is not ideal.

Some useful ratios for managing through financial value added include:

- value added/costs of labour and capital – *this is a measure of managerial efficiency*;

- value added/sales is a better measure of *productivity* than the conventional profit/sales;

- value added/total compensation – this is perhaps the best overall measure of people productivity. This is sometimes referred to as the compensation recovery factor.

The proportion of value added to a particular stakeholder/total value added, is a measure of the contribution to the particular stakeholder. Thus we can compare:

- compensation/net value added is a measure of the employees' share in the wealth pool;

- net profit/net value added measures the shareholder's portion;

- dividends/net value added measures the shareholder's current return;

- taxation/net value added is the government's share;

- interest/net value added is the return to bondholders or banks.

A UK network known as 'The FiSSinG Benchmark Club', now defunct, came up with a core ratio as:

Employee Value Added Ratio (EVAR)

EVAR = operating profit – (employee costs)

employee costs

Where the technical calculation of 'value added' is not available, commercial organisations are more likely to go for ratios involving profits (preferably operating profits) or revenues.

The expert here is Jac Fitz-enz and his Saratoga Institute, and readers are referred to his comprehensive *'RoI of Human Capital'* (2009).

Fitz-enz organised measures at three levels, all of which need to be integrated:

- The overall enterprise – the relationship between human capital and its contribution at the level of the whole enterprise.

- By process or function – leading to service, quality or productivity.

- The 'human capital itself' – by which he means how it is *managed*. This is more about the effectiveness of HR processes.

The latter two are discussed elsewhere in this book, but we will look at what Fitz-enz says about the first, even though it only applies to organisational units that have their own revenue and cost statements.

The most popular productivity ratio in use has been revenue per employee. This is fine for measuring sales people, but is simplistic and it is the cost of people that matters, not their number. So a good ratio would be:

Revenues/Total cost of all human capital in use to produce these revenues

As discussed above, this total cost of human capital is much more than the salaries of 'FTEs'. It includes all the additional contributors and we could also add the cost of unwanted attrition, excess absenteeism, and of office space.

Two ratios that will relate to the Finance function – and get their attention – are:

Human Economic Value (HEVA)

HEVA = Net operating profit after tax – Cost of capital

FTEs or Total cost of human capital

There are always problems with final profit and in general it is not recommended as a measure because of the assumptions and adjustments that may go into it. However, operating profit can be used satisfactorily.

Human Capital Value Added (HCVA)

HCVA = Revenue – (expenses –pay and benefits)

FTE's or Total cost of human capital

This is a preferred ratio as it relates more directly to financial value produced.

Fitz-enz also suggests a ratio for Human Capital Return on Investment, which looks at the financial value added related to compensation costs. It is calculated as:

Revenue – (operating expenses less compensation)/compensation

Targeted changes in ratios such as these should appear more often than they do as objectives of an HR initiative.

PRODUCTIVITY WHERE OUTPUTS ARE NON-FINANCIAL

Everyone in a commercial organisation who is not dealing directly with customers or producing products for them has outcomes of their work which will be at least in part, and may be wholly, non-financial. Likewise this applies to all not-for-profit organisations. Nevertheless, we start from the principle that all outcomes can be measured. We made the point earlier that such outputs and outcomes often need both quantity *and* quality measures.

We will tackle the case of the productivity of an HR function in a later chapter. But let us take a *finance function*. Like most support functions they have five main roles:

- the delivery of an administrative service;

- monitoring for compliance with the law and/or internal rules;

- the achievement of certain financial targets which they own;

- providing advice and guidance to managers in matters of financial management;

- creating new processes, systems, ways of working, use of outside services and so on, which will contribute to better money management.

In the first role the output is a level of service, and the input is the cost of providing that service. The level of service can be measured in process terms – the speed and accuracy of accounting information – and in perception terms by those who receive the service.

The second is measured by incidents of non-compliance and related to the cost of the compliance department – which may be called 'internal audit'. This is an example of an outcome that is 'negative' and needs to be minimised. It could be an index based on the number of incidents and their cost implications.

By the third role we mean items such as 'debtor days', for which there will be a target. Again this may be a 'negative outcome' – namely the cost of exceeding the target set against the cost of the department concerned.

'Providing advice and guidance' must be measured from time to time by a perception survey – covering responsiveness, helpfulness, creativity, accuracy, and so on. It is an important outcome of a support department, albeit it may not be 100 per cent of the job of the professionals concerned. The productivity measure will be the percentage satisfaction of the service related to the proportion of time spent on this activity by the people concerned.

Finally, that part of the activity that is dedicated to 'future added value creation'. An ongoing productivity measure is not appropriate here. The methodology which determines effectiveness is 'return on investment' on a project by project basis. Sometimes the outcome of one year's investment in such projects may not be measurable until the next year or beyond.

How might we measure the productivity of a *research and development* unit? Its outcome is measured in new products. We could measure the volume of new products over a time period, but this just encourages product variations for their own sake. The real desired outcome is products that people want to buy, that is, those that are commercially successful. This is value added both to customers and to shareholders. The problem is there is a time-lag before we know that a product is successful. So we have to choose a time related measure, such as the number of commercially successful products launched between one and two years ago.

This we then relate to inputs using ratios of either:

- total cost of the unit over the period;

- human effort expended over the time period (such as man days);

- total cost of the human effort expended.

A less complex example might be a group of *Quality Assurance Engineeers*. Here their actual work is varied – training, redesigning processes, measuring, and so on – but the stakeholder outcome is clear and is measured all the time – the percentage of products with no defects. This can also be related to any of the three inputs above. It is an example of how productivity could increase to such a high level that their input is no longer needed – as the outcome has become self-perpetuating - and their skills can be redeployed elsewhere.

Some organisations, or parts of them, do not exist to provide the same kinds of stakeholder benefits month by month. They work as 'project organisations', with a series of projects throughout the year. Their value process is the project at the time. It has outputs, inputs and efficiency measures in exactly the same way as we have described.

PUBLIC SECTOR PRODUCTIVITY

In the UK and other countries in recent years, government departments have been set a multitude of targets. Some have been mere activities, but the opportunity to measure productivity has improved enormously. Much care is needed however. In the UK, the Office of National Statistics reported in June 2009, that between 1997 and 2007, a period of substantial extra public spending, that overall productivity – or value for money – fell by 3.2 per cent. A BBC Report said:

> The Office has been attempting to measure the 'outputs' of all the public services.
>
> The ONS admits that is a very difficult task and it has been developing more complex measures of output to assess quality, particularly for healthcare and education, which account for about half of all public service activity. For education, the measure of output now includes GCSE average points scores. For health the measures include clinical outcomes, waiting times and what they call 'patient experience'. In other areas, such as policing and defence, the outputs are assumed to rise in line with the inputs.

National figures are the ultimate consolidation, and the real value is always in the detail. If we want to use such figures to take appropriate action, then we need to measure as far down as we can into the organisation.

1.7 The Drivers of Productivity

We have talked so far about measures of productivity itself. But we need to know which levers to pull. There are four main drivers of productivity:

- How *capable* are the management and employees?

- How motivated and *engaged* are the people working in the group?

- How efficient are the group's *equipment, systems and processes*?

- What proportion of *time* is spent on 'value adding work'?

THE CAPABILITY OF MANAGEMENT AND EMPLOYEES

Management and employees - and as we have indicated, sometimes others too – make up our human capital, and it has a value that can be identified, quantified and increased. Attempts to quantify it financially have generally failed to achieve any acceptance. This has significantly held back what is an important issue – namely if parts at least of our human capital are our most vital asset, it is essential to have a good measure of it. Unlike money as a resource, the value of people and knowledge/technology grows with time. That value has to be found in the quality of leadership-management, together with the skills, knowledge and competencies of the employees.

Many organisations have tried to identify so called 'high-performance' behaviours in an effort to create a strong link between people and performance. However, the focus on behaviours alone, whilst important, is somewhat narrow. A full understanding of what constitutes the inherent value of people is critical to our theme and Chapter 2 is devoted to this subject.

MOTIVATION AND ENGAGEMENT

Numerous research studies have shown that this is the most significant driver of performance, and it therefore has a chapter to itself, Chapter 3. We will just introduce the subject here.

Back in 1968, Herzberg in his seminal article *One More Time, How do You Motivate Employees* distinguished between factors which were 'satisfiers' and those which were 'dissatisfiers'. Both affected motivation. 'Satisfiers', are factors which influence it positively, and, generally speaking one cannot have too much of them. 'Dissatisfiers', however, (which he named 'hygiene factors') are those which cause demotivation if they do not reach an acceptable level – but beyond that level have minimal further effect.

His work led to a growth in 'satisfaction surveys'. More recently, however, we have learnt that satisfaction in itself does not necessarily drive performance and in fact can be correlated with low performance – an easy life may make the workplace congenial but not necessarily productive. It is helpful to do 'dissatisfaction surveys' – to ensure we are aware of any hindrances to motivation and hence productivity. But we need to get beyond this threshold, and understand the factors that lead to what we call today 'engagement'. This is a synergistic alliance with the organisation's goals, and a care and concern that are successful.

Marcus Buckingham and Curt Coffman introduced the word 'engagement' in their book *First, Break all the Rules* (1999). In an article in *Fast Company* (2001), Buckingham says:

> *You can divide any working population into three categories: people who are engaged (loyal and productive), those who are not engaged (just putting in time), and those who are actively disengaged (unhappy and spreading their discontent). The U.S. working population is 26 per cent engaged, 55 per cent not engaged, and 19 per cent actively disengaged.*

In Chapter 3 we examine how we can measure the level of engagement, and also identify the factors that lead to it. We also look at practical studies that organisations have made in the linking of motivation levels with performance.

EFFICIENCY OF EQUIPMENT, SYSTEMS AND PROCESSES

This is where our third major resource comes into play – technology. Although historically it is new equipment that has been bought to improve productivity, many organisations today do not have any other than computers. So for them the issue is systems and processes. Each process in use needs its own measures – how successful is the process in achieving its goal (that is, effectiveness)? How much effort is expended in achieving those goals (efficiency)? Is the resource expended justified by the outcomes achieved? How can we simplify the process to reduce the resource that is needed without losing quality? Some organisations have processes which strangle the value creating process and even subtract value from stakeholders.

Groups of employees within a value creating unit often do not have control over many of the processes they have to utilise. IT systems may be imposed, such as 'enterprise resource systems' like SAP; HR and Finance have their own processes to which they demand conformance. In the public sector processes are often designed remotely from where they need to be applied. Many of the outputs from these provide data but do not add much value to any stakeholders - although the process owners may not see it that way, as often it is protectionism and risk avoidance for them. This in itself can affect motivation – witness the increasing frustration of many public sector professionals in completing paperwork to satisfy ever increasing 'regulatory' or 'quality assurance' processes which just tell them what they know anyway.

THE UTILISATION OF TIME

There was a time when all tasks were carefully examined and timed – it was called 'time and motion study' and was one of the critical management disciplines of the 1950s and 1960s. I myself spent a year with a stopwatch in my early years. With the growth of 'knowledge workers', this has largely disappeared. No wonder the guru of gurus, Peter Drucker, said as far back as 1991, 'the greatest future challenge is the productivity of knowledge workers'. This applies to the vast majority of all jobs today. 'Support functions' are adept at creating *work* (rather than *value*) for front-line people, whether in private or public sector organisations, and the value of this work often goes unchallenged.

However, every role, even in the 'front-line', does not spend every minute of the day adding value. Time is also absorbed in such legitimate activities as travel, training, meetings, report writing, problem solving, and communicating. All of these may be important to the smooth running of the organisation, but they can absorb a disproportionate amount of the time available. In terms of the efficiency of 'the value creating process' this is an important issue.

Accounting systems treat the work done by people as cost items, such as 'wages and salaries', 'overtime', 'bonuses', 'benefits', 'pensions', 'social security' and so on. There is no distinction between the proportion of time spent that is actually adding any value to a stakeholder, and that which does not. Tony and Jeremy Hope, in *Transforming the Bottom Line* (1995), argue convincingly for the analysis of work in this way. They suggest a 'value-adding work index' – which is a product of the degree to which work is 'quality' (in the sense of not having to be redone), and the percentage which adds real value to a stakeholder. An enormous amount of time may be consumed by such things as:

- car travel;

- meetings about internal affairs;

- reviews and updates;

- reading superfluous email;

- managing problems that should not have occurred;

- re-doing work;

- reports and information provision;

- consultation for its own sake (that is, it is unlikely to add value to the decision);

- internal negotiation and cross-charging;

- arguing for resources;

- mistakes, especially when repeated;

- duplication;

- waiting time;

- computer downtime;

- regulatory compliance;

- and readers can add to this list from their own experience. All support professionals are challenged to release value-adding time from their day.

Productivity – and value added - would be transformed if only a percentage of such work was eliminated. Tony and Jeremy Hope (*Transforming the Bottom Line*, 1995) quote an example from a study made by Arthur D. Little over a year of a typical engineer in an American automotive company.

Table 1.5   **Example of work analysis**

Activity	Value adding %	Non-value adding %
Solo work:		
Scrap or rework		10
Valuable work	20	
Make work		10
Meetings:		
Useful	5	
Useless		10
Management reviews		5
Preparation for reviews		10

Table 1.5   *Concluded*

Activity	Value adding %	Non-value adding %
Paperwork:		
Work documentation	5	
Reporting for administrative control and other paperwork		10
Communications:		
Team exchange	5	
Crisis management		5
Miscellaneous		5
TOTALS	35	65

Not good news! Only one third of time spent was value adding, although no doubt the individual engineers are working hard and are relieved when the weekend comes.

There are many consultancy techniques aimed at eliminating non-added value work, although it is a truism of organisational life that one never arrives at total annihilation.

The UK Public Sector was treated to the *Gershon Report* in 2004 – a report on how the Government could become more efficient. It identified six 'work streams' aimed at greater productivity (to be measured in line with the Atkinson report referred to above), and one of them was called 'productive time'. He stated that:

> *Front-line staff are there to deliver services to the user and reducing the amount of time they spend away from these core activities is an important part of efficiency...' and that 'Productive Time can be reduced if people are having to spend too much time servicing the organisation rather than their customers.*

In support of this the Office of Government Commerce produced a paper called *Productive Time – Efficiency Programme – Measurement Guidance*. It stated that:

> *Productive Time initiatives will deliver:*
>
> *1.   For the same input cost, more time for core activities, or,*

2.   *At a lower input cost, the same time for core activities.*

In both instances, the quality of service delivered will be either the same or higher, never lower.

In the real world, there will be instances where all three factors (input, output and quality) will change.

The paper discussed three methods of measurement – activity sampling of tasks, role requirements and service delivery as the outcome.

Activity sampling is the most direct, and will reflect what is actually happening. An example is given of the 'activity analysis' used by the police, where there is a broad categorisation of the tasks performed and that which is deemed to be 'front-line' or in our terms, value adding. Note that analysis at this level is not in terms of every minute or detail, but enough to give a broad proportion.

Table 1.6   Activity analysis

Task	Front-line?
Interview	Yes
Paperwork/case file	Yes
At court (waiting or giving evidence)	No
Investigate	Yes
Community	Yes
Prison	No
Monitoring cellblock	No
Call handling/relief control room	No
Asset confiscation	Yes
Burglary	Yes
Communications	No
Coroner's Office	Yes
Marine	Yes
Personnel/Human Resources	No
Technical Support Unit	No
Vehicle crime	Yes
Call handling/relief control room	No
Monitoring cellblock	No

Adding value would be transformed if only a percentage of the 'non-productive' work was eliminated – provided of course that the time released is transferred to a productive category. It is dangerous to assume this will happen without continued activity sampling – for many people the 'non-productive' tasks may be done in 'overtime'.

Plenty of options will be marketed aimed at time saving – for example, automation, process engineering, restructuring, decentralisation, outsourcing and activity based management. Sometimes the time and effort involved in making the changes outweighs any potential savings for years ahead. It may happen that the new system has just created new opportunities for non-added value work and I have no doubt readers can think of several examples from their own experience.

Nevertheless, the first step is for everyone in a group to share an understanding of what is one side of the line and what is not. This will lead to a 'blacklist' of both necessary and unnecessary evils and every department should have a notice to place on their desks or on the meeting room '*Do Not Disturb – Non-Value Added Work Going On Here – Speed is of the Essence!*' And individuals who care about their personal productivity will do regular health checks on the percentage of their time that is truly productive.

1.8 Creating Future Value - Innovation as an Output

On page 25 we distinguished between delivering current value to stakeholders and activities aimed at delivering a higher level of future value; there are people in all organisations, even if it is only the owner, who have this role, some exclusively. Most managers are expected to innovate and develop better futures. What we might broadly call 'innovation' is the outcome of their work and it will not be reflected in current productivity ratios.

The results of successful innovation are:

- New *services* that add value to a stakeholder.

Not all new services are *directly* aimed at increased revenues or reduced costs. In the airline industry, for example, some business passengers are offered a free chauffeur service to and from the airport. Clearly an additional cost, it is aimed at customer convenience, and hopefully consequent loyalty.

- New *products* aimed at new revenue streams and fulfilling customer needs.

Innovation involves not just the production of ideas, but turning a sufficient proportion of them into *successful* ones. A commonly used output measure is 'the proportion of sales that come from products or services introduced in the last x years where x may be 1-3 depending on the sector'.

For example, 3M use a goal of at least 25 per cent of annual sales coming from products less than four years old.

There are risks with measures like this. What constitutes a new product? Japanese electronic companies are adept in introducing almost continual variations and improvements, many of which are testing the market rather than responding to it. So a useful variation of this is to track *gross margin* rather than sales. We may not know which sales are actually profitable.

Another kind of measure – in, for example, the pharmaceutical industry – is:

- the percentage of sales from proprietary products as opposed to those generically available to all suppliers;

- New and improved *processes* aimed at greater value for a stakeholder.

Here we can look at measures such as:

percentage change in cost per unit or service

percentage improvement in service level for the same cost

savings accruing from employee suggestions made.

We might well want to keep track of the production of *ideas* themselves. We could use measures such as:

number of new patents registered ('patent count')

number of ideas leading to projects

'citations' to patents – these are references by subsequent patent applications, and imply that the original had some usefulness

number of new suggestions made from employees/head

number of process changes made in a time period.

There is always a danger that effectiveness measures for people trying to create a different future are confined to activities only. 'Management Development', for example, aims to create more effective managers and build leaders for the future. Its effectiveness is not measured in terms of the number of events or activities that are run, nor by the throughput of managers. We need measures which tell us we have better managers, better succession capability, or higher productivity in the teams that are being led.

We have discussed measure of the *outputs* of innovation. What about the *inputs*? One measure would be the percentage of employees who have most of their job dedicated to creating futures rather than servicing the present. Good companies have always paid attention to the long-term and to their stakeholders' interests. Porras and Collins (1994), of Stanford University, took 18 'truly exceptional companies in the long run' (visionary companies they called them) with an average life of nearly 100 years. They compared them with similar companies with roughly the same opportunity but which had not achieved the same reputation or performed so well. 'We were looking for timeless management principles,' they said. What did they find? The visionary companies demonstrated continuing focus on 'intellectual capital', and in the following ways:

- A consistent and strong core ideology, with clear values that formed the foundation of their infrastructure.

- A clear vision for the future and 'big, hairy audacious goals' that went beyond the current financial year.

- High premium on innovation – 'try a lot of stuff and see what works'.

- Focus on employee development, and growing their own senior managers.

Many would say with justification that innovation success is closely related to culture, particularly to openness, freedom to generate ideas, and to fail. Above all the provision of time beyond operational demands is what makes the difference. A variety of cultural measurement tools which focus on innovation can be found.

In an excellent case-based report for *Business Intelligence*, Michel Syrett (*World Class HR: 'The New Measurement Agenda' Business Intelligence Report* 2005) devotes a chapter to the measurement of innovation.

He suggests one measure would be the availability of 'strategic competencies' and quoted research by Roffey Park which identified five key roles:

- 'spark' – the creation of ideas;

- 'sponsors' - people who promote and sustain ideas;

- 'shapers' – people who work on ideas and make them useable;

- 'sounding boards' – what Meredith Belbin would call 'monitor-evaluators';

- 'specialists' – contributors of specialist knowledge to the ideas.

To be effective these require a process to surround them and in which the various roles can participate.

Any system of performance measurement must maintain the balance between short-, and long-term gain. The forces for the short-term are strong and easily dominate. A clarity about 'stakeholder *equilibria*' (ref Figure 1.2) will help keep this balance.

1.9 The Contribution of the Individual

Table 1.4 looked at four types of expenditure. Some employees are dedicated exclusively to one or the other, but this is rare – most have a prime focus in one area but in practice need to do some 'maintenance work', and will at least be encouraged to contribute to the future through ideas.

We have already suggested how important it is to understand how time is being spent. The ratio of time spent does not necessarily equate to the same ratio of outputs. The measures of outputs for individuals are often reflected only in a team or group output. Likewise the fruits of worthy time spent on future ideas may be a long way off, if at all, because 'failure' must not be stigmatised in the area of innovation.

Nevertheless, there is an 'individual productivity' that is easily observable. Some people get through work very quickly through their own personal organisational skills. Some are excellent at maintenance work – always on top of their paperwork and email. I had a boss, Don, who was amazing in this respect. Nothing was held up in his in trays or email boxes; his answers were always to the point; and he was never late or unprepared for a meeting. Others *produce results* faster than most – not so much getting through the volume but spending time on the value adding priorities and bringing them to conclusions.

A personal contribution will be the product of:

Role Productivity × Personal Productivity

Let us explain this: for a given role it is possible and useful to set a norm of how much time we would expect to be spent on added value work. If we take a typical week of say 40 hours of a sales person, how much time should be put into present value contribution, how much into future, and how much is required for non-value added tasks? The main task is to obtain customer revenue (say 25 hours of the week). He or she will also be building relationships with potential new customers (measured in the number of new customers over a period), and feeding back a weekly report on how customers are feeling and what their needs area (say 6 hours a week). Then there is time spent travelling, having meetings, doing routine reports, expense reports and so on (say 9 hours). In such a case the 'norm' ratio of value added to non-value added, time in the role would be set as 31/40 = 77.5%.

This norm – which can be revised with time, experience and process changes – provides a comparator and a target setting mechanism. But then every individual in such a role brings different personal skills in the way they do the job, and in the way they respond to the demands and guidance of their manager and work group. The reward system is very likely also to influence productivity – for salespeople, for example, – where efforts are visibly and directly rewarded.

For each individual, we need to know the following (as illustrated in the example of a salesperson):

Table 1.7   Individual productivity

Norms and Actuals in Time Spent: Salesperson			
	Present value contribution %	Future value contribution %	Non-added-value %
Role norm	50	30	20
Individual actual	60	10	30
Outcomes against Targets			
Present value-added targets	Present value-added achieved	Future value-added targets	Future value-added achieved
Revenue £500K	Revenue £700K	New customer prospects identified – 20	New customer prospects identified – 8
Delivery accuracy 95%	Delivery accuracy 90%	New customer needs identified – 6	New customer needs identified – 3
		Loyalty agreements signed – worth £400K	Loyalty agreements signed – worth £250K

This is the kind of data readily available for salespeople or call centre staff, but a multitude of roles – especially in the public sector – have nothing so systematised. It is no wonder they often struggle with what it means to have a high performance culture.

One useful tool suggested in the *Human Value of the Enterprise* seems worth mentioning at this point (Mayo 2001 pp. TBA). It is to develop a ranked order of the value adding contribution for roles, and then *within* a role for the people in them. The ranking could be by percentage of the time available, time spent on added value work. All stakeholders are important, but adding value to customers would generally be considered of a higher priority than to others.

1.10 Summary

Organisations – and parts of them – only exist to provide value, or benefits, to their stakeholders. Stakeholders have different levels of power and influence, and an organisation has to base its priorities on its needs to satisfy their particular 'stakeholder map'.

Stakeholders both provide and receive value from the organisation. This value exchange needs to be kept in equilibrium, lest one party decides 'this is not working for me'. The value exchange is not static, as over time expectations increase and more value is exchanged on both sides. What is important is to understand and be able to measure the value (which may be either financial or non-financial or both) that the organisation provides and receives.

Stakeholder value can be seen as the outcome of a 'value creating process'; this consists of resource inputs, each of which have value; the organisation itself which converts the resources, and the outcomes themselves.

The effectiveness of the organisation in converting the inputs into outputs needs measures in its own right. Those measures can be described as 'productivity', and appropriate ratios should be chosen which reliably and specifically reflect the contribution of people in the value chain. We then need to analyse and measure the drivers of this productivity. Four such drivers were discussed – the capability of people (expanded in Chapter 2); their motivation and engagement (expanded in Chapter 3), equipment and systems efficiency, and time utilisation.

These measures reflect the current value exchanges that exist. However, we are constantly seeking to enhance the level of value in the exchange through innovation – an outcome in its own right and needing its own measures.

We noted that, whereas resource inputs are generally accounted for as *costs*, they have differing levels of value also. It is important to understand what costs are being used for and to associate them with their value producing activity – which will enable a more intelligent approach to cost cutting than is often found.

Finally, we considered the contribution of the individual to stakeholder value and linked this with the way time is spent.

1.11 Challenges for Action

- In which contexts is the word 'value' used in your organisation? What meaning would people give to it?

- How would you draw the stakeholder map of your part of the organisation? What is the relative power that each has?

- For each of these stakeholders what are the components of the value they receive? What measures are in use to describe the level of value? Are there any gaps?

- For the department you work in, pick the three most important value measures to your stakeholders. Are these reflected in your performance management system?

- Within your organisation, to what extent have you identified 'value creating groups' whose value creation effectiveness could be specifically measured?

- How is productivity measured in your organisation? Do the measures used reflect each outcomes rather than the activities of the department?

- What measures of the drivers of productivity do you have? What would be useful to have? Do you have a clear distinction between 'value adding' activities and those that are not? Do you monitor these by periodic time analysis projects?

- What targets and measures for innovation do you have?

- How would you classify the proportion of your input spend in terms of Table 1.4?

- How would you rank roles in your organisation in respect of their value adding potential? Is this ranking reflected in the reward system?

1.12 References and Further Reading

Atkinson Review: Final report. (2005). *Measurement of Government Output and Productivity for the National Accounts.* London: Palgrave McMillan.

B&Q. Cass. (2003). *Unlocking the Wealth of Organisations.*

Buckingham, M. (August 2001). *Think Your Boss Has an Attitude Problem? Fast Company Magazine,* (Issue 49).

Buckingham, M., and Coffman, C. (1999). *First Break All the Rules: What the World's Greatest Managers Do Differently.* New York: Simon & Schuster.

Fitz-enz, J. (2009). *The ROI of Human Capital: Measuring the Economic Value of Employee Performance.* Amacom.

Hamel, G., and Pralahad, C.K. (1994). *Competing for the Future.* Cambridge: Harvard Press.

Herzberg, F. (January 2003). *One More Time – How Do You Motivate employees? Harvard Business Review.*

Hope, J., and Hope, T. (1995). *Transforming the Bottom Line.* London: Nicolas Brealey.

Kaplan, R.S., and Norton, D.P. (1996). *The Balanced Scorecard.* Boston: Harvard Business School Press.

Kaplan, R.S., and Norton, D.P. (2000). *The Strategy-Focused Organisation.* Boston: Harvard Business School Press.

Mayo, A.J. (2001). *The Human Value of the Enterprise.* London: Nicholas Brealey.

Office of Government Commerce. (2005). *Productive Time – Efficiency Programme – Measurement Guidance.* www.ogc.gov.uk

Porras, J.I., and Collins, J.C. (1994). *Built to Last.* New York: Harper Business New York.

Syrett, M. (2005). *World Class HR: The New Measurement Agenda. Business Intelligence Report.*

www.balancedscorecard.org

2

The Value of People Themselves

In Chapter 1 we suggested there were three key resources in the modern organisation which were inputs to a value creating process. Of these, only money is consumed; in fact, people and technology, or knowledge, have the facility to appreciate. 'Human capital management' (HCM) looks at people as value creating assets with an inherent value in themselves that can be enhanced with time. The breadth and depth of that value influences the outcomes we produce. This chapter considers how this can be understood, measured and therefore managed; the higher the value of the human capital available to us, the higher the potential value of the benefits for stakeholders.

2.1 Where Does 'Human Capital' Come From?

Management accounting systems in general use today are not able to take account of either movements in (the operating statement) or the current status (balance sheet) of 'intangible assets'. These are all those assets which an organisation has, other than money (and investments), and physical assets such as buildings, equipment and stocks. Sometimes the term 'intangible assets' will appear in a balance sheet in the form of 'goodwill'. This arises from acquisitions, where the price paid is substantially more than the 'book value' – and this premium has to be accounted for. Accounting rules demand that this amount is depreciated, that is, written down, over time.

That premium, however, is paid for the intangible assets of the purchased company. It is a strange recognition of their value to reduce them down to zero! In reality, this is the last thing an organisation wants to do – it is largely because of the nature of those intangibles that the company was attractive to buy.

Where a company has a market valuation – its share price times the number of shares – history has shown a steady rise over the last 20 years for the 'market-to-book ratio'. For oil and gas companies the ratio is typically 3:1 (despite their heavy physical plant investment) and for high-tech and service companies it may be as much as 20:1 or more. This is a ratio one might expect the business minded HR Director to be constantly aware of (where available) since a vital component is the human capital of the organisation.

The gap represents the value placed on the intangible assets. Sometimes the term 'intellectual capital' is used, to distinguish it from physical and financial capital. Thomas Stewart, previously Editor-in-Chief of the *Harvard Business Review* and an early writer on the subject, defined it in a 1994 article as:

> *Intellectual material – knowledge, information, intellectual property, experience – that can be put to use to create wealth.*

It was at this time in the mid-1990s that various writers sought to understand intangible assets, led by Swedish pioneers such as Eric Sveiby, Leif Edvinsson and the Roos brothers. (A summary of the contributors formed the Appendix to *The Human Value of the Enterprise*, 2001).

The most common division is into the following components:

- Customer (external structural) capital

  This includes assets which enable and/or stimulate people outside our organisation to work with us, and – in a commercial organisation – to buy from us. It includes customer contracts, relationships, loyalty, satisfaction, market share, image, reputation, brands, distribution networks and channels.

  In the public sector, we would talk, for example, about service levels, accessibility, reputation, or the popularity of revenue generating activities.

- Organisational (internal structural) capital

  This includes all that relates to our internal operations and efficiency. It embraces strategies, systems, methodologies, and operational processes. All the recorded knowledge we have is here – patents, know-how, databases, and technology. We would also place here the culture of the organisation, and:

- 'Human capital' (which Sveiby called 'Professional Competence')

This is not just the people *en masse*, but the qualities and talents they bring that are valuable to *our* organisation – loaning their personal 'human capital' to us, their individual capability and commitment, their personal knowledge and experience. But it is more than the individuals alone – it includes the way in which they work together and the relationships they have both within and outwith the organisation.

Baruch Lev of Stern University, New York, whose work parallels that of Sveiby, distinguishes the three categories of 'human resource intangibles', 'organisational intangibles' and 'innovation-related intangibles'.

Figure 2.1 illustrates the relationship between the different forms of capital in an organisation. This dynamic value-creating organism is powered by its human capital. It is people and the way they work together that both maintains the other forms of capital, and also increases them over time.

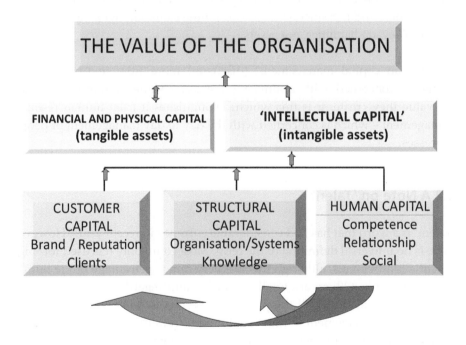

Figure 2.1   Components of intellectual capital

All of the above 'intangibles' are clearly *valuable*, which is why they are referred to as assets. However, their *value* is not generally easy to measure, certainly in financial terms. An American consultancy, Interbrand, has derived a formula for assessing what proportion of the total intangible assets (based on market value) is attributable to the brand, or brands, the company has. The annual list of the top 200 across the world is published on their website. It is possible, also, to place a value on patents and long-term customer contracts, but for most of these assets we will need to look for non-financial measures.

Can we say that people truly are 'the most valuable assets we have'? Or should this engender the cynical response it often gets? Without people, for sure, no value for stakeholders will be provided and increased. In this sense, they are the foundation of the whole value creation enterprise, whether commercial or public. But the clichéd statement is trite, because it is *some* aspects of *some* people which are the assets. There can be people who actually *subtract* value from stakeholders. Examples would be managers who make decisions which are against the interests of a key stakeholder, front-line staff who turn off customers and bureaucrats who absorb time from otherwise value creating people. They are liabilities, not assets.

'Human capital management' (discussed more fully in Chapter 5) is primarily concerned with optimising the asset value of our people, and the value they create. It is this which distinguishes it from human resource management – which is concerned with the day to day management of people processes.

2.2 A Note on 'Talent'

'Talent' is a word that has had considerable currency in recent years. However, there is no universal definition of the term. Most commonly it is used for 'high potential' individuals, although this is a very minor percentage of the human capital available. Others are totally inclusive and regard it as an exercise in managing the talents of all the people. If there is to be anything distinctive about 'talent management' it must be different from the general management of people, so the totally inclusive approach does not add any value.

One attractive definition is that proposed by Tajer and Scott-Jackson of the Oxford-based Centre for Applied HR Research. In this they go through the following steps:

- start with the business mission and key strategies;

- identify the critical capabilities the organisation must have as significant strengths in order to be successful;

- identify the roles where these are major components;

- assess the people in those roles for the extent of mission critical capabilities they possess.

This process is business driven rather than individual driven. It identifies both the roles and the people in them and is particularly useful for 'talent planning'. It would also be a guide to those groups and teams for whom measuring human capital value is a priority.

2.3 Valuing Human Capital

This is still the most underdeveloped area in people related measures. Recent focus has been on measures of engagement, and few organisations have thought systematically about quantitatively valuing their human capital. Would there be any benefit? After all, many organisations have delivered increasing value over the decades without solving this problem – is it a *real* problem?

Years of growth and progress may yet hide a multitude of poor decisions which have subtracted *potential* value from stakeholders, including the owners and shareholders. For example, precious assets and knowledge are often lost through restructuring because they are only seen as costs. There are a number of reasons why we suggest that the effort is worthwhile:

- Most organisations count people only as 'heads' or as 'costs'. There is no corresponding figure for value, and so decisions about them are one-sided. 'Price is what you pay, value is what you get' says the Annual Report of Systematic A/S, a pioneering reporter of data on intangible assets (see page 129). It will always be necessary to adjust levels of employees, but it should be done intelligently. A team leader knows the unique and relative value of his or her people – and could describe it qualitatively. They are known as individuals. But as we go above and beyond the team leader's level, that value is lost in a fog and those individuals just become headcount.

- We need to understand both the *unique* and the *relative* value of individuals and teams. This will guide who we must retain if at all possible, and who it would be good to replace.

- We need to understand and isolate the special characteristics of the human capital available to us which we find are particularly linked to value added outcomes.

- Analysing our asset value will give us a focus for recruitment and training and help us make informed and intelligent investment decisions. We will be able to understand the relative benefits of investing in people compared to that in other assets.

- Most of all, we can 'keep stock' of talent and expertise in a much more meaningful way than counting heads, and know whether the human capital available to us is increasing or decreasing.

It is as important to know how our 'stock' of human capital is changing as it is to understand our cash flow.

LEVELS OF VALUATION OF HUMAN CAPITAL

Four levels of valuation of human capital are potentially useful.

The first is that of the individual. What is the relation of value to cost for individuals? Is it possible to quantify 'the value equilibrium' between an individual and their organisation? How can we 'grow' people such that their value constantly increases?

Secondly, many people work together in teams and groups with a common purpose. We are interested in the value of the team as a whole. This will usually be more than the aggregate value of individuals since there is additional value from the well functioning and cohesive team. But it can also be less than the sum of its parts, if aspects of the way people work together cause friction and animosity and detract time and energy from otherwise valuable people.

The third and fourth levels are at organisational and enterprise level, the latter being defined as the level of the 'public face' – that of annual reports, websites and so on.

Much attention has been given at the fourth level to the publication of people related data, stimulated by some European governments, but no pressure is currently put on valuation itself. Professional accountant bodies have generally decided that this cannot be done financially. However, some academics have sought to find answers and one public company at least regularly reports such a valuation. And then there is the special case of football clubs. We look at these below.

FINANCIAL VALUATION

'Human resource accounting' (sometimes known as 'human asset accounting') is a term better known in the US than elsewhere. The 'father' of this niche of study is Professor Eric Flamholtz, Professor of Management at the Anderson Graduate school of Management in the University of California.

Flamholtz asserted that the aim of human resource management is to optimise human resource value. He defines the measure of individual value as resulting from two interacting variables – a person's *conditional value* and the *probability* that he or she will stay with the organisation. An individual's *conditional value* is the present worth of the *potential* services that could be rendered if the individual stays with the organisation for X years. The conditional value is a combination of productivity (performance), transferability (flexible skills), and promotability. The latter two are heavily influenced by the first element. This is then multiplied by a *probability* factor that he or she will stay for the X years. This gives the *expected realisable value* which is a measure of the person's worth.

He extends the principle to evaluating the effectiveness of development programmes. If a programme produces a measured change in productivity, transferability or promotability, this translates into increased value of the individuals concerned.

There are a number of difficulties with this approach, not least of which is the estimation of potential future services. It also leads to lower values for older and more experienced people who have less time to render future services. There is a case for looking at them this way if we consider value over a future lifetime, but it fails to take account of the wealth of value in past experience.

Lev and Schwarz (1971) devised a methodology of human resource accounting which has been followed for some years by the well-known and innovative Indian IT company, Infosys. For inspiration from a successful model of responsible capitalism, one need look no further than the website and annual report of Infosys, a role model of corporate reporting. Their revenues grew by 29.5 per cent between 2008 and 2009 and for many years their annual reports have included a section entitled 'human resource accounting'. The evaluation of human resources value is based on the present value of the future earnings of the employees and on the following assumptions:

- employee compensation includes all direct and indirect benefits earned both in India and abroad;

- the incremental earnings based on group/age;

- the future earnings were discounted in 2009 as 12.13 per cent, the cost of capital for the company.

Using this, they calculated in 2009 the total human resource value of their 104,800 employees to be 102,133 crores of rupees (one crore is 10m rupees). The employee cost was 12.7 per cent of this. Value added is also calculated (see page 27) as 19,073 crores (2008:14,820). Interesting ratios are derived as follows:

Total revenue/human resources value 2009 0.21; (2008 0.17)

Value added/human resources value 2009 0.19; (2008 0.15)

Value of human resources per employee (%) 0.97; (2008 1.08)

Return on human resources value (%) 2009 5.9%; (2008 4.7%)

These ratios have been consistently calculated over many years of growth and vary around these figures year by year. This remarkable report goes on to calculate a brand valuation and then to restate the balance sheet including the calculated intangibles. The Brand Value is calculated as 32,345 crores.

The general prudence of accountants, and the lack of desire to publish more than is necessary, certainly constrains more attempts to value human capital in this way. Infosys believes fundamentally in transparency as a competitive advantage and provider of confidence to investors. Their results would seem to justify this belief. As an observer, one sees a much better balance of the assets used in the business.

One sector of organisations does place the value of, literally, their key players in their balance sheet, and that is football clubs. This is because players are traded as assets. The British club, Tottenham Hotspur, for example, show in their 2008 report intangible assets as GBP 121m at cost. The intangibles are defined as the costs of players and key management, netted for acquisitions and disposals, and amortised in equal annual amounts over the life of the individual contract. As at 30 June 2008, 'amortisation and impairment' shown as 58.7m, giving a net value of intangible assets as 62.4 m (2007: 71.0m). This compared with tangible assets of 42.6m.

Unlike football players, most employees increase in value with time and we cannot apply accounting rules to them. Note, however, that all these methods start with individuals and sum them together. The corporate sums – our fourth level – only have interest if we can see a trend and compare with previous years, or see comparable figures with other similar organisations. For public sector organisations, such figures have no meaning at all.

In 2005, Herman Theeke published an erudite and wide-ranging article in the *Journal of Human Resource Costing and Accounting*, countering the notion that people could not be accounted for financially. Instead of referring to them as assets he argued they should all be classified as liabilities. He does not, however, work out the details of how this might be done.

When it comes to individuals and teams, it is perfectly possible to apply a financial formula. However, in *The Human Value of the Enterprise* (Mayo 2001) we discussed in some detail the options here, and *concluded*:

> *whereas it would be neat if we could have a realistic, generally accepted, absolute financial formula, this is unlikely to be achieved. There are very real problems in following definitions and methods which fit the principles of economics in valuation. Furthermore the variables to be considered are very complex, and the uncertainty of future predictions immense. We should end up with formulae so complicated that they would be unusable – and to some extent this is what has happened to human resource accounting as a discipline. It has rested largely with the academics.*

One also has to question what we would do with a financial figure, and how it would help us to understand the value of people better, as well as how to increase it. Rather than concentrate on searching for a formula, it is more useful to focus on the characteristics or qualities of people which make them valuable to the organisation.

NON-FINANCIAL VALUATION

Giles and Robinson (1972) were the first in the UK to examine this in a joint study commissioned by the two professional institutes at that time concerned with people (The Institute of Personnel Management), and accounting (The Institute for Cost and Management Accounting). They came to the conclusion that a points system was needed. They developed a factor called the 'human asset multiplier' which they then applied to gross remuneration. They took into account the following factors:

qualifications/expertise   experience

attitudes   promotion capability

loyalty   replacement scarcity

and an estimate of expected future service.

These authors were looking for a multiplier to apply to salary. Although their work is largely forgotten, it does seem to have the most practical and useful basis for understanding individual value, and this was taken forward in the author's *The Human Value of the Enterprise* referenced above.

If we wanted to answer the question '*Does this (or these) employee (s) add more value than they cost?*' we are faced with a comparison between a non-financial evaluation and money. We, therefore, have to define some levels of expectation – that 'in this role, at this pay level, we expect these levels of capability'.(It is traditional in HRM to value *jobs* in order to determine pay levels – but a human capital approach would lead us to put more emphasis on valuing individuals.)

If the answer to the question above is positive we would want to think hard about how we retain them, in both good times and bad. We would certainly want to ask some more questions if it was proposed that they were not needed. There might be some good answers – 'we don't have enough demand for the value they create right now', or 'they could be replaced with people who would give *more* value for the same cost'.

In the case of Infosys, employee costs were 48.0m and added value was 80.3m. *On average*, each employee added 1.67 times their cost. This does not take account of *non-financial* value that employees added to stakeholders. However, there would be great variation between individuals – partly based on their job – their *structural capacity* to add value, and partly based on their individual qualities – their *personal capacity* (as discussed in Section 1.9).

The problem is: for individuals, their manager and those around them know their value and can make a judgement of the *balance* of cost and value, but because it is not written down the knowledge stays down there. Whereas knowledge of their costs is wholly accessible at all levels.

2.4 The Concept of 'Human Asset Worth'

One of the constant dilemmas in HR management is the balance between 'one size fits all' approaches and 'customisation'. Undoubtedly the former has many advantages. Everyone talks the same language, common standards are developed, and comparisons are easily made. But the downside is that we place people and teams into a mould that often does not fit very well and end up with a bureaucratic procedure that *in extremis* loses its original purpose.

In the area of human value we are dealing with tremendous diversity across an organisation. The optimal solution would be to have a common framework with the scope for individual variation within it.

If we look, therefore, at a team of people within a value creating process who broadly share a common set of qualities and capabilities, we can ask:

> *What are the distinctive characteristics of this/these employee(s) which epitomise their special value in creating the outputs for the value-creating process of which they are part?*

I have phrased this question many times to managers in this way: 'Rank all the members of your team in terms of the 'amount of pain you would experience if they were to leave'. What is it that is distinctive about the people at the top of the list, that if you lost them there would be a major hole to fill? And what is it about the opposite end of the list, that if they left, you would be happy to replace them with people who have different characteristics?

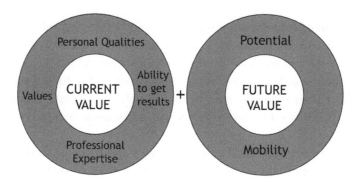

Figure 2.2   The value of people

There are some *personal attitudes* that we always value in any employee – positive attitudes, willingness, being a team player, and reliability. These are often to be found in 'competency frameworks'. We are referring here to those which are more personality-orientated; that is, are generally not developed through training.

But performance is about more than these. The answers will also include:

- Alignment with the organisation – its values, ethos, and mission.

Values may be expressed formally in written (or 'espoused') form, or in an accepted unwritten understanding. In some organisations, but not all, this may be a key factor. Good performing, capable people who comfortably align themselves to our values have particular worth to us. They become 'part of us' and are likely to be loyal to us, and care about what we do.

To expect people to be passionate about their work is quite commonly written into value statements. IBM, when revising their 'business competencies' in the mid-1990s placed centrally, 'a passion for the business'; they recognised that the most potent driver of success was a love for the IT world and what it could do. It is not something that can be forced – but when there, it is highly valued. It is something that should be identified at recruitment. Nando's, a chain of chicken restaurants, is 'passionate about passion'. Pride and passion are two of their values and their website constantly features individuals who are 'passionate nandocas'. They have made their values such a way of life that they are literally 'the passport to working' there.

- Job-relevant capability/expertise – knowledge, skills, specialised experiences and people contacts.

The value of the individual to the organisation is in *all* their cumulative knowledge, skills, experience, and their relevant network of contacts. Many competency frameworks lump all these together under one heading, and that is fine so long a there are relevant subsidiary frameworks which define and measure the detail. No operational manager underestimates their importance. We discuss this in more detail below in Section 2.6.

- Productivity/contribution – people vary in their ability to actually achieve things.

Some people are better at getting results than others – even with the same base level of knowledge and skill. It is to do with the way they prioritise time and effort. We always value more those who 'get things done'.

In Figure 2.2 we define value as a sum of *current value* and *future value*. A manager may not be the best person to assess the latter, and this is where talent management processes need to be harnessed and HR involved.

We are talking here about the potential to undertake a more demanding role in the future – higher or broader responsibilities. A second factor may be 'mobility' – the willingness to take up positions in other locations or countries. We can devise a system for describing potential or mobility (if relevant) that embraces all employees. Note that we are being very restrictive if we only see potential as 'upwards'. We should be just as interested in those with the ability to lead in a technical or professional capacity, and those who can become multi-skilled or multi-functional.

Having identified the factors affecting high performance, we then need to do the following:

- weight the factors for relative importance;

- decide how to rate the factors as observed – both in terms of a scale and a process to apply it;

- design a common display format for them;

- summarise in an overall index of value.

We may call this overall index by any suitable name. In *The Human Value of the Enterprise* (Mayo, 2001) we used 'IAM = individual asset multiplier'. We could use other terms such as 'personal value index' (preferred) or 'human capital index' – or whatever suits the culture of the organisation. What we are reflecting is the truth that every person is an individual, not just 'another head'. He or she brings a different combination of present and potential value to their current role and to the organisation.

WEIGHTING THE FACTORS

We take 100 points and divide them between the chosen factors. In some cases, factors like mobility and values alignment may be entry criteria, and therefore not distinctive. For example, in a medium size software house, when doing this exercise, the value system was so strong and the recruitment process so careful in selecting people aligned with it, that the factor of 'values alignment' was given a very low weighting, and in fact it could have been zero. In a sales team, achieving results may be so dominant that it might be given 30 or 40 points. In a call centre professional skills in customer care may be dominant; in an R&D team, specialist knowledge. What is certain is that each functional team will have a different profile.

The weighting given to 'potential' may be a matter of debate, since a manager may feel this has lower priority. The decision on weighting should be therefore made jointly between a manager and HR.

DECIDING ON A RATING SCALE

The simplest rating scale is 'high/medium/low' and in some cultures this may be preferred to the use of numeric scales. Common numeric scales are 1–5, or a percentage of the ideal. We suggest there is merit in a scale of 0–2 for this purpose: the reason is that the midpoint is 1. A rating of 1 is defined as follows: 'to the best of our judgement this person is delivering what we feel reasonable for what they are being paid'. It is an attempt to define the value-cost equation through describing a reasonable expectation. Those with a summary index of 1 or greater can generally be called assets. Those with less than 1 are not necessarily liabilities, as they may still be adding more value than they cost – but represent an opportunity for either enhancing their value or being replaced by someone of more value.

Here are two examples of using such a scale. The scale is linear – the points illustrated are just markers along it.

Professional expertise

0.5	Has some noticeable deficiencies compared to expectations for this role
1.0	Generally has the balance of capability expected for this role
1.5	In several areas exceeds the level needed for the role; has some unique knowledge and/or relevant experience
2.0	Has considerable breadth and depth beyond the basic needs of the role; known for his/her unique expertise

Values alignment

0.5	Shows little alignment to corporate values or interest in what we are trying to achieve
1.0	Behaviour does not explicitly conflict with values
1.5	Makes considerable effort to align with of our values where possible and has some passion for what we are trying to achieve
2.0	Known throughout as a role model for the organisation's values and achieving its mission

(These examples are quoted from *The Human Value of the Enterprise* Mayo, 2001.)

THE PROCESS OF RATING

When this approach to valuing people is suggested, some recoil at the prospect of obtaining all this information for all employees. Our first focus would be on strategically important groups of employees – within our definition of 'talent' perhaps. *But* we take it for granted that every penny spent will be coded according to our costing system and our budgets are broken down into great detail. Is not our human capital even more important?

In fact, all the factors we have talked about are the essence of an appraisal discussion. Most appraisal systems end up with an 'overall rating' of some kind, called a 'performance rating'. The value of this shorthand, sensitive, consolidation of the detail may be questioned and many recent designs do not have it. We are merely suggesting that having decided the critical factors of value that each is rated separately and systematically.

Clearly a manager is in the best position to do this first. There is always an objection that different managers use different standards. There are many HR schemes that use ranking and there are ways to moderate scorings – using an experienced HR professional; checking them with fellow managers; using peer ratings, and so on.

How often would it be done? This depends on the speed of change of members in the team under consideration. If turnover is very low, once a year may be enough; but if it is more than 20 per cent per annum, this exercise would be reviewed 2–3 times a year.

Suppose we are uncomfortable with rating individuals, especially with the legal frameworks under which employers operate? There are many counter arguments to this discomfort. This is a positive exercise designed to focus on the value of people and to increase it. But if this discomfort persists, one way is to ask a manager to do a distribution on each factor. Thus, on say, personal productivity, what *proportion* of the team would be classified under each quartile of the scale?

An Example

Andrew is the Customer Service Representative for West Scotland for an engineering firm. Andrew is a role model of what the organisation aspires to be and has a very high customer loyalty. He has no potential to grow further in the organisation and his knowledge and skills are very much aligned to the role he has had for many years. He could take another region, but much of his value is in his natural empathy with his clients and colleagues.

The table shows how the factors might work out and what weighting could be given for this subset (that is, field customer service department) of the organisation.

Andrew's 'personal value index' (or whatever we might choose to call it) might be calculated as follows:

Table 2.1   Example of a personal value index

Component	Weighting	Factor value	Weighted value
Capability	0.25	1.0	0.250
Personal Attributes	0.20	1.9	0.380
Contribution	0.25	1.2	0.500
Values Alignment	0.15	2.0	0.300
Potential	0.15	1.0	0.150
Personal Value Index			1.580

A DISPLAY FORMAT

What we need is a picture of the value distribution of a team. This can be given a suitable name. It could be called rather coldly 'the human asset register'. We may prefer something less jargonistic, such as 'people value matrix', or just 'the value of our people – team X'.

The suggested format is as in Figure 2.3. The first four examples are to do with 'current value'; the fifth is about 'future value'. Note that they are just *examples* of indices and factors and each group would have its own.

The Value in a Group

Employee	Personal attitudes(20%)	Capability factor(20%)	Contribution factor (30%)	Values factor (15%)		Potential factor(15%)	"HC" Index (100%)
A	1.7	1.6	1.8	1.6		1.9	1.725
B	0.7	1.0	0.8	0.8		0.7	0.805
C	1.4	1.1	0.8	1.6		0.9	1.115
D	1.6	1.7	1.5	1.0		1.5	1.485
E	1.0	0.8	0.9	1.1		1.0	0.945
Average per employee	1.28	1.24	1.19	1.22		1.20	1.215

Figure 2.3   A people value matrix

Note: The final value in the bottom right box might be known as the '*Human Capital Index*'.

In this team of five people, what do we learn? It is a strong team with all the various qualities important to us averaging greater than 1.0. We are weakest on results achievement, and the team is being sustained here by two individuals, A and D: B and E are weaker members of the team, and B probably should be replaced. We have two people with good promotion potential which is sufficient. In looking for a replacement for B we would probably look primarily for a results orientated person.

A manager may say that he or she knows all this and does not need to put it down in this format. This may be so – but *others* in the organisation do not share that intimate knowledge. This format enables others also (higher management, HR) to see where value is to be found.

In some cases managers may be reluctant to place so many numbers against individuals. An alternative is to present the value effectively as a summary, as in Figure 2.2. This results from the question:

> *'In terms of the contribution level to results, with 1.0 as the reasonably expected level, what proportion of the team would you place in the ranges 0.1–0.5; 0.6–1.0; 1.1–1.5 and 1.6–2.0?'. To do this, of course, the manager will still need to consider each individual, one by one.*

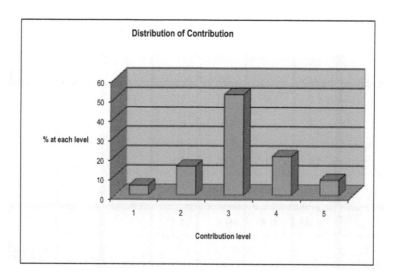

Figure 2.4   Showing team value as a distribution

COMPARING TEAMS

Figures 2.3 and 2.4 give us a team picture and we can devise a summary index of the value of the team. This enables us to compare one team with another, especially where we have several who share a common purpose.

This can be helpful in the following ways:

- It enables us to establish the link between the summary index of human capital and performance, which can be predictive as we invest in the enhancement of the human capital in a team.

- It enables us to set performance targets.

- The detail of all the teams together give us a distribution of useful data on potential, values alignment or any other factor which is deemed important for a particular group.

- It may be able to give us a picture of the flexibility of the workforce, as we see particular characteristics that could be useful elsewhere.

RELATING THE VALUE INDEX TO SALARY

Giles and Robinson applied their 'multipliers' to compensation costs to achieve a financial assessment of 'people value'. Although one might naturally start with the market value of a person, this is hard to ascertain and is not going to be readily at hand. Every individual has a sense of what this is, but our concern is their value to us. What we do know is the remuneration of people and we keep close track of this. It may well reflect accidents of history (either positive or negative), and be under- or over-rated in respect of the market, but it makes the best starting point.

In *The Human Value of the Enterprise*, we suggested the following formula:

HAW   =   EC   ×   IAM/1000
(Human Asset Worth) (Employment Cost) (Individual Asset Multiplier)

EC = Employment Cost was defined as:

Base salary + value of benefits + employer taxes

It should exclude bonuses unless they are in whole or part 'guaranteed'. It also does not include the overheads of providing space and equipment, as this is so variable and is likely to be averaged out on a per person basis anyway.

We divided by 1000 so that the end result would not look like a monetary amount that could be directly compared with cost, as this would be misleading in accounting terms. The purpose is to be able to understand *relativities* and provide a guide to taking appropriate actions.

However, experience of applying the methodology in practice has led more often to just focusing on the indices, which provide sufficient detail and relativities for our purposes.

2.5 The Measurement and Assessment of Capability

This is a critical – and underdeveloped area. Firstly because it represents the core of our human capital, and secondly because a large amount of investment in training and development initiatives will want to measure changes in relevant capability as an intermediate or final measure of return.

The widespread use of 'universal competency frameworks', where every employee at a certain level is expected to shine at a large number of behavioural competencies, makes little sense. It is those which are uniquely critical to the role in question that we want to identify and grow. They will not all be behaviours either.

We suggest 'capability' is a useful all-embracing term, and can be divided into six headings, as shown in Figure 2.5.

This shows two foundational components on which others are built – *qualifications* and *experience*. Then we have *business, technical* and *professional know-how* which embraces knowledge and specialised skills; *personal skills* – which includes attributes and behaviours; and *'know-who'*, the network of contacts that are critical to success in many jobs. These are embraced by the *values* and *attitudes* the individual holds.

Figure 2.5   The components of capability

EDUCATIONAL LEVELS AND PROFESSIONAL QUALIFICATIONS

There has been an explosive growth in 'certification', generally driven by governments and regulators rather than employers. Indeed, the latter are often sceptical about the benefit to them of many qualifications. In some industries, a professional (or regulatory) qualification may be necessary to give a licence to practice. In measurement terms it is simple – the certificate, or a certain grade, was or was not achieved.

For some organisations as a whole, or for some parts of organisations, this may have special importance. In an R&D environment, the percentage of people with higher degrees may be a critical measure and a benchmark against competition; or in Finance, where the percentage who are fully qualified is a measure of departmental strength.

EXPERIENCES

Experiences are the real foundation of learning. Experience gives us both breadth and depth of other competencies, and has value in its own right. It is relatively easy to measure – it has happened or not happened factually. Experiences may or may not be successful in achievement terms, but still can enhance other capabilities. They are obtained through the following:

- being accountable in a function for some results or value added;

- being in a particular type of situation and coping with it;

- a type of project, and learning from it;

- a type of problem or opportunity that has been confronted.

A number of HR and people development initiatives will be aimed at providing experiences for people. What we need are some parameters to describe it. The extent of experience can be described by:

- Time spent – how long has been spent in a situation or job type.

- Scope and stretch – how complex was the experience.

- Parameters of size – revenues, people, countries, and so on.

We can create a number of levels to describe each. For example, if we want to measure experience in project management, or in international roles, we might draw up a table as follows:

Table 2.2   Levels of experience

Experience area	Level	Time spent	Scope/stretch	Size
Project management (delivering discrete results using resources 'owned' by others)	1	< 1 year	Internal, own department External, own department	Budget < £10K; length < 3 months
	2	1–2 years	Internal, cross department	10–100K
	3	2–5 years		3–6 months
	4	> 5 years	External, multifunctional	100–500K 6–12 months > 500K > 12 months
International role (working in contact with, or located in other countries)	1	< 1 year	Regular liaison with people from other countries	1–5 countries involvement; or technical/prof secondment
	2	1–2 years	Responsibility for resources abroad; frequent visits	6–12 countries or management secondment (developed world)
	3	2–5 years	One international secondment	
	4	> 5 years	Several international secondments	13–30 countries or management secondment (less developed world) globally or country leadership

A development or recruitment programme aimed at growing the experience of a team may then track its success using a format as below:

Table 2.3   The experience profile of a team

Area of Experience	Entry			When experienced			Person A			Person B			Person C		
	time	sc	sz	time	sc	sz	time	sc	sz	time	sc	sz	time	sc	sz
International management	-	-	-	2+	2	1	3	3	2	2	2	2	4	3	3
product marketing	2	1	1	3+	3+	3	2	3	3	2	1	1	4	4	3
distribution channels	1	1	1	3+	3+	3	3	2	2	1	2	1	3	3	3
pricing	1	1	1	3+	3+	3	2	3	3	1	2	1	4	3	3
etc.															

This applies the four levels of depth of experience in Table 2.2. It uses columns for time spent, scope, and size; and describes first the required minimum *entry* level; then the level to be expected when experienced, and then the current level of Persons A, B and C.

EXPERTISE – TECHNICAL, PROFESSIONAL AND BUSINESS KNOW-HOW

This includes both *knowledge* and *professional skills*. The latter overlaps with 'personal skills' but covers those where specific training is needed (as opposed to many personal behaviours).

A simple way of distinguishing levels of expertise is to use a five point scale as follows, for a defined field of knowledge or skill:

A = 'Aware' – can speak the language; knows what is involved

B = 'Basic' – has a rudimentary knowledge of the field

C = 'Competent' – is able to discuss and work competently

D = 'Distinguished' – is one to whom work colleagues turn for advice

E = 'Expert' – is known within and beyond the organisation for his/her expertise

This scale embraces 'practical expertise' just as much as intellectual knowledge.

Philips, the international electronics company, uses a variation of this scale. Their four levels are:

I Foundation

II Practitioner

III Expert

IV Leader

For a particular area of expertise these levels can be expanded to describe what is required at the level.

PERSONAL SKILLS

This area covers personal traits, attitudes and behaviours that are demanded by a role, or which generally characterise 'high performance'. They are undoubtedly important and very individual. They are difficult to assess in an objective and consistent way.

Personal behaviours are described in different ways. Here are some examples taken from various companies' competency frameworks:

- a description of behaviours represented by the competency;

- a description of positive and negative examples of the behaviour;

- hierarchical levels of expectation of the behaviour – typically 3–4 levels from that is expected of all employees to that which is expected of leaders;

- levels of demonstration of the behaviour – but not linked hierarchically.

The third bullet is very common, because it appears to provide a mechanism for promotional assessment. However, there are big questions about the validity of this. Firstly, people do not behave consistently in different situations or at different times. And secondly, although more developed behaviours are to be expected in senior roles, quite junior people can display high levels of some behaviours, given the chance. What does happen as responsibility increases is that new competencies come into play, and others become less important for success.

A useful approach to describing behaviours is to specify a series of specific examples which typify the behaviours at all levels and against which people can be assessed for their strength and consistency.

Assessment can be done in three ways:

- on the job observation, assessed in performance appraisals;

- on the job observation, using feedback instruments such as '360 degree' surveys;

- off the job observation, through targeted assessment centres.

Psychological tests indicate the likelihood of behaviours being shown. But people adapt to situations and they are not such a reliable guide as real observation. They can be useful in recruitment when people are not known internally.

PERSONAL NETWORK – 'KNOW – WHO'

'Who' you know can be as important – if not more so (in some jobs) – than 'what you know'. Many development programmes will have an objective of extending internal or external networks.

Depending on the nature of the organisation's activities, we might have some useful measures such as:

- proportion of customers known personally;

- number of prospects we have based on a personal relationship;

- number of competitors for whom we have a personal link;

- number of relevant officials known;

- number of relevant experts outside the organisation who are known;

- range of contacts in other divisions, departments, countries;

- number of employees with management potential who are known (a measure for a management development manager).

This aspect of capability can be defined in the following ways:

- *Extent* of network:

  - level of contacts (upwards, downwards, sideways)
  - internal/external balance
  - national/international.

- *Variety* of contacts:

  - for example: business, political, government, professional, academic.

- *Quality* and *relevance* of relationships:

  - business acquaintance, business provider, social acquaintance, and so on
  - anticipated speed of response, degree of influence.

An index can be created based on a combination of relevant items above, backed by a five point scale to assess the level of this capability.

PERSONAL VALUES AND ATTITUDES

These two areas shape many of the ways a person behaves. *Values* reflect the ethos a person has about their work and their interaction with the people connected with it. They are rarely changed. *Attitudes* are closely related, and are about how people view their world, what some call *mindsets* or *mental maps*.

In general, we would not measure these separately, as they would be reflected in personal behaviours. However, we may want to assess alignment with company values, and this needs to be done using a 360 degree instrument based on what people observe.

2.6 Human Capital is More Than the Sum of Individuals

The model in Figure 2.1 introduced social and relationship capital as additonal aspects of the overall human capital. Others have used the term 'network capital'. The idea of an organisation is to 'organise' the human capital of individuals in ways which produce more than they would as individual contributors. This leads to the much over-used concept of the 'team' which we have used ourselves above for a group of people with a common purpose. Through working and sharing together people are able to create more value for the organisation than as isolated contributors.

However, we need to recognise that many employees do not work in teams – either because they are literally individual contributors, or because the team they belong to is dysfunctional. How can we take account of this in thinking about the value we have?

'SOCIAL CAPITAL'

People are mobilised into teams to create new intellectual capital. They will want to work together and to share and exchange knowledge and ideas, if they trust each other and are enthused by the work itself. They will find reasons to come together, to seek and give help, and exchange ideas. Building such trust may become an investment in itself – through providing opportunities for people to meet together. Project teams, working groups, seminars for exchange – all of these are activities which promote this social capital.

In Figure 2.3, the final index in the bottom right hand corner could be further multiplied by a 'team effectiveness index'. There are a number of ways this could be created. It could result from a 'pulse survey' done by all members of the team on how well it worked together. They could decide what is important to them and then create a benchmark for periodic checking against. A similar scale to that used for evaluating individual characteristics would be ideal.

An example of such a template would be:

We want to be a group where:

- we all have special skills and knowledge that are known and respected;
- we share new learning from any source;
- we put the team needs above personal preferences;
- we celebrate success and work to learn from our mistakes;
- we help and support each other when needed;
- we always talk positively about the group to others;
- we face up to interpersonal difficulties honestly and constructively.

There are many openly available tools for members of a team to enable mutual assessment and team development. One of the better known is by Dr Meredith Belbin, who identified nine different contributory roles, and his questionnaire identifies the primary and secondary roles of each person. Another is the Team Management Index developed by consultants Charles Margerison and Dick McCann. It groups team members under Explorers, Organisers, Controllers and Advisers and has a 15 minute questionnaire for individuals to complete.

There is evidence that *stability* of teams and workgroups who share common goals is related to continuing performance. People learn how to work (and play) effectively together; they come to share similar values, processes, and trust one another; plan for and strive to common purposes – celebrating or commiserating at their achievements together.

A 'Stability Index' can be created such as:

Average length of time of team members/number of changes in the last year.

The higher the number, the more stable the team. However, stability seems a rare commodity in today's turbulent world. But this index could be combined with the survey evaluation to give the full picture.

'NETWORK OR RELATIONSHIP CAPITAL'

This is about the value of relationships that exist within, and beyond, an organisation that makes it function effectively.

The most obvious and important example is the relationships with customers. Customers can interact with a firm quite impersonally, and many transactions take place without any intervention of a human being other than in a mechanical way. But in many businesses it is the personal touch with members of our organisation that makes such a difference to customer loyalty. It is not surprising that when some salespeople or consultants leave a company, they are made to sign an agreement that they will not take with them any clients for a period of time. It is also well-known how difficult this is to enforce especially where the client has the choice of whom to deal with.

The same principle applies to suppliers. Firms like Marks & Spencer (in its heyday) and Procter & Gamble were always known for seeing suppliers as real partners; for creating relationships with them with a view to maximising their common interest. Frequent visits would take place; joint projects and experiments be entered into, data on quality and product effectiveness shared. The cold, adversarial, clause-enforcing relationship that characterises – by contrast – the construction industry produces no loyalty and a constant and expensive struggle for contracts.

Today's businesses invariably involve a range of partnerships and alliances. They may cover research, marketing, manufacturing, shared technology – a host of opportunities present themselves today. Each has its own network of the key relationships of trust that make it all work.

The variety of external and internal relationships is extensive. Their importance means that a firm should have knowledge of them and be very careful before breaking them. Restructuring in the interests of cost saving often takes no account of such 'capital' and, as a result, precious customer loyalty is lost. Copious written explanations of why the change will be 'better' for the other party are unlikely to make up for the loss of a relationship of trust.

It is one thing to look for the positive side, but equally important is the removal of discord and destructive relationships. Enmity between departments that need to co-operate is all too often found and is clearly a liability. Job rotation, inter-departmental 'team building' sessions, secondments – these are some of the ways of creating trust and better working together.

How should this form of capital be measured? Relationships are always between individuals and so, as appropriate, we suggest it should be taken into account in the evaluation of each employee leading to the 'personal value index'.

It should be noted that organisational restructuring is a major source of the *destruction* of the above types of intellectual capital.

2.7 Case Studies in Valuing Human Capital and Linking with Performance

Since the core methodology described in Section 2.5 was originally developed, we have learnt some lessons in its application:

- It is always good to build from where organisations are, despite imperfections. So if they have measurement systems that work reasonably well it is best to build on them rather than abandon them.

- This means using the language in common use to describe the characteristics of people and their contribution.

Case Study One – a Large Retail Bank

This was part of a project to build a 'human capital monitor' (see Section 4.6) for customer service officers (CSO), the name given to the retail bank staff. We describe here how we looked at the value of the people. This is a summary of the section on people value, which resulted from extensive consultation with line managers and focus groups with staff representatives, and utilised existing frameworks as much as possible. Note that, instead of using a 0–2 scale, a points system is used to provide a set of benchmarks of expectations.

The Asset Value of People

The CSO Value components were as follows:

- Business Capability – (skills and knowledge)
- Personal Qualities – (competencies/behaviours)
- Performance – the achievement of objectives under 5 balanced scorecard headings.

Line managers assessed each of these components, collecting evidence of what knowledge and skills have been learnt and applied, how the behaviours required to do the job are being demonstrated and what outputs are achieved. This information was collected through observation and feedback from staff and customers.

Once this information has been collected managers then assessed each CSO against agreed performance scales for each of the components. This resulted in a points 'value' being obtained which was then compared to benchmark standards to determine what level of development was required and in what area.

Business Capability

The generic skills and knowledge a CSO needed were defined as follows:

- Oral Communication

  Uses clear and concise speech to put message across effectively.

- Written Communication

  Selects appropriate information to complete standard letters and application forms. Produces accurate and legible written work at all times.

- Interactions with others

  Uses effective questioning and listening skills to extract all relevant information and identify needs.

- Self-/Work Organisation

  Uses straightforward personal planning to organise own work effectively. Knows where to find things and adheres to deadlines.

- Keyboard/Software Applications

  Uses a keyboard; understanding functions for producing a range of outputs. Carries out basic day to day management of machine under own control, for example, security.

- Organisational Awareness

  Has an understanding of the main activities of own business unit/ area, together with their role within the bank's vision and values.

In the assessment a line manager determined the level of application of these skills using the following assessment:

Level Attained	Description	Points Scored
A	Aware – of what is expected but little experience to date in applying the skills	1 Point
B	Basic knowledge – has received training and has some experience to date	2 Points
C	Competent – is able to apply this knowledge fully in their job	3 Points
D	Distinguished – is known for being particularly knowledgeable and experienced in this area of knowledge	4 Points
E	Expert – knows the area completely, trains and coaches others	5 Points

A benchmark of expected achievement was set depending on how long the CSO had been in their role as follows:

Generic Skills	New Entrant		1–5 Yrs Level		>5 Yrs Level	
Oral Communication	C	3 Points	D	4 Points	E	5 Points
Written Communication	C	3 Points	D	4 Points	E	5 Points
Interactions with others	B	2 points	C	3 Points	E	5 Points
Self Work/Organisation	B	2 Points	C	3 Points	E	5 Points
Software/Keyboard	C	3 Points	D	4 Points	E	5 Points
Organisational Awareness	B	2 Points	C	3 Points	E	5 Points
TOTAL POINTS		15 Points		21 Points		30 Points

Specific Skills

As well as the generic skills, CSOs also require specific technical knowledge, and these were assessed by accredited achievements. The system had three levels, each recognised with five points.

The benchmarks for achievements are:

- New Entrant = Achieves Levels 1 and 2 (10 points)
- 1–5 Years = Achieves all 3 Levels (15 points)
- 5 Years = Achieves all 3 Levels (15 points)

Personal Qualities

These were as follows:

Providing Excellent Customer Service

Exceeds the expectations of external customers through the quality of customer service provided, meeting their needs and demonstrating the added value of the service provided.

Attention to Detail

Ensures that information is correctly processed and that work complies with relevant internal/external rules, procedures and regulatory requirements: checks work and corrects mistakes promptly.

Team Working

Works co-operatively and productively with others; openly exchanges information and supporting colleagues from around the organisation to achieve business goals.

Self-motivation

Puts personal energy and commitment into completing a piece of work and doing it to the best of their ability: looks for ways to meet and exceed challenging performance standards and targets, setting personal goals at or beyond business expectations.

Adapting to Change and Uncertainty

Improves personal effectiveness in response to changes at work by identifying new learning and self-development opportunities that arise from the changes and working towards them.

Delivering Business Results

Focuses attention and resources upon meeting agreed business targets, priorities and objectives. For the service role:

- Analyses customers' real needs and concerns and produces simple solutions, conducts customer research and provides leads to other staff.

Once again to determine the level of application of these behaviours the following scale has been developed:

Level Attained	Description	Points Scored
1	Fails to show appropriate behaviour under normal circumstances	1
2	Shows behaviour, but not consistently so does not always achieve a positive effect	2
3	Shows appropriate behaviour under normal circumstances and typically achieves a positive effect	3
4	Shows appropriate behaviour with conviction and to a high standard under most circumstances	4

| 5 | Shows appropriate behaviour consistently and to a very high standard even under pressure – an example for others to follow | 5 |

The benchmarks for personal qualities are:

Personal Qualities		New Entrant		1–5 Yrs Level		>5 Yrs Level
Providing Excellent Customer Service	3	3 Points	4	4 Points	5	5 Points
Attention to Detail	3	3 Points	5	5 Points	5	5 Points
Team Working	3	3 points	4	4 Points	5	5 Points
Self-Motivation	3	3 Points	4	4 Points	5	5 Points
Adapting to Change and Uncertainty	3	3 Points	4	4 Points	5	5 Points
Delivering Business Results	3	3 Points	4	4 Points	5	5 Points
TOTAL POINTS		**18 Points**		**25 Points**		**30 Points**

Performance

All CSOs have objectives set in five different 'balanced scorecard areas'. Performance in each area was assessed using the following scale:

Level Attained	Description	Points Achieved
1	Contribution significantly below others in the group and requires regular supervision	1
2	Generally acceptable and balanced level of contribution but not always consistent	2
3	An acceptable contributor, well-balanced performance	3
4	Consistently a positive contributor, with some particular areas of strength	4
5	An outstanding and consistent contributor to all the key measures	5

The benchmarks for performance were:

		New Entrant		1–5 Yrs Level		>5 Yrs Level
Service Quality	2	2 Points	3	3 Points	4	4 Points
Franchise Growth	2	2 Points	3	3 Points	4	4 Points
Risk	2	2 Points	3	3 Points	4	4 Points
Contribution	2	2 points	3	3 Points	4	4 Points
People Development	2	2 Points	3	3 Points	4	4 Points
TOTAL POINTS		**10 Points**		**15 Points**		**20 Points**

Value Components – Benchmarks

The table below summarises the level expected for each of the value components for different levels of experience. This is a target to work towards, and the line manager and the CSO worked together to put a specific development plan together that would help each CSO reach the required level.

	New Entrant	1–5 Years	>5 Years
6 Generic Skills	15 points	21 points	26 points
6 Personal Qualities	18 points	25 points	30 points
5 Performance Categories	10 points	15 points	20 points
Achieving Technical Accreditation	10 points	15 points	15 points
TOTAL VALUE	**53 points**	**76 points**	**91 points**

The maximum number of points that could be achieved was:

6 Generic Skills (6×5 points)	30 points
6 Personal Qualities/Competencies (6×5 points)	30 points
Knowledge Achievement – STAR 1–3 (15 points)	15 points
5 Performance Categories of BSC (5×5 points)	25 points
TOTAL VALUE	**100 points**

Electronic Reporting of Value Components

Once all CSOs were assessed a pictorial representation was possible as detailed below:

	Length in Role	Points Achieved	Required Benchmark	% Achievement
Julie	1	45	53	85
Mary	2	60	76	79
Jo	2	50	76	66
Henry	1	52	53	98
Barry	3	45	76	59
Suzie	4	89	76	117
Mark	3	78	76	103
Alan	2	70	76	92
Jane	1	60	53	113
Laura	5	88	91	97
Joseph	6	92	91	101

Case Study Two – a Large International Engineering Company

This company looked at its Leadership Group, defined as the top 650 leaders for whom data was maintained and monitored at Headquarters. It decided that the key areas of value were as follows:

- Contribution plus potential (weighted 50 per cent) – this was used because of an existing regular assessment process which used a colour coded evaluation of both factors.
- Leadership capability (weighted 15 per cent) – five competencies are used to underpin an integrated performance and development programme. These were:
    - Developing others
    - Continuously improving
    - Working together
    - Focusing on the customer
    - Achieving high performance
- Business knowledge and experience (weighted 25 per cent) – this was one area requiring a measurement tool to be set up.
- Personal mobility (weighted 10 per cent) – data on this was obtainable from the succession planning review process.

Case Study Three – University Support Staff

This case concerned a particular faculty group in the university, and was aimed at 100, or so, support employees, providing administrative and technical support to faculty and students. Through dialogue and focus groups, the key 'qualities' that linked most to high performance were identified as:

- service delivery
- job knowledge
- communications and relationships
- proactivity
- ready availability of materials and equipment.

These were broken down into behaviours and questionnaires were devised, using a five point scale, which were then given to undergraduate and postgraduate students, to research assistants, and faculty to assess on the support teams they interacted with.

Correlations were sought with performance criteria such as measured service provision, compliance with procedures, complaints and stock availability levels.

The study also looked at engagement, as discussed in the next chapter.

Case Study Four – Air Industry Service Provider

This study was conducted internally to identify if there was a performance enhancement of 200 general managers based on their behavioural profile.

The HR Director explained: 'Of four typical dimensions of human behaviour – values/principles, skills, temperament and coping behaviours – it is only the latter that we are interested in. It is a high predictor of performance and is where the value lies for us'.

The HR function designed a competency and behavioural model by creating internally validated behavioural profiles demonstrated by high performers. Detailed behavioural interviews were conducted for members in the population around 13 competencies to ascertain the best fit between the model, the person and the predicted outputs the business needed.

The company asserts that that an overall productivity gain of 48 per cent is possible if they could replace all 'average people' with high-performers, and that 40 per cent of this is driven by behaviour alone. Figure 2.6 shows what they found as the 'corridor' between the best and lowest performers and the plotted line is the average of those that had been assessed.

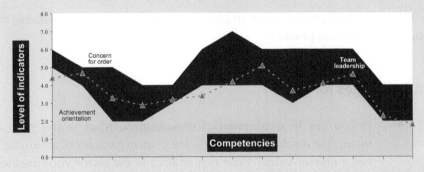

Figure 2.6   Example of behavioural skill profiles and performance 'opportunities'

2.8 Summary

The origin of the term 'human capital' comes from the analysis of intangible assets, which in today's organisations generally form the majority of the value of an organisation. Various analysts have broken down these intangibles into those which form part of the organisation (structural) and that which is inherent in the organisation's people (human).

'Human capital management' is an approach to managing people with a value mindset – focusing on the value they have and the value they produce. It necessitates an approach to measurement of both of these types of value.

Valuing people financially has not become widely used, although there are examples of where it is done at least at the enterprise level. It is always a summation of individuals – and what is more useful in practice is to understand what makes people valuable and to assess the strength of the resulting components.

An approach to categorising, assessing and presenting these components is suggested, and that by documenting them systematically, a number of benefits accrue. It provides a picture of value in a group for all to see, and gives a planning tool to focus recruitment, development, retention, restructuring and, where necessary, exiting.

In addition to individual value, we looked at the additional value that arises from people working together effectively – which can only be measured by perceptions, but is generally strongly experienced for good or ill by the people themselves.

Finally, we looked at some examples of putting the concept of 'valuing our people as assets' into practice.

2.8 Challenges for Action

- If you are in a commercial organisation, what is the ratio of intangible assets to book value for your organisation, assuming it has a market value? How is it relative to the sector your business is in?

- Is the concept of people as value creating assets really understood by senior management? Could they draw the 'value creating chains' across the organisation?

- If someone said 'of course people are valuable, but there is no way they can be valued' – how would you respond?

- Take three different groups of employees – say front-line, functional specialists, and middle managers. What would be the factors you would isolate as the real value creators for each group? What weighting would you give to them? How could they be assessed using existing and additional tools?

- How would you propose to assess the additional value (over and above that of the individuals themselves) from a great team?

- Can you see any obstacles in building a regular 'value review' of employees? How could they be overcome?

2.10 References and Further Reading

Baron, A., and Armstrong, M.. (2007). *Human Capital Management – Achieving Added Value Through People*. London: Kogan Page.

Infosys Annual Report. (2009). Available at: www.infosys.com

Kinnie, N., Swart, J., Lund, M., Norris, S., Snell, S., and Kang, S-C. (2006). *Managing People and Knowledge in Professional Service Firms*. CIPD Research report.

Lev, B. (2000). *Intangibles: Managing, Measuring, Reporting*. New York: Stern School of Business.

Lev, B., and Schwartz, A. (1971). *On the Use of the Economic Concept of Human Capital in Financial Statements*. The Accounting Review. January 1971.

Mayo, A.J. (2001). *The Human Value of the Enterprise – Valuing People as Assets, Measuring, Managing, Monitoring*. London: Nicholas Brealey.

Robinson, D., Hooker, H., and Mercer, M. (2008). *Human Capital Measurement – Issues and Case Studies*. Brighton: Institute of Employment Studies.

Scott-Jackson, W.B. and Tajer, R. (2005). *Getting the Basics Right: A Guide to Measuring the Value of Your Workforce*. London: Chartered Management Institute.

Stewart, T. (1997). *Intellectual Capital*. London: Nicholas Brealey.

Sveiby, K.E. (1997). *The New Organisational Wealth.* San Francisco: Berrett-Koehler.

Theeke, H.A. (2005). *Human Resource Accounting Transmission: Shifting from Failure to a Future. Journal of Human Resource Costing and Accounting,* volume 9(1).

Thomson, K. (1998). *Emotional Capital: Maximising the Intangible Assets at the Heart of Brand and Business Success.* Oxford: Capstone.

Tottenham Hotspur Football Club Annual Report. (2008). Available at: www.tottenhamhotspur.com

www.interbrand.com

www.belbin.com

www.valuebasedmanagement.net/books_lev_intangibles.html

www.12manage.com/methods_margerison_team_management_profile.html

3

Motivation, Engagement and Performance

Employees are in a special position in an organisation. They are the means of adding value to stakeholders, yet are stakeholders themselves. They follow the same rules of 'equilibrium' as in Figure 1.2 – and either side can withdraw from a stakeholder relationship. An organisation has to keep that relationship sound with all the employees it wants to keep; this is the foundation for motivation and engagement which is the strongest contributor to performance.

People bring their personal human capital in all its diversity and we should nurture and develop it. They also bring their own level of intrinsic interest in doing their job and doing it well. It is the working environment in its many aspects that adds to or subtracts from the motivation they start with. The productivity we discussed in Chapter 1 depends, more than anything else, on the extent to which we are able to create an environment that enables people to give the maximum, and enjoy doing so.

3.1 Human Capital and Stakeholders

We have argued that in looking at performance and productivity it is logical to consider the whole human effort being applied to the organisation. This includes subcontracted employees and consultants as well as those on the 'payroll'. But when we consider the stakeholder relationship there are some significant differences. All parties give value in terms of time, knowledge, skills and experience, and all receive both financial and non-financial benefits. This is illustrated in Table 3.1.

Table 3.1   The value exchange between people and an organisation

Type of human capital	Nature of the value offered to the organisation	Financial value received	Non-financial value received
Contracted employees	Knowledge, skills, experience, contacts, values, commitment. Potential	Salaries; bonuses, benefits	Wide range of possible categories
Temporary or subcontracted employees	Specific capabilities, no long-term obligations	Fees	Re-applicable experience; training (possibly)
Consultants	Specific knowledge and skills; cross-company benchmarking; best practice; reputation of the firm; flexibility	Fees	Relationships. Reputation, prestige. Learning; re-applicable methodologies

For subcontractors and consultants the *internal* motivation to do a good job is likely to be stronger because the 'stakeholder equilibrium' is more one-sided than for employees. In other words, they can be let go more easily. The desire to secure the financial value generally outweighs any dissatisfaction with how they are being treated. As suppliers, they generally hold the mentality that 'the customer is right, even when he is not'. For employees, however, the situation is more complex; the commitment on both sides is more complete.

3.2 Employees as Stakeholders

People can be thought of as employees at every level of an organisation, unless they are the actual owners of a business. However, it is often helpful – just as it is for customers – to distinguish the varying interests of diverse groups of employees. Senior managers will look for different kinds of 'value' from the organisation compared to staff at lower levels. As one or more stakeholder groups, they have an interest in the success of the organisation, and they offer and receive value.

The general principle of Figure 1.2, however, applies to all. People 'offer' their 'personal human capital' – in the case of full employees exclusively to the one organisation – in exchange for an agreed combination of financial and non-financial value received in return for their time and effort. They become both an asset – able to generate value for others – and a stakeholder in their own right. When a deal is struck, the financial side is contractual, whereas the non-financial is more in the form of 'reasonable expectations'. In HR literature, this part is sometimes called the 'psychological contract'.

Nevertheless, the 'tipping point' for an employee – which tells them that the value exchange is no longer satisfactory –may be from either the financial package or an element of the non-financial. The financial package includes the mix of salaries, benefits, future pension, bonuses, and maybe equity in the firm if it is available. In the days of defined benefit pensions, basic salary was all important as it was (and still is for public sector employees) the foundation of a pension. More flexibility has come in to this arena during this century, and the total mix may weigh more than the base salary. The package, however, is a key threshold at the time of hiring, but is not necessarily sufficient to clinch the signing of the contract. Each individual is different, but some of the following are likely to be important to them:

- opportunities for personal growth and career development;

- challenging and interesting work;

- responsibility;

- location and ease of access;

- job security;

- work/life balance;

- equipment and resources otherwise not accessible to them;

- being associated with an organisation of high repute;

- status and self-esteem;

- recognition – by the person's managers, or by peers, or even publicly;

- interesting colleagues to work with;

- a satisfying and stimulating environment;

- social events;

- opportunities for travel and the perks that may go with it.

Table 3.2 shows a simple exercise I often use with managers which always illustrates: a) what an important part the non-financial elements play (typically 60–80 per cent); b) how much difference there is between individual profiles, and c) how dangerous it is to assume the mix of my employees is the same as 'mine'. This is the essence of the 'psychological contract'.

Table 3.2   **Value mix to an employee**

FINANCIAL	Points	NON-FINANCIAL (drawn from the above list)	Points
Salaries			
Pension			
Other benefits (financial)			
Bonuses			
TOTAL (=100)			

In exchange for your exclusive services, the organisation provides a combination of financial value and non-financial value. Working on the basis of 100 points, how would you distribute them between the different kinds of value you look for? (The test for ranking is to what extent you would consider leaving if the factor became unsatisfactory to you.)

Each factor that is important to an individual may become the tipping point in breaking the stakeholder relationship, unless a perception of fair value exchange is restored. Employees in a state of dissatisfaction are naturally less likely to be motivated and engaged than those experiencing a 'fair exchange'.

Employees at Accenture, the consultancy, are asked to complete something very similar to Table 3.2, known as a 'Personal Engagement List' and to rank a range of factors such as reward and recognition and quality of life. They then discuss the results with a 'career counsellor' assigned to them by the organisation and action plans are put into place to close any gaps between importance and satisfaction.

In summer 2005 Towers Perrin, a global consultancy, surveyed 85,000 people across 16 countries for their Global Workforce Study: they found that what attracted people to an organisation was very consistent globally. For the UK, the top ten 'attraction drivers' included four financial factors (salary, performance based pay, benefits package, and retirement benefits) and six non-financial (work/life balance, opportunities for advancement, challenging work, learning and development opportunities, reputation of the employer, and work variety).

Professor Lynda Gratton of London Business School in her book *The Democratic Enterprise* provides an interesting angle to employee expectations. She argues that the modern employee looks for – and the more experienced they are, the more they seek these – three forms of personal capital which build themselves as individuals. The first is that they continuously extend their 'intellectual capital' – through training, knowledge sharing and experience. They also expand their 'social capital' as every new post and organisation provides new contacts and networks. Finally, through the processes of work itself – and from interaction with and feedback from people around them – they grow emotionally both in 'emotional intelligence skills' and in personal resilience. This all rings very true for myself and is a significant part of the value I have received from various organisations along the way.

For readers interested in a more technical approach, Thomas Davenport's *Human Capital* is recommended. Davenport (then at Towers Perrin) followed similar thinking to our 'stakeholder equilibrium'. He postulated that an employee loans their human capital to an organisation for as long as they get a good enough return. (Naturally this free market approach assumes a ready and open labour market for the employee's services – not always the case.) Davenport analyses, in detail, the sources of value to employees in four categories: financial rewards, intrinsic fulfilment, growth opportunities, and recognition. He quotes one US study which showed how managers under-emphasised involvement (in relation to what employees saw as important), recognition and interesting work (despite Herzberg's findings about this as far back as 1968), and over-emphasised wages, promotion and working conditions.

He uses the technique of utility curves to plot the effect on perceived value by employees (their willingness to invest time, effort and loyalty) achieved through investment in various areas of HR intervention. Thus – in line with Herzberg – the curve for higher and higher salaries levels off above that which is regarded as 'the fair market rate'. In the case of 'intrinsic fulfilment' (challenge, freedom, fun, lifestyle) the 'commonly found' curve shows a rapid upwards growth after a slow start – small investments produce little effect but significant ones have a major impact. He provides a persuasive case for organisations to build up their own utility curves from experience, thus guiding their investment in people to maximum effect based on the optimum trade-off.

'Individuals need the freedom to build ...'

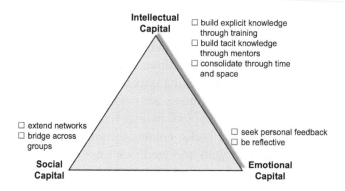

(Lynda Gratton, The Democratic Enterprise. 2004)

Figure 3.1   Growth of personal capital

3.3 Satisfaction, Motivation, Commitment and Engagement

These are all words that are associated with employees' feelings about their work and organisation. For many years the best employers rigorously and extensively checked how their employees were feeling, shared the results, committed themselves to take action, and benchmarked their results with other similar employers. This was typically an annual exercise. (I have been continually amazed by the way some organisations find excuses not to test their employees' feelings because of fear of the results.)

There are a number of questions to be raised about the traditional 'employee satisfaction surveys':

- Often they are 'one size for all' questionnaires which rarely ask how *important* each question is to the respondent – they survey many items that may not be important to individuals even though they are completed.

- The conditions of motivation or otherwise change much more frequently than one year (and many organisations do them even less frequently). If we are testing feelings on one day only, how representative is it?

- They measure stand-alone feelings and are not connected with actual behaviour.

- There is evidence that groups of highly satisfied employees may not be linked with high performance. Their satisfaction may be due to a comfortable and undemanding work environment.

On page 34 we noted the key work of Herzberg, and his distinction between 'hygiene factors' and 'motivators'. The factors he identified have been validated many times – including by myself asking many managerial groups the same questions as he did. Key motivators were achievement, recognition, work itself, responsibility, personal growth and advancement. Most of these are in the first line manager's hands. 'Salary' was marginally on the hygiene side. For the 'hygiene factors', even a small amount below the threshold of acceptability can be significantly irritating and have a negative effect on motivation.

Different groups of employees will have their own priorities on both sides, and we need to find them out. And the conclusion is clear – we need to know what any potential areas of discontent are speedily and ensure they are dealt with, if we want to achieve real motivation.

Figure 3.2 illustrates the connection between the various words. It says there are two starting points on the road to engagement. One is that, by and large, dissatisfaction does not exist. If it does, then we need to deal with it as a priority. The second starting point is the 'intrinsic motivation' people bring to the task. This varies with roles and with personality – but characterised in the diagram with 'I love my job and I want to do it well'. Good recruitment is the key here. This is then subjected to 'extrinsic motivation' – a bundle of factors that may strengthen or, sadly, diminish the intrinsic starting point. With strong factors all round we have a good chance of achieving commitment and engagement, two words that seem genuinely interchangeable.

WHAT IS ENGAGEMENT?

The term came into use with Marcus Buckingham and Curt Coffman's now famous book *First Break All the Rules: What the World's Greatest Managers Do Differently*. They used the terms 'engaged', 'not engaged', and 'actively disengaged' to distinguish levels of commitment. Buckingham's team ran massive number-crunching studies based on the Gallup Company's access to millions of pieces of data from opinion surveys. He came up with 12 core questions, which if answered positively, had a strong link to positive engagement. He then researched how these 'Q12' scores shaped business results. 'The link between people and performance was vivid. The most "engaged" workplaces (those in the top 25 per cent of Q12 scores) were 50 per cent more likely to have lower turnover, 56 per cent more likely to have higher-than-average customer loyalty, 38 per cent more likely to have above-average productivity, and 27 per cent more likely to report higher profitability'.

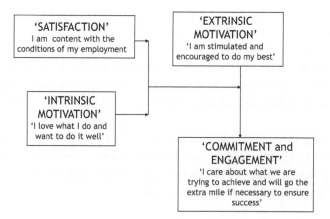

Figure 3.2   Satisfaction, motivation, commitment and engagement

The Corporate Leadership Council, a not-for-profit consultancy, produced a report in 2004 called *Driving Performance and Retention Through Employee Engagement*. They offered three sample definitions:

- Engagement is a positive emotional connection to an employee's work.

- Engagement is affective, normative, and continual commitment.

- Engaged employees are inspired to go above and beyond the call of duty to help meet business goals.

In their study of 50,000 employees globally; 13 per cent were disaffected, 76 per cent neither strongly one way nor the other, and 11 per cent came through as 'highly committed'. They distinguished two types of engagement – 'rational' ('what this organisation is doing is also in my self interest') and 'emotional' ('valuing, enjoying and believing in what I do').

Tim Miller, with Director, Property, Research & Assurance at Standard Chartered Bank, defines an engaged employee as:

- is 100 per cent committed to their role and more productive as a result;

- enjoys the challenge of their work every day;

- is clear on their role and expectations;

- is in a role which uses their skills and strengths;

- applies discretionary effort to the firm.

For Greg Aitken, of the Royal Bank of Scotland, an engaged employee not only stays with the business, but actively contributes to business success. According to him, engagement manifests itself through:

- what employees say – they consistently speak positively about the RBS group to colleagues, potential employees and customers;

- increased retention – employees have an intense desire to be a member of the RBS group;

- the extra effort employees exert in behaviours that contribute to success.

PricewaterhouseCoopers Saratoga, a world leader in metrics consultancy, utilise an 'engagement and commitment matrix'. It is based on six levels of attitude from employees:

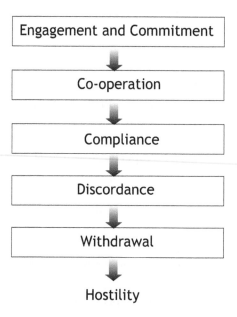

Figure 3.3   **PricewaterhouseCoopers Saratoga's states of engagement and commitment**

These levels are correlated with time usage, work output, attitude to products/services and identification with the organisation.

Kate Feather of consultancy PeopleMetrics, in a 2008 article, summarised engagement well. It is:

- *retention*: I want to stay;

- *effort*: I will give more than is required;

- *advocacy*: I will recommend my company;

- *passion*: I care about what we are trying to do.

In 2008, the UK Government commissioned David Mcleod and Nita Clarke to study engagement in the UK, and this was published in 2009 and is known as the 'Mcleod Review'. By this date most organisations had latched on to the importance of engaged employees so it did not shed a tremendous amount of new light. However, it was very thoroughly researched and is an excellent summary and reference on the subject.

3.4 The Nature of Motivation

We distinguished in Figure 3.2 between 'intrinsic' and 'extrinsic' motivation; the final motivation level that leads to engagement is the sum of the two. The distinction is perhaps best summed up by the often heard statement 'I love this job, BUT....' What we are calling 'intrinsic', is a combination of the following:

- a love of, even passion for, the kind of work my job requires;

- caring about 'doing a good job' – part of a personal value system;

- an internal drive to be successful and make progress.

The process which conditions whether we have people with such 'intrinsic' motivation, or drive from within, is recruitment. We may focus rightly on skills, competencies and experience – but can we assess whether a person will really share our values and get excitement from what the job entails? That is a tough requirement for many mundane jobs, but a constant challenge is how we can build in the *potential* for such excitement into the way we structure jobs. Frederick Herzberg, mentioned above, devoted much of his later work to promoting 'job enrichment', as he seized on the significance of the challenge of work to people.

Professor John Hunt, while at London Business School, developed the 'goal theory' of motivation. Building from Maslow and others, the basis is that every individual has needs to be satisfied but the mix of these needs is different. He developed an instrument called the 'Work Interests Schedule', commercially available, to enable people to self-assess their profile, based on the following areas of need:

- money and lifestyle – split into financial motivation and desire to avoid stress;

- structure – split into clarity about what is required; and avoidance of risk;

- relationships – split into social and team needs;

- recognition and acknowledgement;

- power – control and influence over others;

- independence and autonomy;

- personal growth and challenge.

These provide 10 factors, and the average manager profile is shown in Figure 3.4.

While deep-seated and meaningful, goals both change over time, and can directly conflict with each other. For example, my need for security may marginally outweigh my still important need for autonomy; so I may talk with regret about how, if I didn't have to keep up my mortgage repayments, I would definitely set up my own business.

Different job types fall naturally into these categories. National cultures show variations too in their average profile – some 44,000 respondents have now been analysed. 'High achievers' are strong in the last three areas, and a person's profile varies with age and situation in life.

Clearly a key aspect of 'intrinsic' motivation is the extent to which a job and its surrounding environment stimulate and excite a particular individual. If they do not, whatever we try to do 'extrinsically' is unlikely to succeed in any significant way in building high engagement.

WORK INTERESTS SCHEDULE

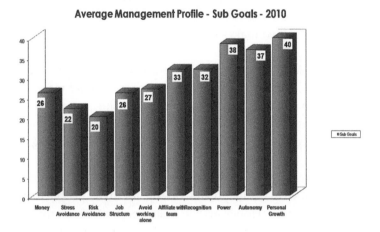

Average Management Profile - Sub Goals - 2010

(John Hunt)

Figure 3.4   Average manager motivational profile from Hunts' *Work Interests Schedule* based on 44,000 results

Source: © John W Hunt, London, 2011.

EXTRINSIC MOTIVATION

There are many factors within the work environment that impact a person's motivation, positively or negatively. There is a tendency to place this burden all on the shoulders of a manager, but it is more complex than that. If I am a non-manager, there are three sets of influences that impact me, and if a manager, four.

The Organisation Itself – The most potent influence on the hygiene factors. How much do I agree with its strategies and plans? Am I comfortable with its values and ethics, both spoken and unspoken? Do I feel its reward and promotion systems are fair? How do I feel about its policies and HR practices? Does its bureaucracy frustrate me? Do 'they' seem to value our work? There may be things that permanently irritate, and from time to time most people experience short-term frustrations.

Internal or *External Customers* – the majority of employees are doing things for other people outside of their own department. Those on the 'front-line' regularly receive feedback from customers, either positive or negative, and it can make a great difference to their motivation. To be continually berated for reasons beyond one's own control does not lead to job enjoyment. On the other hand, being clearly valued makes it all worthwhile.

The Team Below Me – if I am a manager, the team I have around me makes a big difference. True, it can be argued that 'my team is what I make it' – both in terms of who is in it and how they act as a team, but life is rarely so simple. The newly appointed manager usually inherits the group; and its willingness to co-operate, innovate, accept change and help one another makes a big difference.

My Manager – usually has the greatest influence, but we should remember that in these days of virtual and global working, for many people that influence is not as direct as it was. However, the manager controls many of the areas that have the most effect on people. He or she influences (even if not having total control) the nature of the work itself, communication, listening to ideas, training and development, creating team spirit, recognition, feedback, setting targets, availability of resources, and the working environment. The manager also represents and pleads the cause of his people, where appropriate, to the organisation, or to customers. There is always a tendency, I have observed, for managers to be over conscious of constraints on what they can and cannot do, and underestimate the degrees of freedom they have. Small things can make a big difference, both positively and negatively, to motivation.

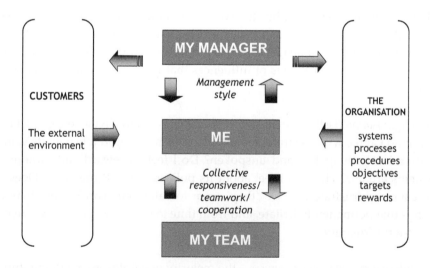

Figure 3.5   A model of extrinsic motivation

3.5 Measuring Engagement

It is important, as always in measurement, to be clear about which measures are of *outcomes* and those that are of the *inputs* which drive those outcomes.

The ultimate outcome that people are engaged will be in the outputs of value to the appropriate stakeholders. We will see the effects of non-engagement on, for example, customer satisfaction, on scrap and rework rates, and on productivity. However, the level of engagement is a vital contributor to that and the evidence that people are engaged is worth measuring in its own right.

We have the following choices, and we need to utilise as many of them as possible to get a balanced picture:

RESIGNATION/ATTRITION RATES

Ultimately disaffected people vote with their feet. This measure is more one of *non*-engagement rather than positive engagement. Nevertheless, it is important data in its own right. Consolidated attrition rates over many types of staff or functions do not tell us much. Nor do rates which are not broken down into the reasons for people leaving – data which seems very hard to come by in many organisations.

We need to know staff loss rates for 'job families' which represent a discrete section of the labour market. This would go along with division by area or department. Typical job families are shown in Table 3.3. Each resignation needs to be classified into two categories which can be subdivided; involuntary (IV per cent), for example, death, retirement, fired, redundant, and voluntary (V per cent). It is particularly important to have sub-categories of the voluntary group. We are especially interested in people resigning for some dissatisfaction – their work, their boss, company direction, and so on. It is best to quote figures as three or six monthly moving averages and to plot trends over one or two years.

The problem is that we are often not told the true reason why someone is leaving as they do not want to leave on bad terms. Many organisations find the 'post-exit' discussion more helpful – at about three months after they have left. It is also important to plot resignations against length of service as this often gives important clues.

Table 3.3   Data on resignations

Job Family	IV%	V%	Target V%	Analysis of Reasons for Voluntary Leavers
Senior managers				
Middle managers				
Team leaders				
Senior professional staff				
Junior professional staff				
Support staff				
Front-line sales and service				
Operators				
Specialist categories				

The question is whether voluntary resignations are exceeding an 'acceptable' level. It is a matter of judgement as to what that is – but to be better than the average for the sector would be a good start. To have a level of attrition that is too low may be unhealthy also and will not necessarily signify engagement. It may imply comfort, inertia, or the existence of disincentives to leave (such as security).

ABSENTEEISM RATES

As for the above, excessive absenteeism is more an indicator of non-engagement than the level of commitment we are after. Nevertheless, it is reasonable to assume that a high level of people not coming to work is telling us something. The average level of *physical* incapability to work is about two and a half days per annum – for many it is zero and others much longer. Above that level, we need to assess whether it is indicating non-engagement or not. There is no doubt that stress related absence has increased considerably – as has the definition and types of stress incurred. Busy, committed people enthusiastic for their work suffer stresses but generally have more resilience to them. It is also the case in some public sector organisations that a certain number of 'sick days' is regarded as a right – and is in effect extra holiday.

The Chartered Institute of Personnel and Development (CIPD) regularly surveys the state of absenteeism in the UK: its 2009 report stated that the average days lost was running at 9.7 (4.3 per cent) days pa (*per annum*) in the public sector, 9.4 (4.1 per cent) in the non-profit sector, and 6.4 (2.9 per cent) in the private sector. The UK Government publishes such data by civil service department in association with RED Scientific, a research firm in Hampshire. In 2007, the highest was the Driving Vehicle and License Agency (DVLA) with 18.7 days pa, and the lowest was the Cabinet Office at 3.3 days. Studying the causes of the difference would be interesting indeed.

The Great Place to Work Institute compared absence rates for organisations listed as 'great places to work', and the labour market generally, across European countries and this is shown in Figure 3.6. UK figures look quite favourable compared to some other countries, but the difference a motivated workforce makes is substantial. This has a clear economic effect which we discuss in the next chapter.

ABSENTEEISM IN EUROPE – AVERAGE vs BEST WORKPLACES

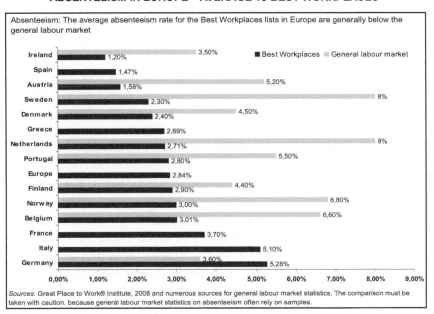

Figure 3.6   The difference engagement makes to absenteeism

Some organisations use a formula known as 'The Bradford Factor'. This emphasises the undesirability of numerous short-term absences which is relevant to the engagement issue. It is calculated by multiplying:

$$S \times S \times D = \text{Bradford points score}$$

where S is the number of spells of absence in the last 52 weeks and D is the number of days' absence during the last 52 weeks.

So, for example, for employees with 10 days absence in one year, differently distributed, the score can vary enormously:

1 absence of 10 days is 10 points ($1 \times 1 \times 10$)

5 absences of two days each is 250 points ($5 \times 5 \times 10$)

10 days of one day each is 1000 points ($10 \times 10 \times 10$)

Long absences generally mean there is a real sickness problem, although increasingly it may be billed as stress caused by some aspect of the work or the working environment.

SURVEYS OF EMPLOYEE PERCEPTIONS AND FEELINGS

The (usually) annual, lengthy, one-size-fits-all survey has its benefits in 'dip sticking' how employees feel about strategies (most have little interest!), company policies and practices, recent changes, and so on. However, motivation/engagement is more immediate and the trend, rightly, is to use shorter, more frequent 'pulse surveys' aimed at this alone. This has been strongly stimulated by the result of Marcus Buckingham's work at Gallup and what has come to be known as the 'Gallup Q12', now copyrighted. However, the 12 questions that Buckingham found made the most difference to engagement are actually 'input' questions and the Gallup assumption (from their research) is that a high, positive score correlates with engagement. These questions are so much in use today that we list them in Table 3.4.

The correlation between a high Q12 score and performance has been repeatedly shown, so one has to recognise its value. However, there are two issues with Q12:

- It benefits from simplicity, consistency and therefore benchmarking – but suffers from the assumption that all employees are actually driven by the same 12 issues.

- It does not actually measure the engagement level – only the inputs which are assumed to lead to the desired output.

With regard to the first point, there is undoubtedly a core set of questions based on motivation theory that will apply to 75 per cent of the people. But if one ran focus groups for a group of sea based oil exploration engineers, or for a group of call centre operators, or for a group of retail store managers, it is certain that they would add quite different issues to the questions about 'significant motivation' and 'significant demotivation'. These additional questions could be the *killer* questions. My own company researched postmen/women and found a very different profile to Gallup's Q12.

So in the interests of simplicity, as always, we have to be aware of false assumptions.

The second point is of greater concern because we do need some absolute measures of the existence of engagement or not.

Table 3.4   Gallup Q12 engagement survey

• Do I know what is expected of me at work?
• Do I have the materials and equipment I need to do my work right?
• At work, do I have the opportunity to do what I do best every day?
• In the last seven days have I received recognition or praise for good work?
• Does my supervisor, or someone at work, seem to care about me as a person?
• Is there someone at work who encourages my development?
• At work, do my opinions count?
• Does the mission/purpose of my company make me feel like my work is important?
• Are my co-workers committed to doing quality work?
• Do I have a best friend at work?
• In the last six months have I talked to someone about my progress?
• At work, have I had opportunities to learn and grow?

Note: this questionnaire requires the permission of the Gallup organisation for use within an organisation.

Numerous consultancies have developed their own survey tools. Towers Perrin, mentioned above, make the distinction between *emotional* and *rational* engagement. They use a set of questions intended to be indicators of actual engagement – but we have put a question mark after those that might be regarded as 'inputs'.

EMOTIONAL ENGAGEMENT:

- I would recommend my company to a friend as a good place to work.

- My company inspires me to do my best work (?).

- I am proud to tell others I work for the company.

- My job provides me with a personal sense of accomplishment (?).

- I really care about the future of my company.

RATIONAL ENGAGEMENT:

- I understand how my unit contributes to the success of my company (?).

- I understand how my role is related to my company's overall goals, objectives and direction (?).

- I am willing to put in a great deal of effort beyond what is normally expected to help my company succeed.

- I am personally motivated to help my company be successful.

In their *Global Workforce Survey 2005*, Towers Perrin found from 85, 000 respondents across 30 countries, that 12 per cent were 'highly engaged', 65 per cent moderately engaged and 23 per cent 'disengaged'. This profile is fairly typical of such surveys. (We mentioned similar figures from Gallup and the Corporate Leadership Council on pages 96–97)

One additional question that is worth asking is:

- If you had a better opportunity to go elsewhere over the next three months, what is the likelihood of you taking it?

The principle of the pulse survey is that it is short, frequent and easily administered. It needs to be analysed by management unit, since every manager creates different climates. It can be a simple paper page or done electronically. Most HR people would recommend it should be anonymous. However, as we discussed earler, and will discuss below, there is both a generic and an individual aspect to motivation – and in the ideal world the survey would be the basis of a dialogue between the individual and the manager. In organisations with cultures of strong trust and openness this is no problem.

One company that has put concentrated and consistent effort, globally since 1999, into understanding the feelings of employees is the Swedish telecommunications company, Ericsson. They do not use pulse surveys but have an annual 100 question survey that is an integral part of the company year. Called 'Dialog', and completed online, it leads to some 20 indices and rigorous action plans. Indices are combined into a 'Human Capital Index' (HCI) which forms part of every manager's objectives and reward plan. The survey includes responses to how managers are seen based on the Ericsson Leadership Model, so that a manager gets a 'leadership profile' annually, based on the views of their employees. They have found a 0.86 correlation between such profiles and the overall HCI. Other indices include 'empowerment' and 'engagement' – and for the latter, they use three outcome questions covering pride in the company, commitment to its goals and values, and belief in what it is trying to achieve.

ASKING MANAGERS

Since we are seeing the key signals of engagement as the application of discretionary effort, managers know well who applies it and who does not. We could ask them, therefore, to rank their employees on a scale of commitment. It would be wise to have another measure in use alongside this.

'GREAT PLACE TO WORK' SURVEYS

The 'Great Place to Work' Institute conducts independent surveys of employees in many countries. (It now has various competitors, often media based, also doing similar things) Their definition of a great place to work is 'a place where employees *trust the people they work for, have pride in what they do, and enjoy the people they work with'*. Their copyrighted model features five areas which they test. The first three are built around 'trust':

- 'credibility' (open communications, competence, integrity)

- 'respect' (recognition, consultation, caring for individuals)

- 'fairness' (equity, impartiality, justice).

Two more areas cover 'pride' and 'camaraderie'. It is a lot of effort, and not cheap, to enter the annual league table; however, very useful data is produced and analysed and achieving a high place does wonders for an organisation's reputation in the labour market.

In the US in 2009, a data management company, NetApp, was the overall winner; the French company Danone was number 1 in the UK and in Europe, as a whole, Microsoft was at the top. Some companies appear consistently, and they are usually companies that are proud of the way they treat their people, and it is instructive to visit their websites.

This type of survey is, of course, only at the organisational level and does not take us down to that of the work unit of each manager.

DOES ENGAGEMENT VARY WITH LENGTH OF SERVICE?

The Royal Bank of Scotland found higher levels of engagement with older people. Analysis of length of service showed employees in their first year *and* those with >10 years service had the highest levels – the group of 3–5 years service was particularly low. Nationwide, a building society, also found a very strong correlation between both engagement and business performance measures with length of service.

3.6 Measuring the Causes of Engagement

What is it then that causes people to be engaged? Gallup's Q12 claims to have found the answer, and many organisations have felt it unnecessary to reinvent the wheel. It is very consistent with other research as to what motivates people, and is very personal. In summary it asks about:

Clear expectations	The right resources
Use of my skills	Recognition
A person not a number	*Care about my development
*Listening to opinions and ideas	My work has meaning
My colleagues care too	Someone is my friend
My progress is discussed	*I keep learning

Interestingly enough, there is nothing here about pay and salary, which is consistent with Herzberg's findings that compensation is more of a 'hygiene' factor. What is interesting is that arguably, 11 of the questions are within the degrees of freedom of a manager to influence, whatever the HR systems or company culture. It is, therefore, very unwise to move to the measurement of engagement without the full co-operation and support of line managers, who need to provide the follow up action.

However, Towers Perrin's *Ten Attributes of the Workplace that Build Engagement* has only three real similarities to Q12 (* above). Their list includes fair pay systems, satisfactory benefit packages, and two on customer satisfaction; 'My manager inspires enthusiasm for work' is about leadership, and another is 'Senior management has sincere interest in the satisfaction and wellbeing of employees'. A report by the Corporate Leadership Council examined over 300 potential 'levers of engagement', and then listed the top 50; of these, 36 were managerial competences.

The Royal Bank of Scotland (see Figure 4.10 for their integrated HCM model) have studied engagement in-depth and identified the following drivers:

- leadership

- reward (financial and non-financial)

- employment security

- recognition

- customer focus

- respect and diversity

- performance and development.

It has used these findings to develop a 'Drivers to Engagement' toolkit, covering surveys, measurement and reporting, applied across the company. Engagement scores are segmented in various ways, including tenure, location and business unit, to allow prioritisation and focus. The group found that engagement increased in line with employees' participation in its flexible benefits plan, RBSelect: employee engagement increased by over 20 per cent when individuals selected three or more options from the plan.

Research carried out by *Human Resources* magazine in 2007 showed that benefits such as flexible working, profit related pay, sabbaticals, duvet days, gifted days and – most of all – home-working, all have an effect on engagement. The latter could make a difference of 13 per cent, comparing up to two days a week from home with none. By contrast, free sports facilities and healthcare made no difference.

IS THERE A 'UNIVERSAL' SET OF ENGAGEMENT QUESTIONS?

The conclusion we have come to now is that a 'universal' template is not the best answer. The main attraction of a 'Q12' is the opportunity to benchmark with others, but one needs to ask seriously what is the business benefit of that? The foundation of our approach to human capital management is to focus on groups of people taking part in a value creating process, groups with their own characteristics. We know that motivation is a very individual matter, and that even within a group, will vary. What is certain is that each job family will look for a different mix. We suggest that each group should be *asked*, rather than some professional in headquarters deciding for them. This can be done by simple questionnaires or focus groups with a group of staff. It is also useful to ask the managers of the staff for their view on what they *think* the answers will be. Questions such as these can be used:

- Through a typical week, what kind of things make you feel good at work?

- Through a typical week, what kind of things make you feel frustrated at work?

- What kind of things make you prepared to 'go the extra mile' when needed?

- Have you felt like leaving over the last year, and if so, why?

Just to show how different answers to these questions can be, here is a summary of the results about what matters to three quite different groups of employees:

CUSTOMER SERVICE OFFICERS IN RETAIL BANK

- feeling of achievement at the end of the day;

- a friendly collegiate atmosphere;

- being helpful to and appreciated by customers;

- recognition for a good job done by management.

Negative influences included undue work pressure, inadequate training, and unhelpful colleagues and managers.

SUPPORT STAFF IN A UNIVERSITY FACULTY

- respect for and appreciation of my work;

- a supportive and capable team;

- having influence and being empowered to do my job properly;

- clarity of role and what is expected;

- changes needed are fully explained to me;

- fair rewards in comparison with others;

- the right training and the opportunity to develop.

FIRST-LINE MANAGERS IN A POSTAL DELIVERY SERVICE

- respect from and appreciation by my manager;

- approachable, listening manager;

- appreciation by my staff;

- positive attitude and flexibility from my staff;

- having the resources needed to do a good job;

- clear and fair distribution of responsibilities;

- receiving helpful feedback.

So the typical 'pulse survey' will have 12–15 questions relevant to the drivers of engagement for the group of people being surveyed, plus 2/3 'outcome' questions such as those on page 108. And as we have mentioned earlier, it is always recommended – since every individual is different – to ask 'how important is this issue for you?'

MEASURES OTHER THAN SURVEYS

The kind of surveys we have been talking about measure how people feel and how they observe others behave, and are completed by individuals. There are some other measures that can be used for some of the levers of engagement.

Leadership and management competences undoubtedly have an influence and these can be assessed using '360 degree' multi-input assessments.

Most people care about the level of *training and development* they receive. In addition to their perceptions, measures that can be used here include:

- days training per person;

- percentage spent on training as a percentage of salary;

- percentage of the group having Personal Development Plans;

- percentage of group having completed Personal Development Plans;

- average time between promotions;

- number of people leaving due to perceived lack of opportunities for growth.

3.7 Engagement and Performance

Measuring engagement in itself does nothing for performance, of course. It is the actions taken to improve it that make the difference. Having moved away from focusing on employee satisfaction *per se*, our interest in engagement is because we believe it drives both better retention of people and better performance, as in value added to our stakeholders. Over the last 5–10 years, a mass of evidence has accumulated to justify this fairly obvious cause and effect.

The first attempt to link the *feelings* of employees with performance was made by Hesketh, Sasser and Schlesinger in their *Service-profit Chain* (1998). This is described in Chapter 4 in more detail. The best known case study was written up in the *Harvard Business Review*, as applied at Sears, the US Retail Company. After research at many stores they demonstrated that a 5 unit increase in employee satisfaction led to a 1.3 unit in 'customer impression', leading to a 0.5 unit increase in revenue *growth*.

Using modern pulse surveys, the way comparisons are made is to rank all the units that have been surveyed according to their engagement scores and then to compare the top quartile and bottom quartile against a chosen performance parameter. The resulting gap indicates what could be possible, if all units were highly engaged.

Gallup in 2007 examined 23,910 business units and compared top quartile and bottom quartile financial performance with engagement scores. They found that:

- Those with engagement scores in the bottom quartile averaged 31 – 51 per cent more employee turnover, 51 per cent more inventory shrinkage and 62 per cent more accidents.

- Those with engagement scores in the top quartile averaged 12 per cent higher customer advocacy, 18 per cent higher productivity and 12 per cent higher profitability.

It is no accident that retail and banking companies are predominant in this work, as they have the benefit of many comparable units in their branches. Standard Chartered Bank, for example, reported that in 2007 they found that branches with a statistically significant increase in levels of employee engagement (0.2 or more on a scale of five) had a 16 per cent higher profit margin growth than branches with decreased levels of employee engagement. They can show significant 'engagement gaps' on a range of parameters – sales productivity, customer fraud, employee retention, and so on. B&Q, the DIY retailer, has similar data – the 'engagement gap' of 'shrinkage', for example, was some £35m per annum in 2006. Figures like this justify considerable investment in better management and in benefits that are important to employees. HR directors who agonise about how to make viable business cases for investment in employees have a lot of evidence to draw on. Engagement levels should also be a measurable objective of many leadership and management courses.

In Chapter 1 we made the case for 'innovation' as a valid output in its own right. A Gallup study indicated that higher levels of engagement are strongly related to higher levels of innovation: 59 per cent of engaged employees say that their job brings out their most creative ideas against only three per cent of disengaged employees.In the public sector evidence is less robust, but that is probably an indication of the lack of output measures. A Towers Perrin study (2007) found 78 per cent of highly engaged public sector staff believed they could have an impact on public services delivery or customer service – against only 29 per cent of the disengaged. This is somewhat soft as evidence, but there is no reason to believe that the link between engagement and stakeholder outputs would not be as compelling as in the private sector.

The Corporate Leadership Council, in the report already referred to, carried out masses of statistical analysis and made this conclusion, which they called the '10:6:2' rule:

- Every 10 per cent improvement in commitment can increase an employee's effort level by 6 per cent.

- Every 6 per cent improvement in effort can increase an employee's performance by 2 per cent.

The Mcleod Review summarises many more examples and the link is now rarely disputed.

THE COST OF THE LACK OF ENGAGEMENT

We have discussed, above, the potential increase in performance that could arise from improved engagement. Headlines abound in the business press about the 'cost' of a lack of engagement. Arguments are made such as these:

> *Let us assume that all Not Engaged and Actively Disengaged employees are giving you 50 per cent of what they are capable of, and we'll assume that the Engaged employees are giving you 100 per cent. We'll also assume an average pay and benefits per employee of $50,000. So 70 per cent of employees are giving back only 50 per cent of what they are being paid. That means 35 per cent of payroll is pure cost.. there is absolutely no return on investment. Using these numbers, that lack of engagement in a 100 person company is costing $1,750,000 (35 per cent of payroll).*

> *(Keith Ayers, Integro Leadership Institute)*

Gallup calculated the annual cost of actively disengaged employees (based on collated Q12 data) in the UK: applying widely used statistical guides, such as standard utility analysis methods, to the £24,002 per year median salary in the UK, yielded £2,048 in losses per worker. Multiplied by 29m British workers who are 18 years old or older, this gives an estimate of £59.48 bn. A separate estimate of £64.7 bn was based on the UK's Gross Domestic Product (GDP) in the year 2007. The GDP figure was divided by the total number of British workers to yield £52,221 worth of goods or services per worker last year. Again, applying standard utility analysis methods, the Gallup statisticians found that a 4.3 per cent increase in output per worker would be attributable to eliminating active disengagement from the workforce. This 4.3 per cent increase, applied against the £52,221 GDP average output figure, amounts to £2,228 per person in the total workforce, or £64.7 bn overall (quoted in the Mcleod Report).

Ayers' assumption of 35 per cent zero return would yield £244bn using Gallup's methodology. What are we to make of these calculations? Gallup's macro economics has more credibility, and it recognises that the increase in output due to eliminating disengagement is quite a small, though significant, number. There is, in theory, no reason why every employee should not be highly engaged and we find teams of people where this is so, what Lynda Gratton calls 'hotspots'. However, we will never eliminate the problem because we will never have perfectly functioning people management throughout an organisation.

For practical use, it seems more useful to create correlations with particular performance indicators than try and calculate a cost in this way.

3.8 Summary

Although we might justifiably regard the human capital of an organisation as all the people available to it, whether formally employed or not, there is a very different psychological contract – at least potentially – with contracted employees. Employees have a special role as stakeholders – and keeping them loyal, productive, and willing to give of their best requires an understanding of what each individual looks for through their work.

People bring to the workplace a basic level of enthusiasm and commitment which varies with both individual personality and the nature of work that they do. Aspects of the workplace, and other people around them either build on and enhance this enthusiasm or degrade it. Satisfaction with the working environment may be described as little more than the absence of dissatisfaction, that is, it is a threshold. Beyond that threshold lies commitment to, and engagement with, the goals of the organisation.

Since we know that high performance is more dependent on these factors than anything else it behoves us to take them seriously, which means understanding, measuring and monitoring them. The correlation between engagement and performance is well proven, and investment in it will have a certain return.

3.9 Challenges for Action

- To what extent has your organisation thought about, and defined, the exchange of value between the organisation and its employees, and indeed other sources of human capital that are utilised?

- Do you have any instrument that regularly checks what is important to each individual and how that is being met?

- What forms of measurement do you have in place for measuring engagement? Are you able to adapt the methods used to take account of the different motivational factors of different groups? Do you distinguish clearly from overall indicators of engagement, and the factors that cause it?

- To what extent is your engagement programme fully integrated in the sense that regular measurement is just a part of it? Is every manager personally committed to its importance and regularly reviewed on actions to improve it? Does HR have its own programme to generate policies and practices which enhance the goal of a 'great place to work'?

- Have you developed models that link engagement to key performance indicators, and that enable you to refine your understanding of the key factors that make a difference?

- Are you therefore able to be predictive, and to focus training and coaching in the most productive areas?

3.10 References and Further Reading

Buckingham, M., and Coffman, C. (1999). *First Break All the Rules: What the World's Greatest Managers Do Differently.* New York: Simon & Schuster.

Centre for Performance Led HR (May 2009). *Engaged to Perform- a New Perspective On Employee Engagement.* Lancaster: White Paper.

CIPD Annual Survey Report (2009). *Absence Management.*

Feather, K. (2008). *Helping HR to Measure Mp: Arming the 'Soft' Function with Hard Metrics. Strategic HR Review,* volume 7(1).

Gratton, L. (2004). *The Democratic Enterprise.* London: Pearson Education.

Gratton, L. (2007). *Hotspots.* London: FT Prentice Hall.

Heskett, J.L., Sasser, W.E. Jnr, and Schlesinger, L.A. (1997). *The Service Profit Chain.* New York: The Free Press.

Krueger, J. and Killham, E. (2007). *The Innovation Equation. Gallup Management Journal.*

Mcleod, D. and Clarke, N. (2009). *Engaging for Success Enhancing Performance Through Employee Engagement.* Report for the UK Government.

PricewaterhouseCoopers Saratoga (2006). *Key Trends in Human Capital – A Global Perspective.*

Robinson, D., Perryman, S. and Hayday, S. (2004). *The Drivers of Employee Engagement.* Brighton: *Institute of Employment Studies Report,* number 408.

Towers Perrin HR Services (2005). *Global Workforce Study.*

Towers Perrin-ISR (2006). *The ISR Employee Engagement Report.*

www.mts.com (Work Interests Schedule)

www.greatplacetowork.com

www.integroleadership.com

4

Integrating and Reporting Human Capital Measures

In the previous three chapters we have looked at different kinds of approaches to measuring output, valuing people, and motivation and engagement. Of course these measures have value in themselves, especially when compared with time and against benchmarks. One question we have to answer is about how many measures we would be happy to report externally. Internally, the high ground is in connecting them together and understanding cause and effect. Then we will be able to pull levers and be predictive rather than just reporting the past.

4.1 Different Audience Requirements for 'People Related Measures'

We can split the audiences into two quite different categories – namely *external* and *internal*. Unless required to meet a regulation, what is reported externally will be driven by public relations considerations. Internally it is matter of performance management.

Table 4.1 shows the diversity of interests in people related measures. It looks at the varying reasons for being interested in them, and how the characteristics of suitable data vary according to the different needs.

This table shows a considerable diversity in the types and levels of data needed to satisfy all the players.

Table 4.1   Audiences for people related measures

Stakeholder	What they need data for	Characteristics of the data
EXTERNAL AUDIENCES		
Investors	To be reassured of a sound future for the company through its management and human capability	At enterprise/global level Focused on the future
Analysts	To make comparisons with other similar companies or against 'expectations'	At enterprise/global level Focused on the future and the present Following ideally standard methodologies to provide sound inter-company comparisons
Journalists	To make comparisons, not just with other companies, but also over time	At enterprise/global level Following ideally standard methodologies to provide sound inter-company comparisons
Governments	To ensure compliance	At enterprise/global level
Benchmark Clubs	To share agreed data in order to understand and learn best practice	At regional/country level Mutually agreed standards of data definition
INTERNAL AUDIENCES		
Senior management	To make internal comparisons between units, and set targets	At business unit/department level Standardised framework and data definition
Other managers	To make good people decisions	Relevant to local needs Correlated with performance parameters
HR function	To measure effectiveness and value added	Cross-organisation agreed definitions
Finance function	To audit return on investments	Standard methodology for RoI, and definitions for calculating 'returns'
Trade Unions	To keep checks on management	Data requirements defined by areas of concern, including political
Employees	Any data referring to them personally	Individual information and assessments

The first obvious differentiation is in the *levels* of data. Even though companies may report business results by operating division, any sections on people have tended to take a consolidated perspective. Thus in the Shell example on page 134, we see an 'overall employee satisfaction rate' of 64 per cent. This is averaged over 109,000 employees and 140 countries – truly 'the average is the enemy of truth'. The more consolidated data becomes the less meaning it has, because of the variations it hides. It is doubtful whether companies will want to volunteer data broken down by unit. A further problem is the difficulty that some organisations would have in collecting many types of data, given geographical and ownership complexities – and the empowerment that local operations may have in choosing their own definition of measures.

Investors want confidence in the future of the company. They should therefore care about good employee relations, investment in training and succession, and employmee engagement. Analysts and journalists would like data that is comparable with other companies. Here we come up against the problem of the lack of standardisation of measures in use. There is a continual tension between standardisation and relevance.

Benchmarking is a popular activity, and it is certainly valuable for the purpose of setting aspirations and targets. Every organisation is, however, unique in its ability to initiate and manage change.

Internally, senior management would generally like units and teams to measure the same things, so that they can get comparisons between them. With statistical data such as headcount breakdown and attrition this is not a problem, and people can work to standard data and ratio definitions. But when we start to look at motivation and engagement, for example, the factors that make a difference are more local.

Managers further down the line, however, are more interested in 'relevance' – data which will be useful in managing *their* business.

It should not, therefore, be HR that decides unilaterally what measures to produce – other than for its own functional purpose (see Chapter 7). They may have powerful information systems that can produce sophisticated data, but each stakeholder in people related measures needs to be considered as to what will help *them*.

4.2 Different Types of People Related Data

One source of confusion for some HR functions is the unhelpful concept of a 'basket of measures' – a mixed collection of measures that are all people related in some way but which are unconnected to any other business measures or logic. To some extent this has been fuelled by the otherwise excellent 'balanced scorecard' approach to performance management – where HR has been asked for some 'people' measures. (Actually the designers of the scorecard talked about a 'learning and innovation' quadrant, rather than 'people' – a much more difficult area for measurement, but arguably more strategic.) So they have often responded with what they have, whether they are the real drivers of performance or not.

Here are seven different types of people related measures:

PEOPLE IN THE ORGANISATION – HUMAN CAPITAL MEASURES

- *Workforce analytics*- this includes various breakdowns of our human capital – by job type, grade, gender, location, ethnic origin, and so on. If we take an inclusive view of human capital it will also include temporary, subcontract and consultant resources.

This category may also include various ratios and trends of attrition (plus reasons), absenteeism (plus reasons), increases/decreases in certain employee groups, and so on.

These measures and derivatives are based on *factual numbers* derived from reporting systems.

- *Financial ratios relating to people and productivity*: this was covered in Chapter 1.

- *The value of people*: this was the subject of Chapter 2.

- *The engagement of people*: this was the subject of Chapter 3.

MEASURES RELATED TO THE HR FUNCTION: THE SUBJECT OF CHAPTER 7

- *The efficiency of the HR function*: here we refer to *service levels* and cost ratios in providing HR services, and to *internal HR processes*.

We could also argue here for measures of value added from the function.

- *The effectiveness of people processes*: these are processes generally designed and overseen by the HR function, but deployed by managers.

- *The investment in one-off initiatives and programmes*: this is about ensuring and assessing a suitable return in the benefits and outcomes from specific HR/training initiatives and programmes.

This chapter will concentrate on the *human capital* measures, and how they can be reported and utilised.

4.3 Workforce Analytics

Perhaps the one set of data we would universally expect is 'headcount'; generally meaning the number of people who have an employment contract with the organisation. It is important because it is the number of people with whom we have a certain kind of stakeholder relationship. In reality, and in these times of flexibility, a portion of these will be part-time and hence we need a parallel figure, which is generally called 'Full Time Equivalents' (FTEs), and is likely to be smaller than the number of people employed.

Depending on the sophistication of data input, we then have the opportunity to analyse the distribution of these people in many ways. We may look at gender, grade, length of service, ethnic origin, location, age, qualifications, time in post, job family, and so on. These may then be cross related or further cut by department and unit, combined into summaries, and expressed as percentages.

Just as in financial analysis, usefulness comes through well chosen ratios. The proportion of overhead staff to front-line staff should be of interest, or, for example, the percent of employees with less than one year's service. For the purposes of talent management, we may be concerned with particular promotion ratios, with the occurrence of secondments, or gender and ethnic ratios in senior grades. If we have information about training days, we can look at training investment as a percent of salaries or average days per person. The choice of what to report will depend on the needs of the stakeholders – and for senior management one guiding factor will be measures which support the business strategy. For senior HR management it will be the people strategy.

Two particular ratios are almost certain to be calculated – namely labour turnover (or attrition) and absenteeism. The latter may be understated in organisations with a high degree of flexible or home-working. For real value we need further analysis – relating turnover to job family, length of service, potential, and so on – and in both cases the classification of the *causes* are critical. It is not enough to divide turnover merely into voluntary and involuntary – information on the reasons behind voluntary leaving is some of the most important we have.

Obviously, no report on workforce analytics should be a dossier of numbers and graphs alone – it is the intelligent interpretation that brings the value. One of those interpretations will be to look at any financial impacts of the ratios, a particularly useful means of achieving senior management attention. There are a lot of spurious and ill-thought through calculations to be found in the press and in organisations, and credibility must be a prime objective.

Here are some examples of where this can be done:

LABOUR TURNOVER

There will always be labour turnover – it is a cost of being in business, and a certain level is needed for healthy movement. The unwanted cost is the excess over a targeted level. So for a particular group, if the target level is 5 per cent and the actual is running at 7.2 per cent, the cost burden is 2.2 per cent. We then have to distinguish between posts filled from within, as opposed to those filled from recruitment. If we had a 100 per cent promotion policy, then in theory the costs of replacements would filter down to the lowest level.

What we need to do is to establish a credible formula for the calculation of a replacement for particular job levels or families. According to the CIPD annual survey of Recruitment, Retention and Turnover (2009) very few companies calculate this systematically. Such a formula would include:

- administration of the resignation;

- recruitment costs;

- selection costs;

- cost of covering during the period in which there is a vacancy;

- administration of the recruitment and selection process;

- induction training for the new employee;

- lost productivity (in terms of value produced, or if this is difficult, a percentage of the employee cost) during the notice period of the resigned employee and the learning curve of the new employee.

This may be simply expressed as a percentage of the employee costs at different levels. For some employees/managers this can exceed a year's salary.

ABSENTEEISM

Headline figures on the cost of absenteeism frequently appear. There is often the assumption that every day lost is a cost to the organisation – based on the value of a person-day. It is true that cost has been incurred for no output, and and the value of that output may be difficult to quantify. But the real bottom line cost should be measured in *additional* money going out of the company caused by the absence. This would be incurred by paying for cover for the person's work. The costs of the person are there anyway, whether at work or not. Often, with knowledge workers, people catch up with work when they return or others cover essential activities in addition to their own – there is no *extra* cost.

As above, there will always be a level of absenteeism so comparisons against a target level should be made, rather than the absolute cost.

STAFF RATIOS

This is particularly useful with ratios of front line staff to support staff. Costs will be based on comparing with a target ratio. If that was, for example, 2:1 and we were operating at 1.8:1 – then we could calculate the cost of inefficiency based on the extra staff required to service the front-line.

STAFF VACANCIES

In theory, a staff vacancy represents a lost opportunity. If we understand the output value associated with a person in a team, then the cost to us is the lost value that could have been generated. However, this assumes that the vacancy is needed and the value would be generated. If we expect every salesperson to generate £x of revenues, then the loss is the *profit margin* on £x of sales. In other cases, work may be covered by existing staff who may or may not be paid for extra time, or by a subcontractor – in which case the cost is the *extra* costs incurred over and above that of an employed person.

HR should establish credible consistent formulae, and decide which costs it will be helpful to regularly report. Such costs are not explicit in most accounting systems – arguably they should be added as 'notes' to the regular cost accounts that managers receive.

4.4 Statutory Initiatives for Reporting

Government initiatives over the last 10 years regarding statutory requirements to report people measures seem to have petered out. By far the most comprehensive was undertaken by the Danish Ministry of Trade and Industry. It was the result of a project co-ordinated by the Ministry and involving 17 Danish organisations who contributed to the project by preparing two sets of intellectual capital statements each. Academic progress about intangible assets and intellectual capital has always been led by Swedish and Danish thinkers and several of these advised the Ministry.

The intention of the Danish concept was to produce an 'Intellectual Capital Statement' (ICS), based on the need to manage, more actively and systematically, resources that deal with knowledge. The main intention of the ICS was to report, externally, a company's efforts to obtain, develop, share and anchor the knowledge resources required to ensure future results.

The ICS recommendations were first issued in 2000 and a second phase started involving some 100 companies, and resulting in 'the New Guideline' published in 2003. The Guideline recommended four elements:

- A knowledge narrative describing how the company ensures that its products and services accommodate the customer's requirements, and specifying how the company has organised its resources to achieve this.

- The second part is to describe the management challenges that, on the basis of the knowledge narrative, the company faces in relation to its knowledge resources. Each action is then tied to one or more of the indicators in the fourth section.

•   Part three summarises initiatives that will be taken to meet the challenges.

•   The fourth part of the statement is about indicators that are appropriate to tracking the kind of resources being discussed.

The report recommends the format for both internal and external use – acknowledging that the latter would be a summary of the key elements.

In 2006 the author surveyed as many of the Danish companies involved in the report as could be traced but this yielded much disappointment. Very few indeed were publishing any data on intangibles and the one that was prepared to speak about it said 'it had proved to be a lot of work for little benefit'. Two exceptions were Systematic A/S and COWI A/S. The former, a software company, published every two years a comprehensive Intellectual Capital Report, divided into 'customers', 'processes' and 'people'. This was guided by Sveiby's 'Intellectual Capital Monitor'. However, they have not done this since 2004. Figure 4.1 shows an extract from that report.

Employee and Competence Profile	2000/01	2001/02	2002/03	Desirable trend
Number of Employees				
Headcount in Denmark as of 30 September	187	257	305	↗
- of this systems engineers	154	208	247	↗
Full-time equivalent employees	150	210	271	↗
Joiners and Leavers				
Systems engineers joining	60	63	55	↗
Systems engineers leaving	18	9	15	→
Employee satisfaction				
Total employee satisfaction (scale 1-5)	3.8	3.8	3.9	↗
'My appraisal is taken seriously'	3.8	3.8	3.8	↗
'My opportunities for further education are good'	3.8	4.0	4.2	↗
'Our work motto: Freedom with responsibility'	4.3	4.3	4.2	↗
% who percieve Systematic as a satisfactory/ very satisfactory workplace	93%	92%	94%	↗
Sickness absence (days per employee per year)	4.9	5.0	4.7	→
Competence Development				
Professional SW competencies (total no. of years)	775	1,118	1,401	↗
- per systems engineer	5.6	5.7	6.0	↗
Training days per employee per year	8.5	14.9	11.5	↗
Training investment per empl. per year (€)	1,817	2,833	2,048	↗

Figure 4.1   Extract from Intellectual Capital Report from Systematic A/S 2004 (see www.systematic.com)

COWI A/S is a firm of engineering consultants. They continue to include an Intellectual Capital Report, based on Sveiby's model, that is, reporting on customers (11 measures), organisational effectiveness (16 measures), and employees (28 measures). Each measure has explanatory notes on how they are calculated. Their 2008 report shows the same measures for the current and previous two years. This includes some unusual indicators such as:

- international travel;

- student 'favourite employer' rankings;

- project management capacity;

- percentage with different kinds of qualification.

At the time of writing, this is the best current example that could be found. Another Danish firm of consulting engineers who was part of the original pilot group was Carl Bro. Their report for 2005 followed the intellectual capital guideline reporting in providing figures and narrative for human and customer capital. However, they have since merged with Grontmij and is no longer published.

The American approach to recognising the importance of intangible assets is reflected in new regulations issued by the Financial Accounting Standars Board (FASB): regulations 141 and 142 concern business combinations and the treatment of goodwill and intangible assets. These are naturally much more accounting orientated, and aim to penalise companies and managers who experienced a loss of their value of uncovered intangibles, through write-offs that immediately reduce earnings. They do not, like the Danish approach, provide anything on internally generated intangibles or intellectual capital.

In the UK, interest was primarily sparked by a taskforce commissioned by the then Department of Trade and Industry in 2003, chaired by Denise Kingsmill. This was presented to the Government in October of that year and entitled 'Accounting for People'. Its key summary was the following:

*'We recommend that reports on Human capital Management (HCM)
should:*

*Have a strategic focus, communicating clearly, fairly and unambiguously
the Board's current understanding of the links between HCM policies
and practices, its business strategy and its performance; and including
information on:*

- *The size and composition of the workforce*
- *Retention and motivation of employees*
- *The skills and competences necessary for success, and
    training to achieve these*
- *Remuneration and fair employment practices*
- *Leadership and succession planning*

*Such reports should be balanced and objective, following a process
that is susceptible to review by auditors, and provide information in a
form that enables comparisons over time and uses commonly accepted
definitions where available and appropriate.'*

(Reproduced under the terms of the Click-Use Licence)

Many suggestions were made for the areas that might be reported, together
with case examples of measures used by companies. However, it did not set
out to be universally prescriptive. It was anticipated that the recommendations
would be incorporated in the requirements of an 'Operating and Financial
Review' (OFR) in legislation concerning annual reports for public companies.
In the event this did not materialise, much to the dismay of the professional HR
community.

In January 2006, the UK Accounting Standards Board made their
recommendations for the OFR in a 'reporting statement'. This is defined as *'a
formulation and development of best practice; it is intended to have persuasive rather
than mandatory force'*.

This document gives extensive guidance to the construction of the narrative
and also to the use of KPIs (key performance indicators). Matters relating to
employees are included. In its 'implementation section', it lists the following
areas as relevant: employee health and safety, recruitment and retention,

training and development, morale/motivation and workforce performance and profiles. It suggests examples of KPIs for measuring these areas.

The UK Companies Act 2006 encourages organisations to report non-financial KPIs, such as human capital, but there is no obligation. Thus at the time of writing, there is no jurisdiction currently demanding that public accountability should be served by metrics on people related measures, other than those relating directly to the directors of a company. Does anyone do it voluntarily?

Researching in 2009, there were very few major companies publishing any significant range of employee metrics, although most include a narrative in their OFR featuring highlights and initiatives in people management and involvement. Some of the resistance to actual metrics is anticipated in the Kingsmill Report (para 60) as:

- commercial confidentiality and sensitivity;

- lack of time and resources;

- seeing no value in such reporting;

- lack of clear guidance and universal practice.

Even Cadbury Schweppes, a company undoubtedly committed to the importance of its people, had minimal people related data in its reports, despite John Sunderland, Executive Chairman at the time, being quoted in the Kingsmill Report as saying:

> An organisation's success is the product of its people competence. That link between people and performance should be made visible, and available to all stakeholders.

Two UK-based companies we feature elsewhere as leaders in using people measures for internal purposes showed relatively little publicly. Royal Bank of Scotland, in a 252 page report for 2007, its last before partial government rescue, showed figures for five years on employee satisfaction and engagement, with response rates, and also data on 'work out events' – a process of employee involvement. Tesco, the retailer, quotes only 'employee retention' (defined as employees who have been with the company for more than one year) as 87 per cent in 2009, compared to 84 per cent in 2008 and a target of 80 per cent.

There are exceptions. We have already mentioned the remarkable case of Infosys. The drive to recognise intangible assets originally came from the Nordic companies and it is no surprise examples can be found from there. UPM Kymmene of Finland is one of the world's leading forestry products companies. For several years this company reported the following indicators (each clearly defined in a note):

- sales per person;

- value added per person;

- remunerations based on incentives;

- training costs;

- average no. of days spent in training;

- personnel turnover;

- no. of man-days lost through strikes;

- no. of man-days lost through lock-outs;

- calculation of key indicators.

Another role model was the oil major, Shell. It has produced, annually since 2005, a very thorough and informative narrative on its people, with many metrics. The 2008 narrative is very similar to previous years, with comparable measures, and is included as an exhibit in Figure 4.2.

DEVELOPING OUR PEOPLE

During 2008, we continued to invest in the development of our staff. Our learning approach focused on deepening professional skills, particularly in technical disciplines. Many activities also focused on improving health and safety performance.

We continued to strengthen skills and leadership capabilities at entry to senior levels within Shell through the Shell Project Academy and Commercial Academy.

We also extended our blended learning, which combines workplace assignments, e-learning, coaching, secondments to projects and traditional classroom methods. The online Shell Open University is the single point of entry for all formal learning courses.

RESOURCING FOR THE FUTURE

Recruiting, developing and deploying skilled people remains essential to our business. In 2008, we recruited more than 5,500 people worldwide from more than 90 countries. These comprised 1,050 graduates and 4,500 experienced professionals with more than half (57 per cent) of these recruits coming from technical disciplines. We maintained our reputation as an energy employer of choice in key target markets such as China, Singapore and Malaysia. Our new graduate campaign, launched in September 2008, brings together under one banner several routes to student and graduate recruitment. It resulted in a significant rise in applications of 30 per cent. We have been able to resource the existing business and the major investment projects in a competitive business environment and in challenging locations. In Canada, for example, the number of people hired in 2008 grew significantly compared to previous years to more than 1,500 – making Canada Shell's single largest recruitment market. While we always seek to attract and develop local talent, our ability to deploy people quickly to major projects around the world remains one of our strengths.

EMPLOYEE COMMUNICATION AND INVOLVEMENT

Communication with our staff and consultation, either directly or via staff councils or recognised trade unions, is important to Shell. One of the principal tools of communication is the Shell People Survey, which provides valuable insights into employees' views. This fully electronic survey was conducted in June 2008, with detailed results made available for line managers to discuss with their staff.

A key outcome from the Shell People Survey is the employee engagement index, which measures affiliation and commitment to Shell. The index covers responses to questions on, for example, job satisfaction and pride in working for Shell. The average score of 74% was up from the last survey in 2006 and continued to indicate a positive level of engagement.

We encourage safe and confidential reporting of views about our processes and practices. Our global telephone helpline and website, which have been in place since 2005, enable employees to report breaches of our Code of Conduct and the Shell General Business Principles, confidentially and anonymously.

Figure 4.2   **Extract from Shell Annual Report 2008**

DIVERSITY AND INCLUSION

We believe our ability to compete effectively in the global marketplace is affected by our ability to attract and retain diverse staff that reflect the countries where we operate, as well as the suppliers and customers with whom we do business. The integration of diversity and inclusion (D&I) into Shell's operations and culture is therefore essential to our success. At the end of 2008 the percentage of women in senior leadership positions had increased to 13.6 per cent from 12.9 per cent in 2007. Women make up 28 per cent of all our professional hires and 18 per cent of recruits for technical roles (both graduate and experienced hires). Women make up 31 per cent of technical graduates. The range of nationalities among our senior staff remains wide. In Asia, considerable progress has been made in identifying, attracting and developing local staff. Local nationals filled more than 50 per cent of senior leadership positions in 32 per cent of our major countries, compared to 33 per cent of those countries in 2007. Our D&I activities continue to ensure that we maintain for all employees equal opportunity in recruitment, career development, promotion, training and reward, including those with disabilities.

Reproduced with Permission from Shell International Ltd

Figure 4.2 *Concluded*

One more admirable example was Smith and Nephew PLC, the international healthcare company. In a 1,000 word narrative for their 2006 report, they covered:

- engagement survey results (90 per cent proud to work for the company)

- internal appointments (28.2 per cent of vacancies, 70 per cent target for management positions vey nearly achieved)

- average turnover for employees leaving the Group within two years of joining was 6.2 per cent (2005 – 4.3 per cent) ranging from 2.1 per cent – 15.2 per cent for the year.

Research in 2009 showed a few more companies quoting figures. UPM Kymmene changed their previous reporting structure in 2008, and showed absenteeism, gender distribution, accident frequency, and the fact that 69 per cent of employees took part in their Engagement Survey – but not publishing the result. British Airways included figures relating to absence and employment tribunal claims. Smith and Nephew followed exactly the same format as in 2006, with a remarkable 95 per cent of employees proud to work for the company.

Figures on internal appointments quoted ranges across the businesses rather than an average figure, and average turnover had dropped to 2.7 per cent. The three parameters chosen by the company would all give investors confidence in the future and in the commitment to the asset value of people.

In 2009 the Association of Certified Accountants and the CIPD conducted a joint study of the annual reports of 40 major companies chosen at random (none of those mentioned above were included). They developed criteria for assessing information and metrics on 'strategic intent', 'governance and assurance' and 'policy and performance'. The first of these was defined in a very people orientated way – including engagement and employee involvement. The company coming out best overall was Vodafone.

Their section on people is extremely impressive, with seven sections of HR reporting and metrics, finishing up with the KPIs listed below:

KEY PERFORMANCE INDICATORS

KPI	2010	2009	2008
Total number of employees (are in year)	84,990	79,097	72,375
Employee turnover rates (%)	13.0	13.0	15.2
Number of women in the top senior management roles	33 out of 228	29 out of 221	26 out of 211
Number of nationalities in the top senior management roles	26	23	20

Source: Vodafone Annual Report 2010

Companies, especially in the US, are struggling with a wealth of corporate governance regulations, and they wish most of all to demonstrate good corporate governance and concern for climate change issues. These are much more likely to win the competition for space and effort in the annual report.

4.5 Other Proposals for External Reporting

In 2002 a report was produced by the Centre for Business Performance at Cranfield School of Management for the Council for Excellence in Management and Leadership (CEML), a UK government quango. The report acknowledged the value of greater corporate reporting and disclosure and in particular, it suggests that 'what investors and other external stakeholders want is insight into the management and leadership talent pool that exists within organisations'. It listed 28 different measures under the headings of morale, motivation, investment, long-term development and external perception. It is unlikely that organisations will be willing to publish so much detail.

Professor Harry Scarbrough of Warwick University authored a report for the Chartered Institute of Personnel and Development entitled, *Human Capital – External Reporting Framework*. This was published just before the Kingsmill Report and was in fact submitted as an input to it. The framework was as follows:

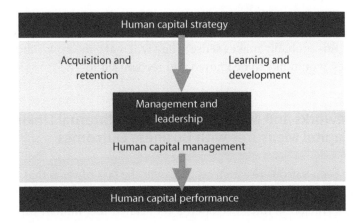

Figure 4.3   The CIPD framework for external reporting
Reproduced with permission.

Professor Scarbrough built on the CEML report. He made some pertinent observations to accompany the framework – for example:

- People are complex and human capital is dynamic – therefore, 'single point' metrics have little meaning and a balanced set of measures is needed.

- Compulsory measures are also not helpful – because what is appropriate for one sector may have little relevance to another, and lead to misleading comparisons.

- On the other hand, using a matrix of compulsory/discretionary vs generic/specific, a small number of sector norms might be created in the centre of such a matrix.

A range of primary and secondary measures were suggested under these headings and this list is as good as any to be found.

There have been other initiatives but it will serve no purpose to list them. Is external reporting ever going to become standardised and a regular part of investor information? It is questionable whether the investment community will ever pay more attention to the people side of organisations than making judgements about the leadership and their remuneration. There are certainly people indicators which signal a healthy, vibrant, engaged, well led, future-building enterprise. I for one would value that information as an investor.

It is unlikely at the present that companies will be forced along specific routes, and this probably makes sense. They will make their own choices based on what they would like to be known and recognised for.

4.6 Frameworks and Models Designed for Internal Linking of Human Capital Measures with Business Outcomes

There have been various research studies over the last 10 years that aim to link 'modern HR practices' to the 'bottom line'. They invariably show positive links. Consultants Watson Wyatt developed a tool called the 'human capital index' based on this. This is a great encouragement to the HR function – although it seems hardly a surprise that if an organisation treats its people well that it will show through in motivation and productivity. Our interest here is not so much in box ticking but in the correlation of real metrics with performance.

During 2003, the Conference Board, a US research organisation, involved a number of organisations in a survey of human capital measurement practices, and how they related to 'business strategy'. Measures used by different companies obviously varied, so they grouped them under broad HR headings such as recruitment and health and safety, and correlated them with cost reduction, revenue growth, customer satisfaction, globalisation, and so on. The highest correlation was +0.365 between diversity and globalisation (as might be expected) and the next was +0.329 between training and cost reduction. The lack of consistent measurement definitions raises questions about the usefulness of this, but the report does quote some significant company examples, one or two of which are mentioned below.

They did find that only 40 per cent of companies had any significant senior management support for initiatives in this area, which reflects the over dominance of financial measures, and the lack of connection of people measures with financial benefit.

In Michel Syrett's report for *Business Intelligence*, referred to in Chapter 1, he started with 'four truths' about measurement which are worth mentioning at this point:

- Having a measure capable of being linked to strategic goals does not mean that it is being used in that way. Measures for their own sake not linked to performance have limited, if any, value.

- Causal links are never self-evident – they have to be proved and re-proved. Moreover, the *strength* of causal links must be established.

- Validity is only achieved if the metric succeeds in capturing what it is supposed to – particularly important when using surveys.

- The right data is useless if it is not acted on – it is not worth the effort if there is no commitment to use it.

Below we look at measurement frameworks that have been developed and linked to performance and/or strategy.

We will categorise these into:

- consultant and academic models;

- institutional models;

- company specific models.

We can only include some examples. Many consultants have developed their own models, though relatively few have explicit links to business objectives. More company case studies can be found in the reports by *Business Intelligence* (2005) and the *Institute of Employment Studies* (2008).

CONSULTANT AND ACADEMIC MODELS

Needless to say, there is a considerable number in this category and we will therefore be selective.

1. The Service Profit Chain

Haskett, Sasser and Schlesinger first published their model in the Harvard Business Review in 1994, and followed up with a book in 1997 which had several practical applications. The model followed a cause and effect logic like this:

Profits depend on profitable revenues. Revenues depend on loyal customers who need to be satisfied customers. Such customers depend on loyal employees who need, themselves, to be satisfied employees. Ergo, the key to sustainable profitable revenues lies with employee satisfaction (or engagement as we would now say).

It was the link between loyal customers and loyal employees that was the leap of logic at the time, recognising the importance of relationships, familiarity and trust in the buying equation. The most famous application in the retail company *Sears* was written up in 1998 in the *Harvard Business Review*, and is shown in Figure 4.4.

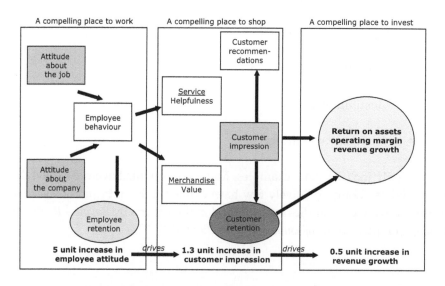

Figure 4.4   The service profit chain at Sears Roebuck

In the mid-1990s Sears achieved a remarkable turnaround, and one of the contributing factors was the application of the service profit chain. After a very bad year in 1992, new CEO, Arthur Martinez, successfully turned round the company financially within a year, but was then concerned about sustainability. He introduced five strategic priorities and multitudes of taskforces worked on these for the next year. One of the results was the three 'C's – 'a compelling place to work, shop, and invest', and three 'P's – 'passion for the customer, our people add value, and performance leadership'.

They expressed the connection between the three 'C's as 'work x shop = invest', and then turned to measurement. Their concern was not to have just a set of measures for a scorecard, but to *connect them* and achieve some dependable predictions. This meant having some rigorous and auditable non-financial measures, which struck many people as utopian at the time. They developed the new measures, and submitted them to *causal pathway modelling*, a statistical methodology which looks for linkages between data. In using a typical 70 question employee survey, they found that just 10 of the questions (6 about the job and 4 about the company) captured the predictive relationship between employee and customer satisfaction. Some of their original measures seemed to have little or no predictive links – including areas like 'empowered teams', somewhat to their surprise.

They were able to conclude that a 5 point improvement in employee attitudes would drive a 1.3 point improvement in customer satisfaction, which will drive a 0.5 per cent improvement in revenue growth. These linkages were regularly audited and checked for validity, and found to be robust.

The findings led to a number of HR initiatives – such as employee education and communication, leadership development, 360 performance reviews, and new compensation and goal-sharing schemes. The costs of each of these is balanced against clear goals in one of the three 'C's, and at the end of the day whichever one is aimed at leads to revenue growth and the bottom line. By 1997, overall increases had been made in customer satisfaction by 4 per cent in the previous year, leading to some £200m extra revenues – success which was well reflected in the share price.

Three researchers at the London Business School were commissioned to test out the validity of the model by a major UK bank. They reviewed data bi-annually between 2000 and 2003 for 1200 branches, a very thorough study, and concluded each link had strong validity.

2. The Balanced Scorecard

The *Balanced Scorecard* (Kaplan and Norton 1996) was described and illustrated in Section 1.4. It was one of the earliest models to recognise that the prime outcome of an organisation (which is financial for a commercial organisation) depended on achieving other indicators too. Their model looked for measures which were both 'lead' and 'lag' indicators, influencing one another, in the four areas of finance, customers, internal efficiency and learning/innovation. This model has proved immensely popular and a majority of large organisations deploy it in some form.

In the Foreword to the *HR Scorecard* David Norton wrote:

> *The greatest concern is that, in the New Economy, human capital is the foundation of vale creation. This presents an interesting dilemma: The asset that is most important is the least understood, least prone to measurement, and hence, least susceptible to management. ... In an economy where value creation is dominated by human capital and other intangible assets, there can be no better starting point for this new science than with the measurement of human resource strategies.*

> By permission of Harvard Business School Press. From 'The HR Scorecard' by Becker B, Huselid MA and Ulrich D, Boston, MA, Foreword xi,x. Copyright © 2001 by the Harvard Business School Publishing Corporation, all rights reserved.

Leif Edvinsson, when at Skandia, kept the four quadrants but added one in the centre called 'people' – and termed his model 'The Skandia Navigator'. He went on to develop a comprehensive set of measures for intellectual capital, and is undoubtedly one of the fathers of human capital management.

Too often, HR departments have been asked to 'supply' some measures for the 'people section', as 'learning and innovation' is frequently renamed. So typically we have measures like retention and absenteeism, with no real rationale or strategic linkage. The authors called this quadrant 'learning and innovation' for a reason – recognising that it was the *knowledge* of people and how it was used that was the real value driver. The HR profession has never seemed to embrace this truth. It is not 'people' (in the sense of warm bodies) that are our most important assets, but the learning and innovation they bring.

Kaplan and Norton's more recent book *Strategy Maps* (2004) develops the theme of linkage. Here the learning and innovation 'perspective' (as it is called) forms the foundation of the value chain, in a similar way to the diagram in Figure 1.4. It is broken down into three categories – human (skills and knowledge of employees), information (explicit available knowledge), and organisation capital (culture, leadership, employee alignment, teamwork and knowledge management). Two thirds of organisations, the authors say, have no real alignment between their HR and IT strategies. On the people side, they see this as focusing on 'strategic job families', and on the strategic competencies required for each.

3. The Human Capital Monitor

We introduced this in the earlier book *The Human Value of the Enterprise* and it is based on the concept of:

Performance = f (Human Value × Engagement)

This formula represents the structure of Part 1 of this book. Most models focus on the link between engagement and performance and few take account of the value of human capital. We suggest that this model needs to be used at the team level, and will have different, but relevant, factors for each team in all

The People Monitor - Group XX		
People as Assets	Commitment and engagement	Contribution to added value
"GREAT PEOPLE" The value of the people we have, using our chosen index	**IN A "GREAT PLACE TO WORK"** Input measures The factors that lead to engagement of this group	**GREAT RESULTS** The measures of *value* for stakeholders or of productivity
Maximising the value Measures of human capital management processes - both inputs and success indicators	Success indicators The measures of commitment and engagement	

Figure 4.5   The human capital monitor (Mayo)

columns. As data builds up, correlations can be made between specific factors and individual measures of added value. Eventually, one can hone in on the few aspects of human capital and of engagement influences that make the most difference.

4. The 'WRDI Institute'

'WRDI' stands for 'Workforce Relationship Development Indicator' and is an approach developed by Colin Beames of Australia. He segments human capital into four quadrants dictated by 'skills value' and 'skills scarcity' as in Figure 4.6. It combines levels of investment for the four quadrants with the required nature of the 'psychological contract' appropriate for the skills group. Quadrant one represents the core assets of the organisation in terms of competitive advantage. The institute has developed methodologies for assessing the strength of, and analysing, the psychological contract, assessing risks of leaving, and relating this to a formula for the costs of unwanted leavers in each category.

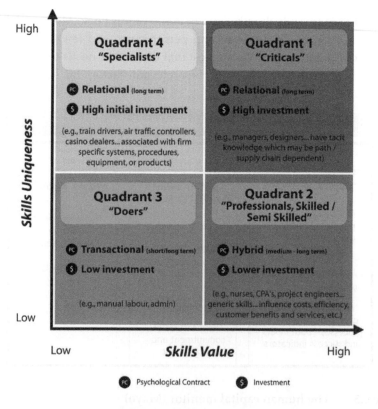

Figure 4.6   WRDI Institute segmentation of human capital

5. The Saratoga Institute

We have mentioned this organisation before; it is part of PricewaterhouseCoopers in the UK. It is probably the world's leading consultancy in the field of metrics and runs a range of benchmarking services. They produce an annual report (see for example *2009/2010 US Human Capital Effectiveness Report*) which summarises the average of a large number of metrics. They have an extensive list available of metrics, very mixed between 'human capital' and 'HR function effectiveness', which we will not reproduce here, but it provides a dictionary from which choices can be made.

6. Valuentis

Nicholas Higgins, who runs the consultancy Valuentis, has bestowed on himself the title of the Dean of the International School of Human Capital Management. He has put a lot of thought into the measurement of human capital and come up with his VB-HR model, which assesses eight 'core drivers of people performance', namely:

- HR strategy

- management

- employee engagement

- HCM architecture

- workforce intelligence

- HR functional capability

- HR service procurement

- HR customer agency

What is described as a 'multifunctional diagnostic tool' and a picture of organisation and HR effectiveness does mix up human capital measures and HR functional performance. The evaluative process is very well articulated and has the superficial attraction of benchmarking, but may be seen as over complex.

Valuentis see four classifications of people related measures:

- efficiency and effectiveness of HR processes;

- aspects of human capital performance;

- analytics that look at causality;

- combining measures and relating to performance.

Higgins has also developed the so called 'Human Capital Reporting Standards', 'Standard Human Capital Reporting Operating Principles' and the 'Human Capital Composite Index' (HCCI). The latter combines a complex set of ratios based on revenues and people costs, and HR practice.

INSTITUTIONAL STUDIES AND MODELS

7. The Chartered Institute of Management

In 2005, the Centre for Applied HR Research and the Chartered Management Institute teamed up to survey directors and investors to find their views on people metrics. Twenty investors were interviewed but only one admitted to taking account of people metrics when evaluating a company. Others implied that meaningful data was hard to find and they would take more account if it was there. Questionnaires from nearly 300 directors were analysed and the three most desirable sets of metrics were those concerned with leadership, employee, motivation, and training & development.

As a result of this work the researchers suggested a three tier model of metrics was as follows:

Level 1: *Basic Measures* – quantitative data and employee profile statistics. The *costs of human capital* (for example, headcount, training costs, salary bill, and so on).

Level 2: *Standard Comparable Analytic Measures* – comparable quantitative data indicating contribution to performance. This can be viewed as the *contribution of human capital* (for example, headcount by value, turnover by value, and so on).

Level 3: *Strategic Measures of Workforce Capability* – capable of reflecting the alignment of workforce capability to business strategy. This relates to the *value of human capital*.

These they put into a table against five areas of HR contribution as in Table 4.2.

Table 4.2   A strategic metrics set from the Chartered Institute of Management

	Leadership	Employee Motivation	Training & Development	Performance Improvement	Pay and Reward Structures
Basic Measures	• Reputation of top team (subjective assessment of visible top team – not comparable) • Vision/ mission/values	• Employee productivity • Staff turnover • Average length of service and deviations • No. of days absence per employee	• Number of days training per employee • Training spend	• Commitment to IiP • Commitment to EFQM	• Total employment costs • Pension liabilities • Directors' remuneration
Standard Comparable Analytic Measures	• % of managers with required leadership capability	• Self-reported employee survey feedback • Evidence of absence management • Communication/ levels of participation	• Training needs against competency • RoI of cost to increase capabilities required to deliver business results	• Balanced Scorecard approach • Individual performance appraisals and personal development plans achieved	• Incentives funded based on company results
Strategic Capability Measures	• % of managers ready to assume greater role • % rating of senior executives amongst key stakeholders (for example, employees, investors or governing boards for public sector) Understanding of leadership capabilities at all levels and assessment of reputation among key stakeholders	• Quality of turnover provides insight into the impact of staff changes • Staff engaged in increasing their capabilities shows motivation aligned to business goals	• People strategy linked to vision/ mission/values • % of staff with deficiency in capability to meet plans	• % of staff with objectives aligned to organisation's strategy and objectives • Ability to improve explicit alignment between individual and organizational goals	• Reward schemes for Strategic roles % of discretionary reward delivered to individuals providing greatest contribution to results

8. The CIPD Model

The CIPD has been active in various developments since its first report on *Evaluating Human Capital* by Scarbrough and Elias in 2002. This work has culminated in the publishing in 2008 of *Human Capital Management – an Online Tool*, based on Baron and Armstrong's *Human Capital Management* (2007). The

CIPD associates HCM fundamentally with measurement and this is a step by step guide to a measurement framework.

The 'tool' provides a methodology for introducing HCM and suggests a model which takes 'business strategy' and the 'business drivers', and against each defines their content, the supporting HR practices, and the data and measures that go with them.

9. The 'Investors in People UK' Human Capital Management Group

In 2005 the Investors in People body in the UK was approached by *Financial Times* journalist, Richard Donkin, to set up a high level group from prestigious organisations with the aim of publishing a set of standards for reporting on human capital management. (The group did not include anyone from the public sector which drew a complaint form Gillian Hibberd of Buckinghamshire County Council, who wrote to *Personnel Today* saying that the public sector had years of experience in measuring and reporting on the contribution of people, and human capital metrics were a 'way of life'.) They commissioned the Institute of Employment Studies to do research on their behalf.

The Group came up with the following recommendations:

- *Overall Performance* – profit per employee; turnover per employee; customer loyalty;

- *Leadership and Management* – surveyed perceptions of management; surveyed employee understanding of the aims of the organisation;

- *Employee Engagement* – surveyed willingness to recommend the organisation to a friend; staff absence; first year turnover;

- *Training and Development* – surveyed employee perceptions of adequacy;

- *Pay and Reward* – proportion that is performance related; employee perception of fairness;

- *Retention and Recruitment* – percentage of unfilled vacancies within three months; offer/acceptance ratio.

This set drew a number of mixed reactions and a final recommendation was never published.

COMPANY MODELS

10. Tesco

Tesco's measurement system is based on the balanced scorecard. The 'Tesco wheel' has been widely publicised in many HCM case study collections and has four quadrants – money, process, customers and people, each with its own sub-measures. This is illustrated in Figure 4.7.

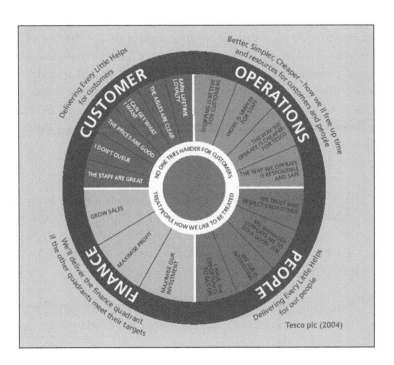

Figure 4.7   Tesco steering wheel (reproduced with permission)
Source: *Human Capital Reporting: A Guide* (CIPD, 2005).

11. Nationwide Building Society

Nationwide Building Society, based in Swindon, has around 16,000 employees located in its administration centres and branches throughout the UK, dealing with a wide range of personal financial services.

Since 2002, Nationwide have been investigating the links between employee commitment, customer commitment, and business performance, largely based on the service profit chain. Nationwide analysed a number of indicators of business performance across their retail areas and divided them into performance quartile groups for the purpose of plotting those groups against parameters, such as employee turnover. At the time, this showed clearly that better results came from those areas with the highest average length of service. As with Sears, they found that a small number of critical questions (nine) in their 'Viewpoint' employee opinion survey were key in identifying employee commitment. This, and length of service, were the most critical factors influencing customer commitment and are significant influences on sales.

Naturally this led to a greater understanding of the drivers of *employee commitment and retention*, and five indicators were found to have the most effect – employees' perception of basic pay levels, average age of employees, levels of resource during peak times, understanding and promoting the values of Nationwide, and role modelling of key management behaviours as highlighted within Nationwide's organisational development programme, PRIDE.

They were able to draw correlations as follows:

- A 5 per cent increase in employee satisfaction through *basic pay* increases customer satisfaction by 0.5 per cent; through *better information* by 0.6 per cent; through '*employee trustworthiness*' by 1.0 per cent, and this in turn increases sales of personal loans by 2.1 per cent.

- Increasing the customer's view that employees are friendly by 2 per cent increases overall customer satisfaction by 1 per cent which increases sales of personal loans by 4.3 per cent.

Nationwide now deploy this model through a line manager dashboard.

These linkages enable predictive results to be expected from investment in any of the parameters. For example, by investing say £100,000 in factors leading to improved retention of staff, over time (if the average improved from low to high length of service) sales of household buildings insurance are predicted to increase by 10 per cent. Assessment and justification of HR projects becomes easier and easier with such predictive correlations – a practical application of cause and effect. Of course the correlations need regular revalidation.

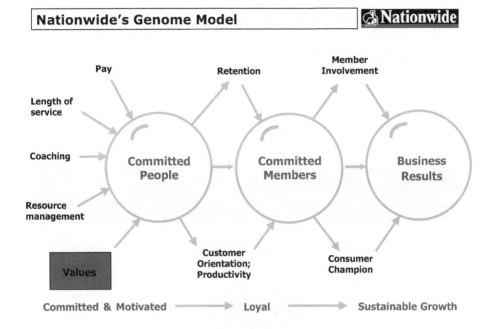

Figure 4.8   The Nationwide genome model

12. Royal Bank of Scotland

The Royal Bank of Scotland Group (RBS) is one of the oldest and largest banks in the UK, having grown by extensive acquisition over the years. At the time of writing it is owned 70 per cent by the UK Government who rescued it during the banking crisis of 2008.

RBS has been a leader in promoting human capital measurement, with top level commitment to the importance of people to its success. Its initial focus was on easily accessible data around engagement, absence, turnover and short-term tenure. Over time it has developed the model shown in Figure 4.9, centred round the 'employee proposition'. It has found that the following employee measures have the greatest impact on business performance:

- leadership index

- engagement index

- customer focus

- image and competitive position

- managing people and change

- efficiency and innovation

- performance management and development.

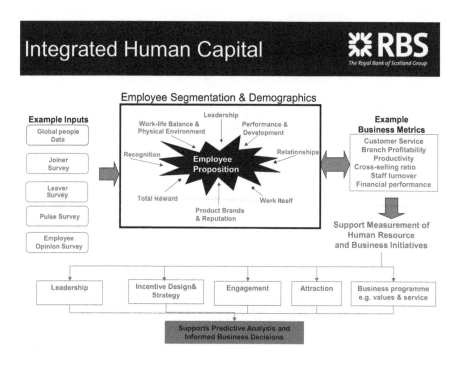

Figure 4.9   The RBS integrated human capital model

4.7 Making Reports a Part of a Manager's Daily Life

The management and reporting of financial resources is well established and managers all receive a statement of how they are doing against their budgets. If they are a profit centre they will receive a profit and loss (or 'operating' statement) which details where they are in relation to their targets and highlights any variances. Their financial 'business partner' will generally have a discussion with them about these, in addition to that they can expect with their boss. These statements cover the last period and the cumulative position since budgets were set. If they are senior enough they will also receive a balance sheet, a statement at a defined point of the assets and liabilities under their control.

The same principles can apply to looking at people. It is likely that it already exists for 'headcount', but this may be the only people related measure that a manager regularly sees. An operating statement will cover a set of measures such as we have described, chosen as relevant and important for the operation in question. It could utilise any of the models described above. It will show the targets that have been set and the measures and movements against them, using a standardised format. Whereas a financial statement is usually monthly, this may be too frequent for many of the measures and quarterly may be more appropriate. Variances would be discussed and actions agreed.

A balance sheet can be prepared also. It will not be solely numerical, and will include qualitative data. Examples of what might be included are illustrated in Figure 4.10.

It may not have all these items for every manager, but can be adapted as needed. It provides a basis for an action plan for reducing or removing the liabilities.

THE 'PEOPLE' BALANCE SHEET

On the Asset Side	On the Liability Side
People and teams who add value to our stakeholders	People and teams who 'subtract' value from our stakeholders
Areas of capability superior to our competitors	Areas of capability inferior to our competitors
Aspects of our people policies and practices that motivate and retain our key 'assets'	Aspects of our people policies and practices which cause dissatisfaction and the 'wrong' people to leave
Aspects of our culture which support us in maximising value to stakeholders	Aspects of our culture which constrain us in our ability to maximise value to our stakeholders
People measures that are 'good' = better than target	People measures that are 'not good enough' = below target

Figure 4.10   Model of a 'people' balance sheet

4.8 A Guide to the Journey

How does one get started on this journey? Here we outline a step by step guide to building a workable, helpful metrics model to focus on the management of human capital.

Most organisations are not starting from nothing. They will almost certainly have some data on headcount, some analytics of the workforce, labour turnover and absenteeism. There will probably be some opinion survey data and some performance ratings ... and there may be much more.

Step One – identify what we have at the moment and distinguish between that which can be classed as 'human capital measures' and that which is about the effectiveness of the HR function. Draw up a matrix of each measure against the following:

- who owns the measure;

- its frequency;

- who is a stakeholder in it – that is, who uses it;

- whether it is 'corporate' or local;

- what it is correlated with (if anything);

- a judgmental rating on a 1–10 scale of its value – its reliability, credibility, and usefulness.

Step Two – through analysing the business strategy, and that part of the HR or people strategy that relates to human capital, brainstorm the measures/ratios that would be helpful in monitoring the success of the strategies. Decide at which organisational level these need to be best monitored and which groups of employees they would apply to.

Step Three – from the same sources, decide which groups of staff are 'mission-critical', and represent pools of particularly valuable assets. This will include the senior management group, and those identified with leadership potential, but also operational groups with vital business or technical skills. (Later the models can be extended to all employee groups.)

Step Four – now we want to take each of those groups and look at what we have and what we would like to have. Where desirable measures are missing we need to make a prioritised plan to build them up. It may take a year or two to complete the picture.

Step Five – decide on the reporting format and the process for dialogue with the managers who own each group.

Step Six – as data builds up, start correlations to provide some intelligence about cause and effect and the measures that managers really find useful for action.

Throughout this process, it is important to involve line managers. They may need to be helped to understand why some measures will really assist them in managing for high performance, but HR should never produce measures for their own sake. The test over time is 'where and when did this measure/trend/ index help us to take action that benefited the business?'

THE BUSINESS INTELLIGENCE MODEL

In 2005, Michel Syrett's report for *Business Intelligence* on 'The New Measurement Agenda' concluded with a roadmap for implementation with nine milestones:

- collecting the data;

- data collation;

- choosing the methodology;

- training HR Staff;

- integrating into strategic operation/review cycle;

- internal reporting;

- external reporting;

- formulating a dedicated human capital model;

- balancing internal and external priorities.

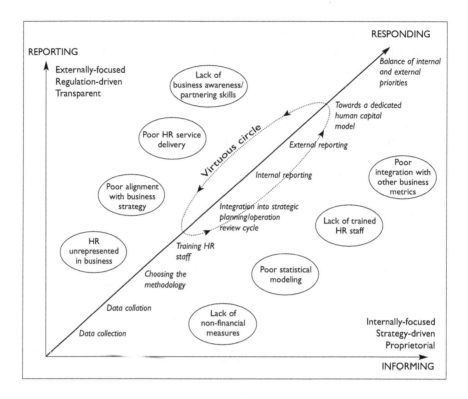

Figure 4.11   The business intelligence roadmap

This roadmap is illustrated in Figure 4.11. The model needs an earlier step which is about the initial choice of measures, based on business and people strategies.

4.9 Assessing the Progress That Has Been Made

The flurry of activity regarding external reporting in the early part of the decade, that was stimulated in the UK by the 'accounting for people' taskforce and in Denmark by the recommendations on reporting intellectual capital, has died away. What we have is voluntary reporting under a 'business and operating review'. Whereas most companies will say at least something about their people and key people initiatives, only a few will volunteer numbers and fewer still provide consistent reporting on those year by year. This may be frustrating for analysts and commentators.

There have been several think-tanks, such as the Corporate Leadership Council, set up with leading companies to try and define the measures that could be used both externally and internally. These have been supplemented by models, proposals, and advice from consultancies and bodies such as the CIPD and Investors in People.

More progress has been made on the use of people measures internally. The large HRIS systems – such as Oracle, SAP and Peoplesoft – are becoming more ubiquitous and promising more and more by way of analytics. The most influential factor has been the realisation of the links between engagement and performance, strongly stimulated by the entrepreneurialism of Gallup and its Q12 survey. The in-company research studies have been largely confined to banks and retailers, with the benefit of multiple branches for comparison.

HR is beginning to step aside from the accountant's shadow, and recognise that there is more to life than the simplistic bottom line, establishing their own expertise on non financial measures. Much of what HR is doing is about the future, and it is a positive future that encourages investors and lifts the share value. HR must identify and build the 'strategic outcomes' that make up the cause and effect maps that lead to high performance and to long-term sustainability.

But the pressure from senior management is weak, and HR is often understandably cautious about pushing forward an initiative that puts itself more clearly in the spotlight. Whatever HR provides, at the end of the day the key test is, 'did the audience for which the data was intended find it useful for their purpose?' at whatever level it is provided. This leads to a focus on unit and team measurement scorecards rather than top level consolidation.

We cannot pay rhetorical lip service to the asset value of people without some substance about understanding and growing that value. 'Human capital management' demands both measures and approaches to people management that are built to support their 'value creating' capability.

4.10 Summary

In this chapter we considered how to create a strategy for reporting and integration of human capital measures. We looked at the different audiences for measures and how external interests were very different from internal. The former is intimately tied up with public relations; the latter with both short- and long-term performance.

'HR metrics', as it is sometimes called, is often a very mixed bag and we attempted to get some order into categorising different types of measures – particularly distinguishing between measures about the people themselves, and those which related solely to the HR function and its work. A wealth of 'workforce analytics' is available through modern HR information systems: but choices should be made based on what is strategically or philosophically important – working on the premise that 'less can be more'. What is important is to calculate and publicise the hidden costs implicit in many of these measures in a credible and consistent way.

We went on to study the situation on external reporting requirements, which are minimal in practice, early initiatives having been shelved. Of more value though are internal integrating frameworks: and we looked at academic, institutional, consultant, and company models.

We concluded that any organisation that views its people (or a critical part of them at least) as vital value creating assets must ensure they are highlighted in measurement and performance systems of the organisation. What gets measured gets attention. And the opportunity to understand which people based levers really drives high performance is one that must be taken, and will add enormous value in itself.

4.11 Challenges for Action

- To what extent has your organisation analysed the different audiences that might benefit from people related measures, and thus constructed a strategy for reporting externally and internally?

- Do you have a clear distinction between different types of measures – particularly between 'human capital measures' and those which relate to the effectiveness of HR as a function?

- How are people measures integrated into your organisation's performance measurement framework?

- Have you chosen which workforce analytic indicators and ratios are critical for your organisation?

- Have you clearly defined the financial implications of these indicators and ratios where appropriate?

- What links have you studied between various measures and performance? Are you able to rank parameters about people and the way they are managed against their effect on performance? (Team by team?)

4.12 References and Further Reading

Baron, A., and Armstrong, M. (2007). *Managing Human Capital – Achieving Added Value Through People.* London: Kogan Page.

Brown, D. (2004). *Capital Vetters – The Case for Human Capital Reporting. People Management.* September 2004.

Centre for Business Performance. (2002). *The Case for Corporate Reporting: Overwhelming or Over-hyped?* Cranfield: CBR. [A report to CEML]

CIPD. (2008). *Human Capital Management – An On Line Tool.*

CIPD Human Capital Panel. (2007). *Developing Performance Measures.*

CIPD/ACCA. (2009). *Human Capital management – An Analysis of Disclosure in UK Annual Reports.*

European Commission. (2006). *Reporting Intellectual Capital to Augment Research, Development and Innovation in SMEs.* June 2006.

Fitz-enz, J. (2000). *The ROI of Human Capital.* New York: Amacom.

Gates, S. (2004). *Linking People Measures to Strategy. Research Report from The Conference Board.*

Heskett, J.L., Jones, T.O., Loveman, G.W., Sasser, Jr, W.E. and Schlesinger, L.A. (1994). *Putting the Service-profit Chain to Work.* Harvard Business Review. March – April 1994, pp. 164–174.

Heskett, J.L., Sasser, Jr, W.E., Schlesinger, L.A. (1997). *The Service Profit Chain: How Leading Companies Link Profit and Growth to Loyalty, Satisfaction and Value.* New York: Free Press.

Incomes Data Services. (2004). *Human Capital Measurement Report.* October 2004.

Kaplan, R.S., and Norton, D.P. (1996). *The Balanced Scorecard.* Boston: Harvard Business School Press.

Kaplan, R.S., and Norton, D.P. (2000). *The Strategy-focused Organisation.* Boston: Harvard Business School Press.

Kaplan, R.S., and Norton, D.P. (2004). *Strategy Maps – Converting Intangible Assets into Tangible Outcomes*. Boston: Harvard Business School Press.

Mayo, A.J. (2001). *The Human Value of the Enterprise – Valuing People as Assets*. London: Nicholas Brealey.

Robinson, D., Hooker, H., and Mercer, M. (2008). *People and the Bottom Line*. *Institute of Employment Studies*. Brighton, Report 454.

Rucci, A.J., Kirn, S.P., and Quinn, R.T. (1998). *The Customer Profit Chain at Sears*. Harvard Business Review, January 1998.

Saratoga Institute. (2009/2010). *US Human Capital Effectiveness Report*. www.saratoga.com

Scarbrough, H., and Elias, J. (2002). *Evaluating Human Capital*. London, CIPD.

Schmeisser, W., and Lukowsky, M. (2006). *Human Capital Management – A Critical Consideration of the Evaluation and Reporting of Human Capital*. Munich: Rainer Hampp Verlag.

Scott Jackson, W.J., Cook, P., and Tajer, R. (2006). *Measures of Workforce Capability for Future Performance – Volume 1 Identifying the measures that matter most*. Chartered Management Institute.

Syrett, M. (2005). *World Class HR: The New Measurement Agenda*. Business Intelligence Report, London.

Tsikriktsis N., Westbrook R., and Funk, B. (2004). *An empirical testing of the Service Profit Chain: Replication and Extension* [Private commission].

www.vodafone.com/static/annual_report10/business/people.html

www.smithandnephew.com

www.ba.com

www.systematic.com

http://www.frc.org.uk/images/uploaded/documents/Reporting%20 Statements%20OFR%20web.pdf (ASB Reporting Statement for OFRs)

www.upm-kymmene.com

www.cowi.com

www.valuentis.com

www.wrdi-institute.com

PART 2

Human Resources Professionals in Partnership with the Business

In Part 1, we focused on human capital – those assets which maintain and grow value in an organisation. In Part 2 we will look at the role that HR professionals have in supporting management in the value creation process.

Ever since Professor Dave Ulrich published his book, *Human Resource Champions* (1997), a certain pretentiousness has crept into the function. It has become preoccupied with 'transformation', which could be described with some justification as a desire to abandon administration to others and concentrate on 'strategic work'. This does not necessarily equate with the expectations of others in the organisation. Often a positioning has been created which is beyond the capability of the staff involved.

It is from Ulrich's work that the term 'business partner' has evolved, almost ubiquitously across the world. It is a strange term in some ways. Most operational managers would not see a support function as a partner in their 'business', and the very word 'partner' implies some jointly agreed arrangement. And are we talking about *personal* partnership with managers (in which case most so called partners are too thinly stretched) or one between departments? Nevertheless, although the description raises questions, the underlying principle of 'HR professionals' focusing on helping business people succeed, is admirable. The question, however, is 'with whose agenda do we start?' Is it HR's predetermined professional agenda, or the business priorities?

The opportunity to make a difference is enormous. In these four chapters we will look firstly at what a true partnering with business managers should be like. Secondly, we look at the creation of people strategies which are driven by the business needs. In Chapter 7 we look at the application of rigorous performance measures to an HR function, and in the final chapter what all this means for the capabilities of the HR professionals involved.

5

The Contribution of the HR Professional to More Effective Business Performance

In Chapter 1 we looked at the process of value creation in an organisation and the place that people have in it. As the function that exists to support people in the widest sense, we will now look at HR and how it works with business managers to achieve both an effective organisation, and effective people management: it should do this through bringing its professional knowledge and skills to support the capabilities of line management through active partnership with them, and contributing to their success.

5.1 Stakeholders and the HR Function

In Figure 1.2 we illustrated the principle of 'stakeholder equilibrium'. That principle operates for an organisation, an individual, and all levels in between. How does this stakeholder balance work for a support function like HR? Every function or department has its own stakeholders, with whom they give and receive value. Survival should depend on the balance of value that the department contributes. Organisations are sometimes surprisingly slack in understanding the truth of such value equations, and act only on crude cost grounds to downsize. But if a function like HR cannot articulate the value it provides, it places itself at a disadvantage as a mere cost target.

The secret of maintaining a position of strength is to ensure that the value equilibrium with each stakeholder group passes these tests:

- the nature of the value passing between the parties is understood;

- the value can be measured on either side;

- the expectations of the level are agreed and regularly reviewed;

- the capability to deliver the value is there on both sides.

An HR stakeholder map is shown in Figure 5.1. Each stakeholder can be taken in turn and these questions answered using a format such as Figure 5.2.

Figure 5.1   The stakeholder map for an HR function

Stakeholder:

The Value I give to them	The Value they give to me
MUTUAL EXPECTATIONS *I will...* *They will......*	The Capabilities I need to fulfil this

Figure 5.2   Format for summarising stakeholder relations

We noted also that stakeholders have different levels of power in relation to one another and are often in tension between themselves. We can look at those surrounding the HR function in terms of: a) the power they have to exert pressure on the function (positive pressure), and, b) the effect of each of them withdrawing their support (negative pressure). Senior management is high on both counts. They can, and should, shape the agenda of the function and set its targets. If they withdraw active support and leave the function to float according to its best ability, HR has no power base and has to rely on its own strength alone. It is inevitably vulnerable to being caught in cross-fires between other stakeholders.

Employees have relatively little power to exert by comparison, and withdrawing their individual support for HR and its activities makes little difference. However, in some industries, trade unions representing employees collectively can be very strong and exert both positive and negative pressures. The support of managers is very much needed for implementing policies and initiatives. Suppliers also can cause temporary chaos by withdrawing support, but have relatively little power to exert pressure. A way of mapping stakeholder power is shown in Figure 5.3.

All organisations, large and small, have to battle to keep a stakeholder focus, as the natural tendency is to be absorbed with themselves. But losing our grip on the healthy maintenance of the critical stakeholder 'value *equilibria*' is the path to disaster.

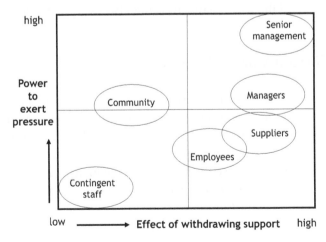

STAKEHOLDER POWER IN RELATION TO AN HR FUNCTION

Figure 5.3   **Stakeholder power in relation to an HR function**

5.2 How an HR Function Adds (or Subtracts) Value

Though it is a vitally important concept, the term 'adding value' is frequently used in a rather vague way. Firstly, 'adding' in this context requires the preposition 'to' – that is, value is added to whom?

We don't so often hear the term 'subtracting value', but it is just as important as its positive opposite. In the financial sense it means losing or wasting money, but as we know 'value' is both financial and non-financial.

There are numerous ways in which HR professionals can add value to the different stakeholders and we look at this in detail in Chapter 7; the possibilities are summarised in Table 7.1. But value can be taken away too. Some people related areas which have a direct financial implication include (for example) increasing absenteeism through greater stress, absorbing manager's time in bureaucratic procedures and meetings, or recruiting people who do not last. Every time HR takes managers' time and involves them in one of their initiatives, we are taking that time from another activity. This is seen most starkly in, for example, a professional service firm, where the maximum amount of a partner's time should arguably be spent in revenue earning, every hour is accounted for, and each hour on internal matters takes an hour of revenue (assuming the work is available). I once facilitated an away day for a group of 13 law partners which was potentially worth £31,200 in the revenues they could have earned – to which must be added the costs of the day itself. This focuses the mind on the value that needed to be achieved from the day. In fact, there are many opportunities for value to be taken from one or more stakeholders – and the way it happens is not always very obvious.

5.3 A Brief History of the HR Function

As an enterprise grows, the first overhead requirement is someone to keep track of its finances. In today's world pretty soon it will need help with IT, and with the ever increasing requirements for compliance with regulations of one kind and another. At some point later the administration and welfare of people may justify some resource – to save the time of other managers, and to advise them, even coach them, in some areas of good people management. Meanwhile, the few managers running the business carry on recruiting and firing, deciding on training if needed, setting targets and managing performance, and organising staff events.

Time moves on. The organisation has grown and it is impossible for the top management to keep track of everyone personally. The people administrator has evolved into a full blown department; complexity has multiplied; managers now leave it to this department to do most things to do with people. The department is not only absorbed in administrative detail, but every now and again its more senior members go to seminars and bring back ideas they want to try out on their organisation. So they start taking initiatives and persuading managers to get involved in developing competency frameworks, resourcing assessment centres, doing team-building and so on, which all seems quite interesting. The department recruits energetic, idealistic trained youngsters whose enthusiasm is infectious. They are all so busy that they have lost most of their accessibility to the employees, and start talking about 'putting people management back where it belongs – with line managers'. Those members of the function with business and professional credibility are highly valued by some senior managers and their advice is sought on a range of issues.

Inevitably as they grow they become the target of criticism and for 'overhead review'. Pressure to keep costs – and especially headcount – down may be accompanied by demands for outsourcing as much as possible. They begin to agonise about being appreciated and about being seen to 'add value'; about whether their position in the organisation truly reflects the importance of people, and frequently network with other HR colleagues for ideas and reassurance. They start to read the works of Dave Ulrich and his many protagonists and words like 'HR transformation' and 'strategic partnership' enter their language. Ulrich inspires them with his thrusting positive picture of how really important they could be.

5.4 The Contribution of Dave Ulrich

Dave Ulrich, Professor at the University of Michigan, is the undoubted dynamic and globally acclaimed champion of the HR function at the time of writing. In his most popular book entitled *Human Resource Champions* he prefaced it in 1997 saying 'the next ten years will be the HR decade'. His book set out explicitly to focus on what HR delivers rather than the detail of what it does as a department.

HR, he said 'must recognise and correct its past. It has spent more time professing than being professional'. His mission was to explore how HR can create competitive organisations through a partnership between managers and professionals with a body of detailed knowledge about people and organisations. The foundation of his approach was to see the contribution of HR placed in four quadrants, as shown in Figure 5.4.

The two dimensions used here are 'people and processes' and 'day to day vs. the future'. He denoted the quadrant representing the future and 'processes' as 'managing strategic human resources', distinguished from the 'management of infrastructure' which is effectively about people administration.

He defined four roles to go with these quadrants as in Figure 5.5.

FUTURE/STRATEGIC FOCUS

Management of strategic human resources	Management of transformation and change

PROCESSES   PEOPLE

Management of infrastructure	Management of employee contribution

DAY TO DAY FOCUS

Figure 5.4   The dimensions of an HR function (Ulrich 1997)

Role	Deliverable	Metaphor	Activity
Management of strategic human resources	Executing strategy	Strategic Partner	Aligning HR and business strategy
Management of infrastructure	Building efficiency	Administrative Expert	Managing processes and services
Management of employee contribution	Increasing commitment & capability	Employee Champion	Listening and responding to employees
Management of transformation and change	Creating a renewed organisation	Change Agent	Ensuring capacity for change

Figure 5.5   The dimensions converted to roles

Ulrich is at pains to point out that the concept of business partnership is the sum of all these roles, emphasising that contributing to strategic issues is but one part. Indeed at a conference in Rome in 2008, where some criticism was directed at his 'unworkable business partner model', he justifiably defended himself by saying he had been misinterpreted. His key message, then and now, was for HR to become more business orientated.

At the time of writing there are many surveys which ask HR people how much time they spend on 'being strategic' as opposed to being involved in administrative matters. The implication always is that the latter needs to decrease and the former to increase – that the mark of arrival is when most of the time is spent on 'strategic' matters.

One example is a report by the respected HR consultants, Mercer Human Resource Consulting. In an article entitled *Delivering on the Promise of HR Transformation* Philip Vernon summarises a global research study that covered 1,100 organisations worldwide. HR transformation is described as 'moving from a high cost low-value function to a low cost, high-value business partner. HR moves away from administration and towards a more value added strategic role'. The findings were that 50 per cent of time was being spent on administrative and compliance issues and less than 15 per cent on 'strategic, value based interventions'. The implication clearly is that this is bad news and shows how slow transformation is happening.

There does not seem to me to be too much wrong with these figures – if we are measuring an HR function as a whole. Administration and compliance has to be done, and done at as low a cost as is consistent with delivering an acceptable service. The standards of delivery of that service should be high, since mistakes and delays cause immense irritation and have a high 'price of non-conformance' (to use a TQM – total quality management – term). How much time do managers themselves spend on 'being strategic'? How often do we review strategies in organisations? Annually: or when a crisis forces us to do so? Significant changes in strategy are a relatively scarce event – implementing chosen strategies is for every day.

What has happened in the urge to be strategic is that the 'employee champion' role has diminished – the 'human face of HR'. Call centres for queries, pockets of professional excellence, 'business partners' preoccupied with management issues. The recent emergence of 'engagement' professional is rebalancing this to some extent, but their focus is a process rather than personal contact.

ULRICH'S REVISED MODEL

In his 2005 book, Ulrich and others revised their original model, although this has not generally replaced the original in the practice of organisations. This model is illustrated in Figure 5.6.

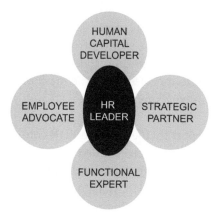

Figure 5.6   Revised HR roles model (2005)

Source: By permission of Harvard Business School Press. From *The HR Value Proposition* by Dave Ulrich and Wayne Brockbank, Boston, MA, Figure 9-2, p. 200. Copyright © 2005 by the Harvard Business School Publishing Corporation, all rights reserved.

The four roles have become five, and are described as follows:

Strategic Partner: HR professionals with knowledge of:

- business

- change

- consulting

- learning

    – who 'partner' line managers to help them reach their goals through strategy formulation and implementation.

The *Strategic Partner* role is defined as:

- Reactive 'devil's advocate': asking challenging questions about strategy direction and the organisation's ability to make it happen.

- Active strategy maker: exploring how corporate resources can be aligned to meet demands of current and likely future customers.

- Development of the senior management team: helping to raise standards of strategic thinking.

- Strategy implementer and change agent: aligning HR systems and processes to accomplish the organisation's goals and vision.

- Diagnosing problems: separating symptoms from causes and setting an agenda for future.

- Facilitators and Integrators of action and learning.

- Functional expert: repository of specialist knowledge in:

  - foundational HRM practices – such as recruiting, promoting, outplacement, measuring performance, rewarding, training and so on;
  - organisational effectiveness practices – such as work process design, the design of physical setting of work, internal communications, organisational structure, knowledge management and others.

Employee Advocate: this is the role of:

- caring for, listening to, and empathising with staff needs;

- developing and implementing policies which treat people 'fairly';

- managing work conditions and health & safety;

- ensuring effective channels of communication;

- resolving grievances;

- managing diversity and ensuring mutual respect;

- helping manage performance issues.

Human Capital Developer: the focus on staff, more than 'processes'. This involves:

- taking a future focus as well as the 'present';

- setting up 'development experiences' for staff;

- coaching leaders by building trust, sharing observations, affirming changes;

- concern for behaviour and attitudes;

- concern for the development of a person, and of effective teams.

HR Leader: providing functional leadership:

The focus here is on effective leadership and management of the function and ensuring delivery and results. It includes maintaining and monitoring the broader 'HR community' in the organisation, ensuring actions are integrated, and the mutual reinforcement of HR practices and policies. Ulrich also includes here the development of effective leaders throughout the organisation.

We have spent a little time summarising Ulrich's contribution as it has had such a major influence on thinking in the HR profession. It also provides a necessary backdrop to what follows – as we rethink the contribution of HR to human capital management. Although widely adopted, Ulrich's ambitions for the function have met a number of difficulties. One is the level of capability that exists in the typical HR function to be truly business orientated. The second is that the understanding of these higher value added roles cannot be unilateral – if it is not shared by management, it will not be utilised.

5.5 What Does it Mean to 'be a Strategic Business Partner'?

In 1980 I secured my first 'HR Business Partner' role. Of course that was not my job title – this was 'Personnel Manager'. But I was responsible for the whole function in a subsidiary company of 2000 people in an international IT group, a member of the management team and reporting to the Managing Director. Soon after starting I booked an appointment with Tony, the MD, in order to agree my objectives for the coming year. I sat down and he looked at me quizzically. 'Andrew', he said, 'I asked you to join us because I know you know what you are doing in managing your department and I trust your judgement to recognise any needed changes to our Personnel and Training. I will judge you by the extent to which our other colleagues around this table *find you helpful in achieving their objectives*'.

After two years our subsidiary was 'restructured'. Tony invited me to take a marketing role in one of the new offshoots. With much trepidation I accepted and spent the next two years so immersed in the excitement of my particular business objectives that I found – to my dismay – that I was looking on the Personnel department as a 'necessary nuisance': all the activities that had engaged me so seriously before seemed irrelevant. It was getting new customers that mattered. I eventually did go back to HR, a much wiser man.

Two lessons remained with me, as I returned to HR. The first was that HR's agenda is but a small part of the line manager's preoccupations, and the second was that to be a valued partner (or colleague, as I would have said then) I needed to focus on what managers were trying to achieve as the priority, rather than what I wanted to accomplish professionally.

There is a lot of confusion as to what is exactly meant by 'business partnership'. Some take it to mean anything that is not 'transactional' – the modern word for dealing with administrative, procedural and legal issues. Ulrich described the (strategic) role as overcoming five challenges:

- 'Avoiding strategic plans being on the top shelf' – turning strategic statements (such as values) into a set of organisational actions.

- 'Creating a balanced scorecard'. This is about having a scorecard for the HR function that measures its performance, and also taking a lead on people related measures.

- 'Aligning HR plans to business plans'. The word 'aligning' hints at separate creations and then seeing how they match, which is what often happens. Ulrich explains it more as 'integration' of the plans.

- 'Watching out for quick fixes' – and here he condemns indiscriminate benchmarking and going for what is popular for its own sake.

- 'Creating a capability focus within the firm' – the emphasis here is on building core competences, those which are vital because of the business we are in, and those which give us competitive advantage.

Ulrich proceeds to emphasise what he calls 'organisational diagnosis' as the heart of strategic partnership – analysing what factors make for effectiveness and generating ways to assess and improve those. We will develop this aspect later in this chapter.

The CIPD, in its 2005 paper written by Peter Goodge, states that business partnering involves the restructuring of HR into 'three specialist sub-functions:

- Shared services – a single, often relatively large, unit that handles all the routine 'transactional' services across the business. Shared services typically provide resourcing, payroll, absence monitoring, and advice on the simpler employee relations issues.

- Centres of excellence – usually small teams of HR experts with specialist knowledge of leading-edge HR solutions. The role of centres of excellence is to deliver competitive business advantages through HR innovations in areas such as reward, learning, engagement and talent management.

- Strategic partners – a few HR professionals working closely with business leaders, influencing strategy and steering its implementation. The task of strategic partners is to ensure the business makes best use of its people and its people opportunities. The role is to highlight the HR issues and possibilities that executives don't often see. It is also aims to inform and shape HR strategy, so that HR meets organisational needs'.

This has indeed become the currently accepted model of the 'modern' HR department, although it seems to be little different from the 'generalists, specialist and administration' format that one was used to in the 1980s. Technology has undoubtedly enhanced administrative delivery, and the range of contribution of an HR function has been extended – but the concept of experienced functional managers being aligned to business teams is nothing new.

Following this model, which Ulrich himself denies originating, has not always led to a more effective HR function in terms of value added. The main reason is that it has been linked with cost cutting, and the number of so called business partners who actually interact with business managers is often woefully low. They do not have time to seriously partner with anyone, in terms of spending time with individual manager needs. The so called 'three legged stool' also runs the risk of ignoring one of Ulrich's four quadrants – namely being an 'employee champion'. However, the modern emphasis on engagement, well being and social volunteering has become a 'specialism' of its own.

It seems inappropriate for individuals to use the term 'business partner' if they are not a member of one (or more) business teams, not just 'assigned' to them, but actively working with the team members. To apply the term to any HR professional working in the field may not be helpful – many use 'HR Adviser'. They cannot escape from doing some administrative work as managers see them as 'the HR person'. And HR people do generally like to be helpful.

We would expect to find true business partners as members of business unit teams, public sector service departments and agencies, country operations – any unit which has some autonomy in determining its direction and dealing with its clients. In addition to the top management team of an organisation, this would typically be at least at the first level below, and maybe at one below that. The value of having dedicated HR Business Partners will be seen in their ability to contribute to the areas discussed below in this chapter.

5.6 Partnership from the Other Side

Partnership requires two parties to agree to work together and to lay out their expectations of one another. There cannot be unilateral declaration of being in a partnership, except in our imagination.

Any professional wants her or his skills to be wanted and utilised. The opportunities in the arena of people are unlimited, since it is people that make up an organisation. The question is where our starting point is. We can market our skills and try and convince people to use them. We can tell them where we want to be. Or we can start by listening to the needs of our desired partner(s) and think about how we can respond to them. Productive partnerships are built on meeting real needs, delivering what is promised, and mutual personal trust.

Let's imagine we are a CEO and are thinking about the role of 'people professionals'. We call in the HR Director and say the following:

> Look, you know how much I value our people. I do mean it when I pay tribute to them in the annual report, you know. And that's why I think your function is important too. But as you well know, overhead departments – especially if they are centralised – always come in for some stick. Just because people are important doesn't mean everyone will knock on your door. More probably than any other department you have to earn your credibility. I know you guys want to be strategic and really help the business, and that's great, but you won't be able to do that without the managers wanting it too.

> Make no mistake, the number one is that you have to be on top of the basics. The last thing managers want is hassle about administrative stuff and the last thing I want is my managers spending precious time on such problems that shouldn't happen. Administration should be so good it is invisible. Now I want you to do that at the minimum cost of course, but I don't want an apparently low cost solution that looks good on your budget but actually causes a lot of hidden costs because it creates inefficiencies and frustrations and wastes people's time.

> Now I also want your people to be eyes and ears, not in any sneaky way, but being in some way a conscience for our integrity and values and sensitive to things that are going wrong. You have got to have systems of tracking where our culture is, why people are leaving us, how they are feeling and so on. And be aware of problems in the way the organisation works and in what managers are doing. This means that your best people need to be attached to business teams, and be part of the regular conversations about how the business is doing and the challenges the teams have. They have got to understand what their colleagues are talking about, understand our corporate priorities and be able to use their knowledge to help managers achieve their goals in the most effective way through their people. Whenever we have change

programmes or a new set of goals, they must sit down with managers and get a plan for what these mean for people and how they are going to support them.

You are in the privileged position of being able to see the big picture and take a longer-term view, as I am. So I expect you to suggest areas of people and organisation development where we can work better together and where we can have processes that combine the strengths that each part has for the greater good of the whole. I don't want us to just follow fashions or 'me too' initiatives – we don' t want to be 'leading-edge' in people management for its own sake, but because its going to make us a better organisation delivering better value to our customers. So I want innovations, but only where they are clearly justified by their benefits.

Lastly, back where I started, I do know that our people are our most critical resource, especially those with special talents. So I want lots of effort into ensuring we have the best: the best leaders, the best managers and the best at every level, not only the best, but motivated and engaged and committed to give their best. So you need to understand how we do that and get policies and processes that deliver it. And I want you to build a reporting and measurement process that tells all of us in clear, understandable words and figures how we are doing and what we need to do better.

'OK?'

As we approach the different stakeholders in our function, we will get different demands and stories. HR will find, as does an organisation as a whole, that conflicting demands of partners have to be balanced.

One of these will be the finance function. What would the Finance Director say if we asked about their requirements? Maybe something like this:

HR is an overhead function. It is my job to keep overheads as low as possible. I like low employee headcount because it reduces our long-term liabilities for pensions and redundancy payouts. But if that is compensated by excessive expenditure on subcontract staff, consultants and outsourcing contracts we must remember it is the total cost that affects the bottom line. I know we have to attract and retain good people but I don't want us to pay more than we need to in the market. I want you to encourage people to work from home because that saves us expensive premises costs. And I am often worried about what we pay out in bonuses because I am not sure we get any more out of people than if we had no schemes at all!

I'd like to see HR calculating the financial effect of some people issues such as absenteeism and labour turnover. We don't report these as separate cost items as you know but I need to rely on your professional expertise to know where the true hidden costs are and work with us on how to cost them on a standardised basis.

The whole area of measuring intangibles is a problem for us. We obviously know the costs of what we spend but we don't distinguish in the people area between what really is a cost and what is perhaps an investment. If you are doing things that you think are investments, such as some of your training programmes, then you ought to do investment appraisal just like we do for the more tangible investments. Otherwise we'll continue to see all people expenditure as costs, and it's our job here to keep all costs as low as possible!

When we get into mergers, acquisitions and divestments I need your help quickly and discreetly to evaluate people related financial liabilities…

Now if we went an operational manager, such as the manager of customer services, we would get quite a different slant on their expectations. It might go like this:

Success in my job is all about people and getting things done right and fast. It's a tough job dealing with customers all day long, who have usually only phoned or written to complain or to ask questions —most of which are answered on the instructions they don't read.

The last thing I want from HR is policing and nannying – I want to be able to use my own common sense. And the first thing I want is speed. I want all the admin stuff dealt with accurately and fast. I want replacements for those who leave, waiting on the doorstep. I want training to be 'just in time' – no fancy nonsense, just targeted at what my people need to know about the products and how they can improve their interaction skills.

Please keep your processes simple and easy for busy managers to use. I want a helpline I can call when needed for instant expert answers. I want a pay and bonus system that is geared to success in our departments' objectives. And I'd like one good HR person who really understands the life and pressures in this department to be a colleague on tap and able to advise me on any problems; maybe even help me with planning and so forth.

And so the HR department, as they go round their stakeholders, could draw up a summary of the various demands and expectations. This is the way to figure out the skills and resources that are needed – not behind closed doors in HR departmental meetings.

5.7 How the Professional HR Partner Contributes to the Business

How could we categorise what these people are telling us? They are saying firstly that they expect HR to support them. They want an efficient administration service, good professional advice, information, help when needed, and to be kept out of trouble. This is the foundation of the HR function, and we explore it more in Section 5.8.

But there is more than that … the essence of partnership is belonging to the business team – being a part of it and contributing to the decisions it needs to make. Any member of a business team must wear two hats and be concerned with two sets of interests, which may sometimes conflict. First, they represent their own unit or function, and second they represent the collective interest of the team. Many a CEO has sought help with the latter – 'how can I get people to stop thinking only of their own area and think about US?' is the cry. The HR member of the team has a people-professional perspective to offer but also will only contribute effectively if they understand what is going on. It is somewhat ingenuous and naïve to take this for granted – not all businesses are easy to understand from a technical point of view. But the underlying business model – what generates margin and profitability – should be fully comprehended. Given at least that, and knowledge of the business strategy, this second area of partnership we might call 'team decision making'. In Section 5.9 we look at the some of the areas that are typically on the agenda of business teams and how HR can contribute.

There is another vital role, which is leading. Not leading the business itself, but suggesting ideas and proposing initiatives that lead the organisation to be more effective. This is not because they want to try out some other organisation's great programme, nor because it is the topical issue of the day, but because it is right for the organisation. (Ulrich, in his new model described above, does not actually include under 'HR as leaders' this aspect of leading towards a better organisation.)

CEOs always have their own focus of interests. Some are technical and are inspired by product ideas. Others are financially orientated and focused exclusively on the bottom line. A few are so interested in people and organisation that they drive the HR function personally. This is both a blessing and a curse as we can imagine – hopefully more of the former. Without such a CEO, if the HR Director does not lead in the areas of organisational change and people management processes, no one else will. Unlike his or her line colleagues, they see the whole picture. This is a tremendous responsibility – to propose investments in people management and people development that will bring good returns in their benefits for the business. We discuss some of these opportunities in Section 5.10.

These three areas of 'partnership' contribute value in different ways. The first adds value, day by day, to managers and to teams in the organisation by helping them achieve their goals. The second adds value to the management team through an individual contribution of wisdom and judgement and ensuring people perspectives are taken into account. The third area is about creating a more effective organisation for the future. 'Adding value' is not just an expression that means 'being valued and respected', although the two are obviously related. Value should be something that can be measured, and every contribution should be seen in terms of a measurable value level.

They can be summarised as three connecting circles in this way:

Figure 5.7   The nature of partnership between HR and the business

5.8 Providing Support to Management

We will go through a number of different kinds of support that can and should be offered.

TO TEAM MEMBERS AS INDIVIDUALS

The essence of partnering is supporting managers to achieve their business goals faster and more effectively. Persuading them to participate in an HR driven agenda will be appropriate from time to time, but if that is all that is done, this is certainly not true partnership. One joint outcome of working *together* should be optimal management of people in the organisation.

HR people often decry the people skills of many managers and go down the 'they really oughta wanna' route. The truth is that in most organisations people are initially promoted for their expertise, not their leadership potential or people management skills. Many develop these as they progress, but not all. The right solution is to ensure there are parallel career ladders, for professionals as well as managers. Meanwhile, we have the managers we have. Some need more support than others. What matters is that the combination of manager and HR partner together provides the excellence that delivers value to employees. This is shown in Figure 5.8.

It is a myth and tradition, borne out of hierarchical thinking, that there is something sacred and unique about the manager's role with people. If people management is not his or her strength, then partnership is about supporting them as needed. Maybe they are not good at giving appraisals? Why should an HR expert not help with the feedback task? This personal support extends to coaching, advising, helping with people decisions, and generally 'being there'. Some HR ideologists would vigorously contradict this view, saying that 'people management should be back where it belongs – with line managers'. To which I would respond 'Is it great people managers that we need or great people *management*?' If the latter, then lets work together towards it.

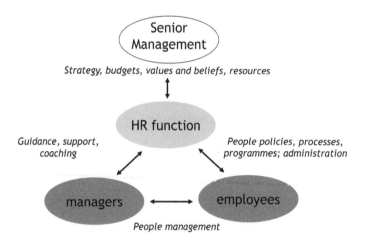

Figure 5.8   A partnership for people management

SUPPORT TO THE BOSS

HR members of business teams often have a unique role – which is that of counsellor to the boss or 'team leader'. I mentioned Tony, my first significant such boss earlier – and one of the things he said to me was 'the thing with you is that you don't have an agenda – everyone else around the table is trying to wheedle something out of me or play politics against a colleague'. Well, true or not, this gave him confidence in me as a confidant, and many the after-hours discussions we had about the business and the players in it.

It's a very personal and delicate support that the HR team member can give here. Delicate, because to be seen as the boss's mouthpiece, or the 'spy', will destroy any confidence other team members have. There are boundaries of confidentiality on both sides that must be made clear and not trespassed.

Behind the scenes it may be, but it gives many an HR team member a strong sense of importance and contribution.

PROFESSIONAL SUPPORT TO THE TEAM

Apart from supporting individuals, there is the day to day role of HR. The HR Business Partner may not be the one who actually does the administrative or routine advisory tasks, but they will ensure that they happen efficiently and effectively. They will fill any holes and resolve any difficulties. They will also:

- Provide data and information to the team – workforce analysis, market surveys, cost information, statistics, and benchmarks.

- Monitor employee opinion and engagement and not only analyse the results but suggest collective and local actions.

- Initiate (see Chapter 6, page 240ff) and implement projects that will support business goals.

- Manage processes jointly with team members such as recruitment, appraisal, selection, feedback, pay management, bonus systems, and so on.

- Provide consultancy – problem solving and generating ideas.

- Organising learning programmes which support business or individual/team requirements.

And maybe do more depending on the scope of their role.

5.9 Decision Making in the Business Team

As mentioned earlier, this is the wearing of 'the two hats' – both the professional HR one and concern for the collective good of the team to which we belong.

Here are some of the contributions the HR representative (in common with all other team members) should be expected to make:

- helping define vision, values and principles;

- helping define business strategies;

- business performance management and review;

- mergers, acquisitions, partnerships and divestments;

- organisation and resource restructuring;

- corporate governance;

- collective response to issues and problems;

- initiatives for change and investment.

And particularly for the HR member (*as the servant of the team*):

- responsibility for 'team maintenance', that is, the healthy functioning of the team itself.

We discuss each of these in turn below.

HELPING DEFINE VISION, VALUES AND PRINCIPLES

These may be well established, or even dictated by a parent organisation, and not up for discussion. However, when they are, it's a matter for the top team – even though they may involve others in the process. The HR member has a role of 'the conscience' of the organisation and may be aware that what exists has little credibility, or currency, in the way the organisation really works. It is better not to have values or principles published at all if they are regularly flouted. In this case the HR member may challenge the team to address the issue and propose a process for doing so. As we will see in the next chapter, they are a very important guide to the creation of a people strategy.

Some organisations have values and principles that are stale and have lost currency. They are not a part of everyday life. Just as the Finance Director is the guardian of financial propriety, so HR is the guardian of culture. They have an ongoing role in reviewing and assessing the validity of such statements, and analysing what should be done. This may be a relaunch, or going back to square one and starting again.

HELPING DEFINE BUSINESS STRATEGIES

One sometimes hears statements like 'people are so important that HR should be leading the company strategy' – or similar grand ambitions. This is nonsense. Nevertheless, there are several invaluable roles to be played when it comes to the formulation of business strategies. Here is a summary of them:

- At the time when the planning process is underway, there is an important part of the *analysis* that the HR function should contribute to. Where relevant to the particular business goal, HR should conduct its own 'PESTLE' (political, economic, social, technological, legal and environmental) analysis on people related factors as it scans the relevant environments and looks ahead. It may also have useful knowledge of competitive activities to bring to the table.

- *Testing and validating* each strategy, from a people and culture perspective, is a vital and difficult role. Difficult politically that is, since one does not want to appear negative and it is not easy to go against the tide. A good example is a planned acquisition – how many disasters would have been avoided if HR had fully understood the potential cultural and engagement issues and made other senior managers aware of the risks? All business strategies need to be tested against our capability, resource availability, cultural constraints, and employee acceptance. Management needs the full picture for their final decision.

- HR has a role in ensuring decision makers *are trained in strategic thinking*. Leadership development programmes must include this so that each contributor is familiar with the processes and tools in use.

Typically, strategies are reviewed annually and/or when there is a major restructuring of the business through acquisition, divestment or planned downsizing. Whereas people like Arie de Geus (*The Living Company* 1997) taught us that the right approach to strategy is to review it continuously, in practice we are mostly concerned with daily implementation. If we are big enough, we have some specialist resource called the Strategic Planning Department, but even they normally work to a timetable.

In the next chapter we briefly discuss the formulation of business strategy – and go on to look in detail how people and organisation strategies support it. To make a contribution, the business team member needs to have a good grasp of strategic planning principles and tools; of the industry or sector that they are in, and of the key dimensions of the particular business. Each team member has a particular specialist contribution to make – and those representing support functions have the task of challenging, or playing 'devil's advocate'.

When strategic and business plans fail to be achieved, it is more often than not because ambitious targets were not matched by the resource requirements needed to make them happen. There are tangible resources like money and equipment, and 'intangible' too, such as organisational and individual capability. The challenging of strategies makes for a healthy process and should not be considered 'negative thinking'. The Finance function will challenge proposed levels of profitability or expenditure. Likewise, HR should challenge strategies and their timescales for feasibility, using their knowledge of human resource availability and people related issues. Once all is agreed HR will take them one by one and build the people and organisation strategies outlined in Chapter 6.

What are the areas of challenge that HR might have as a checklist? Many of these may not be obvious to the proposers of the strategy, yet can so easily derail it. They will consider the following:

- Cultural dissonance – does the plan call for requirements that run counter to prevailing cultural norms? Broad assumptions that ambitious line managers like to make, that 'we'll ride through that when we get to it' do not usually succeed. We may require extensive 'cultural transformation' and that takes a long time and requires a deliberate plan.

- Resource availability – how feasible is it to have the right resources available at the right time? There may be constraints of availability. The business is not served well by rushing to 'get bodies'; we need the *right* people.

- Organisational capability – will the existing structure support or work against the proposal?

- Management and employee capability – is this going to require new levels or new types of knowledge and skill? Where will it come from and how long will it take to achieve it?

- Employee engagement – is what is being proposed going to create employee resistance? Of course it is HR's job to manage that, but anticipating and planning for it in advance may affect the time targets of the strategy.

Thinking through these issues clearly will help HR when it comes to preparing its own supporting strategies, but they are a second step. The business strategists may need to revise their goals as a result of these challenges. It is better for all concerned – and not least for outsiders to see – that a good, but perhaps more cautious, strategy was implemented and achieved, than for an ambitious one to fail.

BUSINESS PERFORMANCE AND MANAGEMENT REVIEWS

Everyday life for a management team is not about 'strategic thinking' – it's the day to day achievement of targets and managing problems. Organisations review performance in different ways, but it is common for each business unit to be reviewed periodically by the whole management team. Depending on levels, it may be two way – both being reviewed and doing the reviewing.

Such events look at achievements against targets, forecasts, actions taken, actions needed, deciding priorities and reviewing projects and investments.

Having sat through literally dozens of business reviews, and trying my best to make a helpful contribution as both HR Director and business team member, I know it is not easy. Firstly, the reviews may both have heavy agendas and a lot of attendees and airtime is at a premium. Secondly, there is often game playing taking place and the rational objective voice is treated as naïve. Then, even though the people issues may be obvious, many managers have an unwillingness to recognise and address them. Because of the pressure of time in this type of meeting, the HR person may well be making notes of issues to help with 'off-line'.

There are different levels at which a contribution can be made. At the operational level, sometimes the 'excuse my ignorance' question can be helpful, but it runs the risk of being irritating especially if overused. Unless the

HR person is firmly grounded in the operations of the business (through their own experience) it may be hard to add value. In a commercial business, at the financial level, any HR person that calls her/himself a business partner should be able to hold their own. That means understanding the figures, making intelligent analysis and suggestions, and being able to comprehend cause and effect on the bottom line. In a non-commercial organisation they should be completely *au fait* with what drives, and what works against, the achievement of the organisation's objectives.

Naturally, we expect a contribution in areas that concern people, and the HR team member would ensure there is a specific part of the agenda devoted to this:

- There will always be items to be reported on that are owned by the HR function – change projects, initiatives, resourcing targets, response to new external constraints (such as laws) or opportunities (such as a new government incentive).

- There is an 'organisation and people' dimension to every problem. HR people should be particularly skilled at cause and effect analysis – to see in every task or problem what issues of employee capability, motivation, organisation, and resourcing may lie behind an issue.

- There should be regular performance reports on what is happening to 'human capital'. Business reviews should have on the table sets of people related measures that are relevant to the performance of the organisation, using one of the models outlined in Chapter 4.

INVOLVEMENT IN MERGERS, ACQUISITIONS, PARTNERSHIPS, AND DIVESTMENTS

The business strategy may state its intent to seek these, but each is a project in itself. Often partnerships and divestments are carefully planned ahead, but mergers and acquisitions are more opportunistic and happen quickly. The HR Business Partner will ensure she or he has the capability to respond to such needs. In the last major acquisition that I was involved in, the CEO instructed all the top team to immediately delegate the running of their departments to their 'number two' in order to work full-time on the acquisition. That was a challenge to some of them!

These opportunities represent a classic example of team decision making, as many functions play their part in the whole. The reasons for the appalling failure rate of mergers are well known. They are almost always to do with people and cultural issues. Sometimes the basic strategic reasoning was wrong in the first place, but more often than not a major cause is that there is undue pressure to demonstrate the benefits promised, which are frequently expressed as savings in the number of people.

It is beyond our scope to discuss in depth the major role that HR plays in such situations (but see Chapter 10 of *The Human Value of the Enterprise*, 2001). The HR team member's role, however, is again one of devil's advocacy, and because of the frequent clouding of judgement in the excitement of the deal, it can be a hard one to play.

The most common cause of failure is cultural dissonance, but it is also in the loss of key people. In acquisitions a hefty premium is normally paid for the intangible assets. Those that are not actually named as individual people, such as customer reputation and operational systems, are nevertheless dependent on people somewhere. Hasty decisions which result in the loss, voluntary or otherwise, of critical staff have to be resisted.

ORGANISATION AND RESOURCE RESTRUCTURING

This of course happens in the situation of mergers and acquisitions, but may happen for other reasons. The HR team member will often be in on the proposal from the beginning, sometimes even before it is presented to the team. Their role is to ensure that each member is involved and has an input, and that any conflicts or overlaps resulting from the change are resolved. On behalf of the team they may prepare the implementation and communications plan.

CORPORATE GOVERNANCE

The representatives from Finance, Legal and HR all share the responsibility to ensure that the organisation has, and is seen to have, good corporate governance. HR has a number of specific roles – in director appointments, remuneration and performance reviews; in processes and reporting for health and safety, and (often) diversity. Needless to say, the highest standards of integrity and principle are required here. In the story of Enron (*Conspiracy of Fools*, 2005) there is no mention of any HR influence of significance – but then the last thing top management wanted was to be challenged.

COLLECTIVE RESPONSE TO ISSUES AND PROBLEMS

All kinds of issues arise in an organisation during a year, requiring a wise and considered response. There are stories and rumours in the media, competitive activities, customer and supplier issues, operational difficulties, natural disasters, political interference ... and so on. Many of these do not come to the level of the team, but when they do each member has to contribute to the collective wisdom in coming to a solution. The personal credibility of the member for HR (as for any other) will be made partly at least on the contribution they make.

CHANGE AND INVESTMENT DECISIONS

In some organisations a separate sub-committee may be convened for investment decisions regarding the commissioning of projects with a future return. HR has two important roles here. The first is to be able to apply RoI methodologies to projects that they propose (see Chapter 7), and the second is to be able to make an intelligent appraisal of other projects. For both, they need a sound understanding of the financial appraisal process. In addition they should be expert in the quantitative estimation of non-financial benefits and hidden costs.

'Hidden costs' are the cause of many projects going wrong: if we consider an office relocation, a restructuring, a plan to outsource, a new IT system, and certainly a merger proposal, it is often the case that only the obvious implementation costs are compared with projected savings. Protagonists usually put forward their proposals optimistically. The HR member should know from experience the risks of such projects and have at their disposal sets of relevant figures. These would be for such areas as loss of productivity, loss of people, rebuilding of relationships, costs of retraining, and so on. Without being in any way negative, they can draw on similar experiences within or without the organisation to make sure that the full picture is taken into account.

Large IT projects are notorious for going way beyond time and budget; especially, it seems, in the public sector. It is not HR's job to stop projects but rather to bring in a perspective of the effect on people and what that might do to performance as a result. Sometimes it is the role of the responsible HR person to say 'I cannot support this and this is why'.

MAINTAINING THE TEAM

A study of Belbin's 'team roles' tells us of the importance of a role simply called 'team worker', which falls naturally – at least positionally – to the HR person. This is a role of observing how the team is working together and intervening appropriately. In many senior teams we may have a group of people who happen to be reporting to the same person, but who mentally share very little. A typical example would be a group of country/regional operations reporting to an international Vice President. They are probably in no way dependent on one another; even though they may have some bonus based on 'corporate results' – which seems to them to be 'the luck of the draw', compared to the (probably) much larger portion of remuneration based on their own area.

This is frequently the case in public sector organisations. In local government, for example, each department delivers its own unique service, requiring its own professionals and methodologies. Each line director has an interest in all corporate policies, but otherwise is very departmentally focused. CEOs often bewail this fact, even though it is totally understandable, and turn to HR (who may turn to consultants) to 'do something about it'.

Team or no team, in the strict sense of the word, the HR member will be sensitive to how the group is working. There are significant risks. Though other colleagues may accept a special confidential link with the CEO, their own confidence has to be maintained and a political tightrope navigated with care.

'Team maintenance' is ensuring that the team is functioning well. The signs of concern are when members hold back information, create mini-alliances, hide or fail to control emotions, get into personal conflicts, show low participation – or fall easily into 'group think' for fear of voicing contrary views. This last is sometimes known as the 'Abilene Paradox', where the story is told of a family group in Abilene, Texas, who thought they had a unanimous decision to drive 50 miles, in great heat, for lunch – only to find out afterwards that nobody really wanted to go in the first place. A more common example is illustrated by the *Challenger* space shuttle disaster in 1987, when a lone protesting voice about a safety issue was overwhelmed by the political urgencies to launch and to maintain good customer relations: the whole crew was killed.

The HR member may feel uncomfortable about tackling these issues personally and, rightly so, since he or she is one of the team members. However, they will be continually sensitive to what is happening and suggest appropriate (external) help when it is needed. Often some of these problems are caused by the CEO's style and persona, and some private counselling may be possible.

5.10 Leading – Towards Greater Organisational Effectiveness

What we mean here is proposing, initiating, gaining support for, and managing change; changes that will make the organisation function better. Ulrich's original model included 'change agent', but this is now absorbed in 'strategic partnership'.

There are, and have been, many CEOs who have a personal passion for the way the organisation should work and harness the HR function to make it happen. Jack Welch at GE (General Electric) spent an extraordinary amount of time in management development programmes at Crotonville, and on succession planning meetings. John Browne, when at BP, drove the agenda for knowledge management. Alan Leighton, at Asda and the Royal Mail, showed his passion for the employee voice. Sometimes they pick up ideas from books or from 'CEO Clubs'. But it is rare that they drive the complete people and organisational agenda. Whilst HR is responsive in supporting CEO initiatives, it is their job to take the overview.

TAKING THE INITIATIVE – OR NOT...

Most organisations are rabbit warrens of initiatives: added to those taken by each operational unit to improve themselves come numerous projects and programmes from the support functions. All of these divert the time of line managers from their operational tasks. So proposing an initiative should not be done lightly.

HR people are not usually short of ideas. Many are avid attendees of networking groups and seminars, we may hope largely in search of 'better ways of doing things'. Generally they are some of the best consumers of business books, and have an immense range of consultants to draw on, many of whom have been practitioners themselves and who court them assiduously to try out their ideas.

Many organisations seem permanently hungry to find out what 'world class best practice' is, and in some ways this is healthy. Those who believe life is a continuous search for improvement cannot accept that the 'best' has yet been found by definition – what we mean, is 'good practices that have worked for one or some organisations'. There are dangers here. One is that practices are copied too readily without adaptation to the culture and needs of the receiving organisation. The other is that they are not properly prioritised in terms of the business benefits.

Initiatives for creating a more effective organisation, which should be the name of the game, fall into two categories. One is through reacting to a problem that exists. A wise professional once gave me invaluable, yet so simple, advice – 'always ask what is the problem you trying to solve?' This is the first test of any initiative. The second category is that we believe that a proactive change would give us real benefits. In this case we must be very honest about assessing the cost and benefit balance for the proposed change. We must ask 'what will happen to the business if we don't do this?' Another aphorism to pin up on the support function's wall is 'one person's professionalism is another person's bureaucracy'.

THE DECISION PROCESS

Needless to say, any proposal for an initiative requires intelligent preparation based on sound knowledge. The HR professional will be keeping in constant touch with the progress of the business through monitoring achievement and attending appropriate meetings, as well as regularly having informal chats with the operational managers.

When a need for an initiative is perceived, some diagnostic work will need to be done (well directed Masters' students from local universities and business schools can be very useful here, doing the research as their dissertation). This may take the following forms:

- Benchmarking against other competitors. This is always better than the 'general' benchmarking, but competitors in HR include other industries drawing from the same labour pools.

- Seeking opinions and perceptions of the present situation and checking out some possible alternatives. This can be done through online surveys, or using the opportunities provided by training events and other diagnostic tools.

- Researching cost information – maybe using the help of the Finance department.

- Collecting anecdotal comments or putting together incidents of commonly experienced problems.

Once data is established, a case must be put together. In Chapter 7 we discuss the detail of doing this. We should be very clear about which stakeholders will benefit and how, what metrics will demonstrate the benefits, and all the costs involved.

THE POLITICS OF GETTING COMMITMENT

The basic rules will be well-known here, and there is no need to elaborate extensively. The hindsight of experience provides the following guidelines:

- It helps considerably to achieve support before a decision meeting from key players. This is likely to include the Chief Executive, but should go further. If possible, any team members most likely to object should be won over in advance. This might include the Finance Director if significant expenditure is involved.

- The benefits need to be 'baited' in a way that will appeal; that will enable the team member(s) to see a gain that is important to them. Thus if absenteeism is a headache for operational directors, then a proposed stress management programme would perhaps start with the savings that could result and how operations will be made smoother.

- As always, piloting an initiative with a supportive line partner is a good strategy. If successful, others will want to take it on board. Otherwise, not too much has been lost.

LEADING ON CULTURE

The HR business partner should be at the heart of their organisation, seeing it as a whole and particularly conscious of how it works, or does not work, together. They have – or have access to – expertise in the areas of:

- aspiration and reality in terms of organisational values;

- describing behaviours that support the values;

- the nature of organisational culture and how it can be assessed, changed and developed;

- the causes of internal competition and political game playing.

A strong consistent culture is an asset to any organisation. Porras and Collins, in *Built to Last* (1994), studied what makes organisations consistently successful, and this was one of the factors. However, restructuring today is so prevalent that it is increasingly rare to find cultures immune from 'contamination' – by a new broom CEO bringing in their own new ideas, or through mergers and acquisitions. When Jim McNerney was passed over for taking over from Jack Welch, he became the first external CEO of 3M, a company with a very strong culture and reputation for innovation. He showed considerable concern to keep as much as possible of those cultural strengths, and to add to them with a few ideas from GE; notably the six sigma system of quality control. There are many more cases where great cultures have been destroyed, especially through mergers – where there is always one dominant partner. Mobil's innovative and empowering culture was subsumed by Exxon's systematic control; Digital Equipment's engineering excellence by Compaq's cost management – books have been written, filled with such examples.

ESTABLISHING A CULTURAL VISION

Culture is 'the way we do things around here'. There will always be layers of subculture within an organisation of any size, based on location and nationality, history, dominant figures of the past, and so on. But many of the ways in which we do things – systems and processes – are dictated from some central point.

There are plenty of tools available for describing or comparing cultures, most of them founded on two dimensions – the concern for people vs. the concern for the task to be done, and how these are balanced. People can be asked how they experience various indicators of 'the way things are around here' and then secondly, how they would like it to be. Deeper analysis can be done using tools like the 'cultural web' which identifies not only the way things are but the factors that have caused it to become like that.

Most people can fairly quickly come up with some things they would like to change in their organisation. Since culture change is difficult and lengthy it is not to be undertaken lightly. What we need to be sure of is that aspects of culture are not barriers to achieving our goals. So a recommended process, to be done at the time of setting or reviewing the organisational strategy, (see next chapter) is for the senior team to do the following:

- imagine it is five years hence, and we have been successful in achieving our goals over this period;

- take each stakeholder in turn and describe what it is like for them to interact with the organisation;

- come up with a series of statements which describe this desired culture;

- rate each of them high, medium, low for the importance of their impact;

- score them out of 10, or by using traffic lights, on how close the organisation is now to those statements;

- analyse the scores and make a plan for strengthening the strengths and moving forward on critical deficits;

- use the set of statements as an instrument for periodic checking on progress.

LEADING ON ORGANISATIONAL CHANGE

It is well-known that new leaders like to change the organisation to establish their own mark and/or beliefs, and in this case HR is briefed to get on with implementation. The HRBP with courage will try and influence proposals if they feel they will be counter-productive and at least ensure that they work together with the new leader in formulating proposals, as well as implementing them.

Most managers and employees accept the organisation they are in as a given, and live with its imperfections. They are often quite unaware of how difficult their organisation is to deal with from outside. The team member for HR will carry a checklist of the characteristics of an effective organisation, and be constantly on the look out for breaches of these. They will include such indicators as:

- clear accountabilities without overlap and duplication;

- efficient flows of communication and knowledge;

- each department has a clear strategic line of sight to the business strategy;

- performance targets are not in conflict;

- processes that cross organisational boundaries work efficiently, especially if customer related;

- customers see one organisation not several;

- spans of control are consistent with effective people management.

This latter is of particular interest to HR. The tendency to delayer organisations and increase the number of people being looked after by one manager or supervisor (on cost saving grounds) has put people management processes under much strain.

LEADING ON LEADERSHIP AND EXECUTIVE DEVELOPMENT

Having spent 15 years on behalf of a major business school designing and delivering leadership development programmes, I am constantly disappointed at the level of thought that goes into many of the requirements that land on the desks of the schools. The first question I ask is 'To what extent is the programme designed to develop individuals as leaders, as opposed to supporting an organisational change programme?' A common answer is 'well, both really'. Yet the learning objectives are very different, and so will be the structure of the solution. It is also very natural for HR people to see all development in terms of soft skills, and take for granted that their managers know all they need on strategy, finance, marketing, supply chain management, and so on.

The business minded HR professional will ensure that the specification of off the job executive development programmes is based on careful analysis. A programme aimed at supporting organisational directions will be derived from one of the following:

- An analysis of business strategies and their implications for executive capability.

Examples here would include changing the business model, entering new markets, the need to comprehend rapid external change, gaining competitive advantage, or preparing for a future discontinuity in the way things have been traditionally done.

- Organisational and cultural change initiatives which require new mindsets, knowledge and skills.

An organisation wants to be different in the way it behaves. It is radically changing its structure – perhaps to a matrix or horizontal configuration – and needs everybody to understand how to work with the new model. Or it is seeking to transform its culture and needs leaders to role model the vision. Perhaps a recent merger has taken place and there is a need for executives to share a new common vision and way of working. In the public sector, a government initiative may require significant change in ways of working.

- There are persistent problems that indicate a lack of attitude, knowledge or skill.

Employee surveys might indicate that people feel disempowered and over controlled. Or the company is continually losing out against competitors in a certain market. Perhaps people are pulling in different directions and need to share a common focus.

All of the above require some *collective* learning. Often the same is assumed for the entire 'leadership' population – but there will almost certainly be requirements for subsets of this for specialised needs.

From time to time the HR Business Partner will assess these three areas, for their part of the organisation as a whole and in its sub-units. Before rushing to expensive prestigious programmes, they will carefully analyse, with expert help as needed, the options available to achieve the learning objectives. Some requirements may be met by well facilitated events managed internally.

Sometimes, as with all 'training', the real reason for embarking on it is motivational and the event itself is actually more important than the outcome – time away with colleagues, perhaps a nice certificate at the end, and a positive feeling towards the organisation for investing in me/us.

The essence of leading in this area is not just seeing the need, preparing a case and making it happen. It is a continual role of involvement and participation, and ensuring the objectives are being achieved. The HR Businses Partner will not delegate this role to a more junior colleague or to the L&D (learning and development) department.

LEADING ON RESOURCING STRATEGIES

The labour market is, or should be, bread and butter for the HR function. In some countries, including the UK, it has changed radically over recent years. The norm of full time employment contracts and exclusive work relationships remains the most common form of work arrangement, but is supplemented with many more flexible and global options. The initial sourcing of people at many levels has become internet based.

Workforce planning, based on the business plans, is an essential discipline and it is HR that will shape the methodology and templates. They need to ensure we have clear policies for the distribution of human effort that is needed to deliver results – which includes outsourced effort, temporary workers, subcontractors and consultants, and for the targeted levels of internal promotion. They must be aware of external factors affecting these, as well as having a clear understanding of the flows of people through the organisation. They will be able to calculate demand for different skills over the planning period, assess the availability of supply, and prepare strategies to close the gaps. A lot of money can be saved in recruitment and/or redundancy by effective workforce planning.

LEADING IN REWARD, RETENTION AND MOTIVATIONAL STRATEGIES

HR is expected to lead on matters to do with pay. But when it comes to retention the issue is much more complex than how much people are paid. In Table 3.2 we explained a tool for assessing the balance of an employee's expectations. It is said that 'people leave people, not organisations' and that the onus for retention is firmly in the individual manager's court. Nevertheless, it is mostly HR that will suggest new ideas which increase retention – for example, service related benefits, share options, career workshops (most people leave because they can see no way forward), and project assignments.

LEADING ON PERFORMANCE MANAGEMENT

Finance or strategy departments set up targets and systems such as 'the balanced scorecard', but performance is delivered through people: so called 'performance management systems' are actually a problem in many organisations. According to an IRS study, 78 per cent of organisations in 2005 were redesigning their 'appraisal' processes. Something must be wrong after all these years. My own view is that many systems try to do far too much in one event. But it is the job of HR to try and get it right.

This is an area where HR is in danger of perfectionism. The only useful criterion is that 'the process fulfils its purpose'. We must, therefore, be clear about what the purpose(s) is/are in the first place – and as before, this is not to be decided by HR, albeit may be proposed by them: organisations are littered with over sophisticated, ultra complex, performance management systems that cause pain all round.

I recall a major US-based pharma company whose European HQ asked me to help them review their HR strategy: a key strand of this was a new performance management system (sent from the US), and they were very concerned how they 'would sell this to the line'. Their concern was justified – it was based on a complex competency framework. But my first thought was, 'isn't there something very wrong if we are worried about this? Surely every line manager wants to help improve the performance of their employees?' And, worryingly, 'did anyone check this out with the line management?'

Nevertheless, understanding what leads to high performance for both individuals and teams is a fundamental professional contribution of HR.

LEADING ON 'TALENT MANAGEMENT'

If there is one area that CEOs and top people in HR seem to share as a priority, it is what is popularly called 'talent management'. It is a term that has many interpretations. The first question to arise is about the comprehensiveness of the word 'talent'. Its definition needs to be agreed by all concerned, albeit HR may make the original proposition. It is then the task of HR to propose and initiate the processes needed for the acquisition, retention and development of those that fall in to the categories of 'talent'. This will include definitions and assessment of potential, succession planning and career management. HR can set the framework, but talented people work for managers in different parts of the organisation, and processes must be as enthusiastically owned by operational managers as by anyone in HR.

LEADING ON KNOWLEDGE MANAGEMENT

To some this might seem strange for HR to be involved with – isn't 'knowledge management' the job of the IT department? It certainly helps with the management of 'explicit knowledge', but most, of course, resides in people. And even the technological tools that IT provides require the right motivation to ensure they are used effectively.

Knowledge management can be defined as:

> *The management of the information, knowledge and experience available to an organisation – its creation, capture, storage, availability and utilisation – in order that organisational activities build on what is already known and extend it further.*

In *The Human Value of the Enterprise* (Mayo 2001) I outlined 'Fourteen Building Blocks of Knowledge Management' (Chapter 8, p. 205). There are a number of potential interventions by HR:

- raising the consciousness of the need in an organisation.

The HR Business Partner could arrange for an expert to provide a short seminar or could conduct some research to demonstrate the nature of the problem. As usual what gets management's attention first and foremost are figures.

Here is a set of survey questions that could be used:

Can you think of an occasion where you found someone else in the company was doing the same project as you? If yes, give a few details including the approximate cost of the project.

Can you think of any sales project that was lost because we lacked enough information about the customer's needs or about what competitor's could offer? How much money was the deal?

Can you think of any situation that 'went wrong' and afterwards you discovered that a) either the same mistake had been made before, or b) it was due to inadequate utilisation of existing knowledge? What did it cost?

How much time do you spend a month (% approx.) searching for information?

Do you have ideas for a better company or a new product/service that nobody seems to listen to?

Can you think of any external relationships that have been lost, and because of this we have lost sales opportunities? What was their (approx) impact?

Can you think of any situations where you could not respond to a request through lack of available knowledge and skills? What did you lose as a result?

Would you say it is normal for people in your area to freely share their knowledge and experience? Both within and beyond their own unit?

Once the case is made and accepted, HR may be asked to propose the resources and organisation needed. Many organisations today have a Chief Knowledge Officer, with a small staff. Their role is to set the framework of processes, culture and technology and to work with units in their implementation.

- Effective knowledge management is probably more about people and culture than anything else.

HR must lead in defining the nature of any culture change and managing the journey to achieve it. A typical set of change requirements is as follows:

From	To
Blame culture	Problems/mistakes seen as learning opportunities
Information shared on need to know basis only	Information freely available to all
Innovation requires permission	Innovation and experimentation expected
No time taken for reflection and experience sharing	Such time is normal and expected
Knowledge comes down only from above	Relevant knowledge is sought from people at all levels
'Not invented here'	Interest in learning from anywhere
'Knowledge is power'	'Shared knowledge is power'

These are attitudes and mindsets, and patience will be needed to change them. Processes, which incorporate knowledge sharing steps, have a major effect. Just as important is the reinforcement of desired behaviours by senior management and the reprimanding of the undesired.

- In addition to attitudes, some skills may need to be sharpened – including questioning and listening, delegating and empowering, information search and retrieval, report writing, using tools such as virtual discussion groups, and storytelling.

LEADING IN COMMUNICATION STRATEGIES

Whether internal communication is the responsibility of HR or not (it very much should be in the author's view), it is such a vital component of people management that a constant monitoring would be done by HR. Where needs emerge, either in upwards or downwards communications, HR would actively propose solutions. They may also propose completely new channels for piloting or full-scale adoption.

LEADING IN PEOPLE RELATED MEASURES

This is a major theme of this book, and we have observed that managers often are simply not aware of how better people measures would help them manage better. Since the test of any intervention is that it will be seen as useful by managers, the introduction of new measurements needs the same approach as any other proposal in this 'HR as leading' category.

5.11 Summary

We believe Ulrich made a seminal contribution to understanding how HR could be more in tune with, and more helpful to, the business. But his concept of 'strategic business partner' had been hijacked beyond the balance he intended. Our approach, the 'SDL' model of business partnership, arguably introduces some additional elements which emphasise the involvement in the business – taking part in business decisions, and some of the areas for leading the organisation to be more effective. Table 5.1 shows a comparison of the two models.

Table 5.1   Ulrich's roles and the SDL model

Ulrich Role (original)	Ulrich Role (2005)	SDL model
Strategic Partner	Strategic Partner	S,D,L
Change Agent		S,D,L
	Human Capital Developer	S,L
Employee Champion	Employee Advocate	S,D,L
Administrative Expert	Functional Expert	S,L
	HR Leader	L

HR is often seen unfavourably – as consumed with administration, or as a policing and compliance function with little concern for business priorities. It can be seen as the inventor of complexity that diverts management time, a source of impenetrable jargon, or pretentious beyond its importance. Yet this chapter shows the immense contribution that professional HR can make to help and improve the business of an organisation. We will extend this contribution in the next chapter as we look specifically at the creation of 'people strategies'.

5.12 Challenges to Action

- Has the HR function a clear view of its stakeholders, the value that is exchanged between them, and the relative power they exert? Does value for their stakeholders feature regularly in departmental conversation?

- When was the last time that HR asked its significant stakeholders what they looked for and expected from the function?

- Does the HR function have a clear understanding of the accountabilities and synergistic partnership that should exist between them and managers?

- Has the HR function fully defined its areas of contribution?

- Are those who are designated 'business partners' fully competent to play the role of business team member as well as HR representative?

- What mechanisms exist for HR to keep in tune with the daily progress of the business?

- Has HR a defined process for suggesting initiatives for change towards greater organisational effectiveness?

5.13 References and Further Reading

Ashkenas R., Ulrich D., Jick, T., and Kerr, S. (1995). *The Boundaryless Organisation*. Jossey Bass.

Baron, A., and Armstrong, M. (2007). *Human Capital Management*. London: CIPD.

CIPD. (2005). *Business Partnering – A Guide*.

Dalziel, S., Strange, J., and Walters, M. (2006). *HR Business Partnering – How to Diagnose Gaps, Develop Capabilities and Become a Business Partner*. London: CIPD.

De Geus, A.P. (1997). *The Living Company*. Harvard Business School Press.

Eichenwald, K. (2005). *Conspiracy of Fools – the Story of Enron*. Random House.

Holbeche, L., and Carroll, P. (2006). *Business Partnership – A Fresh Approach. Developing HR Strategy*.November 2006.

Hunter, I., Saunders, J., Boroughs, A., and Constance, C. (2006). *HR Business Partners*. Gower.

IRS Employment Review, *Appraisals: Not Living Up to Expectations*, Issue 828 July 2005

Kenton, B., and Yarnall, J. (2005). *HR – The Business Partner – Shaping a New Direction*. Oxford: Elsevier.

Mayo, A.J. (2001). The *Human Value of the Enterprise*. London: Nicholas Brealey.

Porras, J.I., and Collins, J.C. (1994). *Built to Last*. New York: Harper Business.

Ulrich, D. (1997). *Human Resource Champions*. Harvard Business School Press.

Ulrich, D., and Brocklebank, W. (2005). *The HR Value Proposition*. Harvard Business School Press.

Ulrich, D., and Eichinger, R.W. (1998). *HR with an Attitude. HR Magazine*, June 1998.

6

People and Organisation Strategies Derived from the Business Strategy

In this chapter we want to separate out and examine the contributions of HR that are genuinely to do with strategic decisions, the essence of being a 'strategic partner', but not something one does every day. We will look at four subsets of this, which are quite different activities.

They are:

- *Contributing to the overall business strategy.*

- *Ensuring there are strategies for people and organisational effectiveness that is appropriate for the organisation, and policies/processes which support them.*

- *Developing and implementing a series of people and organisation initiatives/programmes that directly support the current business objectives.*

- *Developing and implementing a strategy for the effectiveness and efficiency of the HR function.*

The term 'HR strategy' often refers to one document written by the HR function, and generally internally focused. We shall show how quite separate components need to be created.

In a conglomerate organisation there have to be both global and local strategies, the latter adding to, but not in conflict with, the former. The principles outlined in this chapter apply to all levels, but parent company strategies and policies may be an overriding input.

There have been a number of models proposed for preparing an HR strategy, notably those of Lynda Gratton, Schuler, and Boxall/Purcell. We acknowledge their significant contribution but have not discussed them below as we have developed our own model.

6.1 The Overall Business Strategy

It is worthwhile defining terms here, as different interpretations are often made when it comes to the plethora of words used in planning. This chapter will use terms in the following way:

- A *mission* describes what the purpose of the organisation is and what it is there to do. It is sometimes referred to as the 'statement of purpose'.

- A *vision* is an end-point of where we want to get to in the long-term – maybe what we will be known for and/or a position we aspire to.

- *Values* describe how we want to behave as an organisation, or what we want to be known for, both internally and externally. This may (and should) include beliefs and principles about how we will do business – how we will treat our employees, our customers, our suppliers or the public.

- *Goals* are specific targets on the way to the vision, usually over a time period of 2–5 years.

- *Targets* are the measures that apply to the goals.

- *Strategies* are the routes we choose to achieve the goals.

- *Policies* are about how we will do certain things, consistent with our values.

- *Processes* describe the series of steps to be followed in implementing the policies.

- *Plans* are detailed actions for implementation in the foreseeable period.

A NOTE ON MISSION, VISION AND VALUES

When an organisation starts into life, it often does not worry about defining these descriptions of what it is and what it wants to be. The 'mission' is understood by everyone, the 'vision' is to survive and grow, and the 'values' evolve through the way the founders work together. There comes a point, once established, where some more explicit statements are valuable. This may include a stated philosophy, or set of principles for running the business. Once articulated, these will form an umbrella to both long-term and shorter term strategies. Business strategies will aim to make progress towards the vision; people strategies will be shaped by the values and principles.

Mission and vision statements can be confusing, partly caused by the lack of clarity in the English word 'mission'. So some 'mission statements' are really visions. At worst both can be convoluted paragraphs, or banal meaningless statements that have little grasp on the hearts and minds of employees. The website devoted to Dilbert (www.dilbert.com) has a mocking 'mission statement generator', which randomly puts together a series of buzzwords to create what Dilbert calls *'the long and awkward statement that demonstrates management's inability to think clearly'*.

This is a common type of statement that is neither one thing nor the other:

> *ABC Global Statement of Purpose: 'The purpose of ABC Global is to honourably serve the community by producing products and services of superior quality at a fair price to our customers; to do this so as to earn an adequate profit which is required for the enterprise to grow, and by so doing provide the opportunity for our employees and shareholders to achieve their reasonable personal objectives'.*

This neither states what business ABC Global is in, nor where it is heading; but makes a stakeholder statement that any respectable organisation could sign its name to. (This was a real statement by a famous company, but now has been replaced by a 'Set of Principles', so it seems unfair to publicise its name.)

A vision statement is a long-term goal, generally not with a specific date attached. Sometimes the impossible can still be inspiring – such as the World Bank who describe (and refer to) their dream as 'a world free of poverty'. A vision should be easily memorable, and at least potentially achievable, but sufficiently stretching that it cannot be reached immediately. Gary Hamel and C.K. Prahalad used the term 'strategic intent' which conveys the sense of a vision well. One of the most famous of all was of Komatsu in the 1970s and 1980s – it was simply 'Karu C!' meaning 'Encircle Caterpillar!' Every employee saw this on the doormat as they entered work every day and they certainly had no difficulty in remembering it.

A vision needs focus; many companies create statements similar to the one above, which say they want to be 'preferred by everybody', 'leading in everything'. The well-known triangular 'customer value proposition' suggested three *foci*:

- *Product leadership* – always at the leading edge of technology; constant experimentation; creativity highly valued.

- *Operational excellence* – the best cost and quality combination.

- *Customer intimacy* – close and responsive to customers; building loyalty and relationships.

Though many try, it is very difficult to lead in everything, since conflicts arise. To be leading in product innovation automatically means that you cannot be the lowest cost provider. Furthermore, as we will see below, each focus requires quite different types of organisation, culture and HR practices.

For the purposes of creating strategy, we need to adopt the 'TMT' approach to the grand top level statements, namely 'This means that...we will or will not...' It is this next level that gives us the real guidance.

Companies today tend to be more explicit in their statements of what they want to achieve, as this example from Ericsson shows:

> We believe in an 'all communicating' world. Voice, data, images and video are conveniently communicated anywhere and anytime in the world, increasing both quality-of-life, productivity and enabling a more resource-efficient world.

We are one of the major progressive forces, active around the globe, driving for this advanced communication to happen. We are seen as the prime model of a networked organization with top innovators and entrepreneurs working in global teams.

Nokia refers to its 'strategic intent' as:

Taking a leading, brand-recognised role in creating the Mobile Information Society by:

 – *Combining Mobility and the Internet*

 – *Stimulating the creation of new services*

Both of these provide very clear guides to "what we will do and what we will not do.

After mission and vision comes 'values'. Porras and Collins in the aforementioned *Built to Last* (1994) emphasise very strongly that sustainable companies have a core ideology, which they define as 'core values' + 'purpose'. Core values are defined by them as: *'the organisation's essential and enduring tenets – a small set of guiding principles; not to be confused with specific cultural or operating practices; not to be compromised for financial gain or short term expediency'.* Clear unequivocal cultural beliefs symbolise continued success.

Such values and principles provide continuity in a changing and turbulent environment, particularly where people come and go. They need to be clear, relevant and memorable, not vague motherhoods that people cannot relate to in their daily work. They must be taken seriously, particularly by leaders, and suitable reinforcements are in place for what is desired and what is not. The acid test is when difficult decisions must be taken, especially in a commercial company, if they will affect profits. Do the values and principles win? The rise in concern for good, visible corporate governance has led to an explosion in statements of 'how we do business,' although the best companies always had them. One of the most famous is Johnson and Johnson's 'Credo'. No hunting needed on their website for what they believe – it is right there on the home page.

One of the most explicit and public documents which shows how values and culture are linked to strategy is the (publicly available) 14 page document entitled *The Nokia Way – Values in Action.*

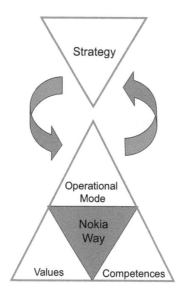

Figure 6.1   The Nokia Way

This document describes, amongst others, their desired flat networked organisation structure, their many multifunctional teams, the focus on innovation and speed of execution. It talks about 'value-based leadership, the values forming a common bond and language as well as a shared philosophy'. These values have not changed for many years and are:

- customer satisfaction

- respect for the individual

- achievement

- continuous learning.

The document goes on to describe the company's ethical principles, its environmental responsibility and corporate citizenship.

If values are being articulated for the first time, they should reflect the best of reality rather than a set of words and aspirations from a break out room or away day. A medium size software house undertook a project of creating a capability dictionary as a foundation of 'people–matching' processes. In the model used, values – and the behaviours associated with them – formed the core and were considered 'the passport to working here' for every job. The company had grown organically over 10 years and had a very coherent, young culture. The steering group for the project (all members of the management team) articulated what they saw as the core values, but then – without publishing their conclusions – a series of focus group discussions were held throughout the organisation to see what employees felt they were. Remarkable consistency resulted, and the eventual six that became the core truly reflected the reality of the culture.

6.2 Building an Integrated Business Strategy

There are endless books on strategic analysis, and this is not going to be another one. However, in order to understand the contribution that HR can make we need to be aware of the basic steps in the process. Strategy is essentially about choices. Costas Markides, Professor of Strategy at London Business School, simplifies it to:

- What will we do AND what will we not do?

- How will we do it AND how will we not do it?

- Who will do it AND who will not do it?

These choices can only be made as a result of analysis. Strategies are often put together without any consideration of alternatives, merely following an ambition, a dream or a fashion. The test of a strategy is to ask the question 'Why have you chosen that path?' and to go on doing so until an answer demonstrates that there were alternatives, criteria and choices. Since we are always resource-constrained we can never do all that we would like.

My students studying for the Masters degree in HRM fall into the same trap. They prepare an 'HR strategy' which includes every best practice they have ever heard of, so generic that you would not even know the sector of the business it refers to, and ignoring any resource constraints. Useful strategies are clearly specific.

Strategy can rightly be referred to as a learning journey, adapted and flexed according to experience. (Indeed many smaller companies would say that is all they do.) Such a mindset will prevent us doggedly pursuing a path that is not achieving our goals. Circumstances may force rapid re-evaluation of existing strategies – such as happened to the airline industry after September 11 2001. But normally the core direction of our strategy needs some 'legs', as they say in journalism. It should be reviewed regularly but not continuously changed in substance unless there is a radical intervention in the marketplace (or policy change in the public sector). Analysis is the relatively easy bit; implementation is the key and it takes time. One of the (many) problems of continually changing bosses is that every new boss wants to restructure the organisation and rewrite the strategy. The evidence suggests clearly that continuity and consistency win in the long-term.

Professor Robert Davies devised a helpful model and series of steps which illustrates well the continual learning involved, as in Figure 6.2. We must start with understanding where we are and where we want to get to. Most organisations will have several goals, and the process needs to be gone through for each one. Each goal needs to be defined in a clear and measurable way with a timescale. The steps are then in two sections:

- *Strategy choices* – involving evaluation and inquiry, seeking information as to what works towards our goal and what works against it; thinking beyond extrapolation of what we have done before and innovating – thus generating alternatives from which choices can be made.

- *Strategy implementation* – obtaining commitment, designing detailed plans and putting them into action.

Many tools are available to help with analysis. Perhaps the best known is a four quadrant representation of strengths, weaknesses, opportunities and threats (SWOT). The external world can be scanned using a 'PESTLE' analysis – assessing the factors that might influence our organisation under the headings of:

- political – what is happening politically in the country or countries that will affect our particular mission?

- economic – what is the state of the economies in which we operate and the forecast for them?

- social – what are the social trends that might affect our business?

- technological – what advances and trends in technology do we need to take account of?

- legal – what current and forthcoming legislation will affect us?

- environmental – what environmental considerations must we take account of?

For a commercial business we will also be interested in *competition*. Professor Porter of Harvard devised the now famous 'Five Forces' model to help analyse competitive forces – these being 'customers', 'suppliers', 'rivals', 'substitutes' and 'new entrants'.

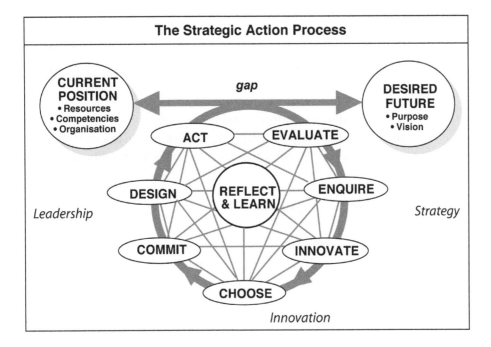

Figure 6.2   The strategic action process (Robert Davies)

Source: Reprinted from *European Management Journal*, 11(2), Robert Davies, Making Strategy Happen, pp. 201–213, Copyright (1993), with permission from Elsevier.

STRATEGIC ALIGNMENT

The business strategy makes the big decisions (ideally with clarity and with clear goals attached), and they lead to all kinds of supporting strategies from other functions. They also have to make decisions and choices, of two kinds. The first is what they must do to directly support the business strategies. The second is a set of professional choices that functions have to make themselves in the best interest of the organisation. Thus, we rely on Finance to manage our bank account 'strategy'; we rely on IT to make choices about disaster and data security management; and on HR to choose the best ways of recruiting people.

It is a challenge for all organisations, large and small, but especially for those that are diverse and complex, to be 'joined-up' – that is, to be internally 'aligned' in a cohesive way so that the parts clearly fit into the whole. The challenge for any support function is in two parts:

- To what extent are supporting strategies aligned *vertically*? Is what they contain consistent with and directly supportive to the stated business directions? To what extent are we working in partnership with operational managers to help them with their goals?

- To what extent is our functional strategy aligned *horizontally*? How consistent are our policies, processes and initiatives with those of other functions? How internally consistent is the functional strategy itself?

ENSURING VERTICAL ALIGNMENT

Alignment does not mean that functional strategies are prepared independently and then checked out for alignment or 'business linkages'. All sub-strategies should be essentially *driven by* the main strategy – they are part of a connected system. There is a great danger of lip service here, making tenuous links between what we really would like to do and suitable supporting phrases in the business plans. Professionals in HR and IT particularly tend to read and network more than most, and they are very conscious of the latest ideas and so called 'best practices'. They may well believe strongly that what they would like to do is beneficial to the organisation, but the question is whether it is the best choice for achieving our goals. We can do a lot of 'things that are right', but the question is whether we are doing the 'right things'. Trainers are particularly susceptible to the trap of 'I have a great idea for the organisation', and they often suffer from a lack of business knowledge and orientation as well. They have their own interests and values, and even when genuinely seeking to help with business problems they may rely on their preferred comfort zone of solutions.

Figure 6.3 shows the steps needed in an integrated and systematic strategic planning approach.

This starts with top level strategies and goals and systematically works down to the detail of what operational and support functions will do to implement them. The operational strategies in the centre create their own needs for functional support. This combines with the box on the right called 'desirable functional requirements' into a general prioritization exercise which yields the final support plan.

In Chapter 5, on page 185, we outlined the contribution of the functional business partner to strategy creation.

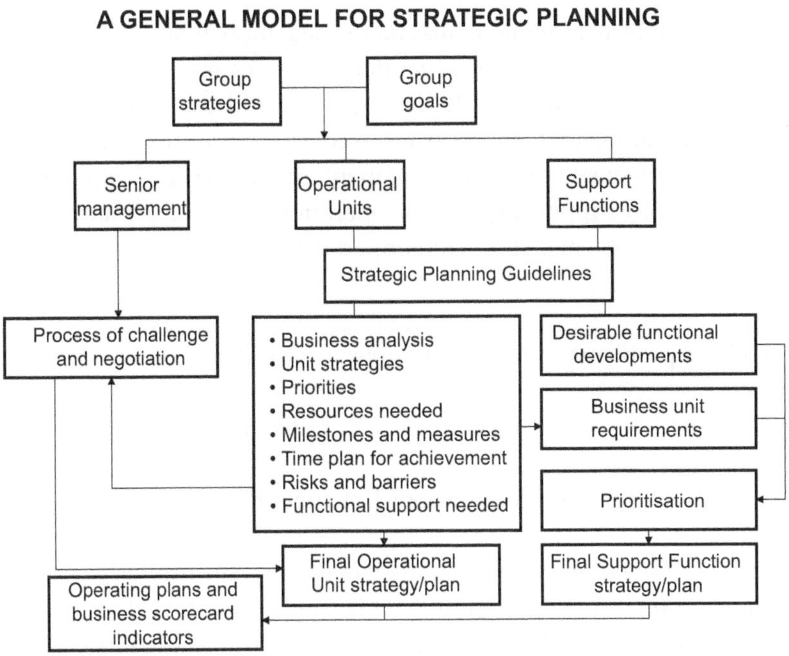

Figure 6.3   A general model for integrated strategic planning

A REALITY NOTE

Before we go further, we cannot ignore the fact that it may be difficult to actually *find* any business strategies for HR/L&D to link into. Some organisations are so short-term (and consistently routine) in their business cycles that life is very 'here and now'. In this type of environment, just articulating the strategy as being 'responsive and market driven' can often help managers and employees to successfully operate. Others struggle for a long time to find the strategy to choose. If this is the case, it does not mean we cannot have a 'people' strategy, since we still have people and have to decide how we want to manage and develop them. But in this case HR will need to use more personal judgement and intuition, and must ensure any conclusions are checked out by the business leaders.

6.3 Strategies for Organisational Effectiveness, People Management and the HR Function

We explained at the beginning of this chapter that more than one people related strategy is needed. We need to separately consider issues of organisational effectiveness, issues about people management and the choices for the HR function itself. For the first two we want to consider three time dimensions – a) that which complements the semi-permanent mission, vision, values and long-term strategies; b) supporting current operational objectives; and c) dealing with issues and problems. This is illustrated below:

Figure 6.4 shows how these dimensions link together.

The '*Organisation and Culture*' strategy needs to come first, as so many other things depend on it. What structure, culture and ways of working are needed to make us effective in achieving our business vision? These must be defined by the senior management team collectively, even though an HR function may provide the process, co-ordination and facilitation for doing so. We want to answer the following:

Figure 6.4   Business strategies driving functional strategies

- What do we believe is the best kind of structure to deliver our customer proposition?

- What do we want employees and customers to experience in our culture?

- What will the role of support functions be, and how will they work with operational units?

- How will we design and manage key processes such as internal communication, performance management and managing knowledge?

The 'People' strategy consists of policies, processes and programmes to do with managing people in the following five core areas:

- Resourcing – having the right people in the right place at the right time.

- Rewards and Benefits – how people will be compensated for their employment and their contribution.

- Learning and Development – having the needed capabilities for today and developing them for tomorrow; talent management.

- Employee engagement and communication – providing an attractive and satisfying employment experience.

- General people administration and legal compliance policies.

6.4 The 'Continuing' Strategy

The *'Continuing'* strategy is the one that fits with our mission, vision, values, beliefs, and long-term business goals. It is like an umbrella, under which operational and tactical decisions are taken. Even if it is not explicitly written down it is there – seen in our current organisation structure, in the culture that has developed, in the people policies and processes we have. Often it has just 'grown' over time and under the direction of various senior players. The question to be asked is whether it is truly aligned across the top of the diagram in Figure 6.3. Every time any factor in the long-term business strategy changes is a trigger – to re-examine the organisation, its culture, and its people management practices, ensuring they are fully supportive of where the business wants to be. A significant merger or other restructuring would require the same review. (In practice, whenever the CEO of an organisation changes, or the HR director, it is natural for them to review and often change the strategy in order to make their mark.)

Table 6.1 shows the factors that will influence our strategies, most of which will change very little – although the last two require regular review. Each of these is discussed overleaf:

Table 6.1   Factors to be taken into account in building strategies

Factors	Organisation Strategy	People Strategy
Parent company mission, vision, strategy, goals and principles	Yes	Yes
Our mission and vision	Yes	Yes
Our values and business philosophy	Yes	Yes
Core business strategies and goals	Yes	Yes
Industry sector developments	Yes	Yes
'PESTLE' factors (see pp. 214)		Yes
Strategic capabilities needed		Yes
Principles and policies of people management		Yes

As we go through each of the influencing factors we ask the questions – what *implications* does this have (if any) for the organisation, culture and the way in which we manage and develop people?

PARENT COMPANY MISSION, VISION, STRATEGY, GOALS AND PRINCIPLES

Before we look at each of the individual factors, it is important to note that many organisations do not have complete degrees of freedom in setting strategy. If they are a subsidiary or a public body, there is usually already an umbrella set up for them by their 'parent'. Whereas going through the strategy setting process for their own business or organisation is still vital, some things may be given. This is most likely to be in the area of values and principles.

MISSION AND VISION

First of all, our strategies are driven by the statements of what the organisation wants to be. It goes without saying that *the mission and vision* will shape our organisation. On page 210 we listed three types of value propositions – below we illustrate how they would result in different people and organisation strategies:

Value Proposition	Organisation Strategy (examples)	People Strategy (examples)
Product leadership	Creative stimulating working environment Respect for the individual Low on bureaucracy; high on flexibility High proportion of R&D people Frequent knowledge sharing	Loose job descriptions Pay for expertise Personal space Flexible working
Operational excellence	Focus on minimal costs Process engineering Emphasis on continuous improvement Command and control	Emphasis on effective teams Performance related pay
Customer intimacy	Great service the dominant value Organise from customers inwards High level of empowerment	Individual wellbeing and satisfaction a priority Personal recognition Flexible working Personal skills pre-eminent

There are natural characteristics of the *business sector* we are in that provide much commonality between competitors or similar organisations. Thus, we find in the UK that financial and legal service firms have many common characteristics since they fish in the same ponds, have the same types of client, and ,therefore, employees have expectations as they move from one to the other.

CORE BUSINESS STRATEGIES AND GOALS

By this we mean the longer term and significant strategies. These will always be broken down into steps which become individual manager objectives, and we will come back to those in Section 6.4.

However, at this stage we need to examine them for their impact on structure and culture and the five areas of HR practice to ensure we are both consistent with the strategies and supporting them.

Typical strategies in this category, which all take time to achieve, might include:

- Internationalisation;

- Growth by acquisition;

- Growth without acquisition;

- Achieving dominance in a sector of the market;

- Setting up new businesses, agencies or operational centres;

- Running down, transforming or divesting existing businesses;

- Major cultural shift;

- Outsourcing activities.

We will apply the methodology outlined in Section 6.4 to discover the people and organisation implications of these and make them part of the strategy.

INDUSTRY SECTOR DEVELOPMENT

In some industries, the profile of human resources has radically changed over the years – mostly driven by technological change. For example, retailers have had to develop website purchasing options, airports invest heavily in security, and police change their recruiting policies under the pressure of social change. In preparing any people strategy we must look carefully at the trends in our sector, and particularly see if we need to have new or different approaches to aspects of people management.

VALUES AND BUSINESS PHILOSOPHY

These are perhaps the most significant of all in shaping our people and organisational strategies. Increasingly companies are defining their 'principles of doing business', to demonstrate good governance.

Once values and principles are decided (see discussion on these above), the implications of the values can be summarized as an intermediary stage towards our strategy and policy definition. We could use a table such as Table 6.2.

Table 6.2   'If this is our value, it means we will...and we will not...'

VALUE	Organisation and Culture		Resourcing		Rewards and Benefits	
	Will	Will not	Will	Will not	Will	Will not
#1						
#2						
#3						
#4						
#5						
#6						
VALUE	Communication and Engagement		Learning and Development		General HR Administration	
	Will	Will not	Will	Will not	Will	Will not
#1						
#2						
#3						
#4						
#5						
#6						

Each time we re-evaluate our strategy an audit needs to take place to test what we do in practice to see if there are any conflicts. We would look at:

- our structure

- all our policies

- all our processes

- typical recent decisions

- our learning and development programmes.

Conflicts may lead us to two types of conclusion. One will be that we need to make some changes to be in line with the values. Another may be that the value is unrealistic for us. I once observed an international public sector organisation develop its values and they came up with 'PRIDE' – 'performance, responsiveness, integrity, diversity and empowerment'. Any audit that followed would require an extensive organisational transformation for these to be realised in practice. In fact the organisation had a reputation for the *opposite* in at least three of these proposed values.

We have mentioned that 'Principles of Doing Business' are becoming more and more common, both to be defined and to be published. There is a natural overlap with values. They are worth writing down because there really are choices to be made and, left to individuals, they will be made differently.

EXTERNAL FACTORS – THE PESTLE ANALYSIS

This needs to be done in all the fields in which the organisation operates, and specifically in our context to the employment arena. In many countries this changes fast although professionals normally keep up to date regularly. Table 6.3 shows some of the factors we would be monitoring.

Table 6.3   Some PESTLE factors concerning people and employment

POLITICAL	Government papers and policies Local government priorities Opposition policies and papers National consultation bodies
ECONOMIC	Economic growth forecasts Employment forecasts Tax changes Skills availability
SOCIAL	Demographic changes Educational policies Social trends and expectations
TECHNOLOGICAL	Internet developments, especially social networking HR support tools Connectivity issues Security issues
LEGAL	Employment legislation country by country Human rights legislation Data protection
ENVIRONMENTAL	Legal requirements Good citizen expectations Publicity regarding company practices

STRATEGIC CAPABILITIES

The *strategic*, or *core capabilities*, needed for us to be successful are critical, to be maintained and strengthened. These are defined as: a) those areas of fundamental expertise which enables the organisation to be in, and stay in, its field; b) those capabilities we must have in addition to support our strategies; and c) those areas which distinguish us from competition (if relevant) and give us an advantage. The first we must have to survive; the second to make progress; and the latter we need to stay ahead in the race. Organisations sometimes find it quite difficult to identify any of the latter. If we aspire to be 'leading' in aspects of our market, we will need the very best expertise we can get working on those aspects – since, as we saw in Chapter 1, these are the prime assets that drive value. People who are experts in these fields form a 'talent pool' of their own.

An identification table will be useful as in Table 6.4. Each capability can be reviewed by colouring red, amber, or green, or marking out of 10, to indicate our comfort with the level – quantity x quality – that we have.

Table 6.4   Strategic capabilities analysis – some examples for an airline

Type of Capability	Which Job Families?	Mission Critical	Needed for Future Strategies	Competitive Advantage
Knowledge	Strategy planning	Transport industry change and economics	Global warming technologies Carbon offset analysis	Being ahead of the game – innovations
Skills	Operations managers Yield managers Cabin crew	Plane and maintenance scheduling Pricing Safety procedures Emergency handling	Maximising alliance benefits	Turnaround times Flexibility Productivity
Behaviours	Ground staff Cabin crew	Customer experience	Flexibility	Exceeding customer expectations

These capabilities will particularly shape our strategies for recruitment, reward and retention, and continuing training and development. By definition, the expertise must be continually acquired and updated; excellence must be maintained aand individuals with these strategic capabilities must be regularly assessed for their expertise.

6.5 Principles and Policies of People Management

Less common is a defined set of 'principles of people management', yet a shared agreement on this is clearly foundational to having a people strategy.

We have mentioned earlier examples of CEOs who have their own personal passion for people, and who are not confined to mere platitudes. Yet it is quite rare to find corporate statements of belief in any more detail other than paragraphs containing commitments 'to develop people to their full potential' or something similar. One company that sat down as a management team in 2001 to create such a set of statements was the international healthcare company, Smith and Nephew. The operating style of the company is very much one of empowering its subsidiaries and it therefore works with an umbrella of principles under which different applications may be made. Adding to their long standing values of *Performance, Innovation and Trust* the team came up with this statement:

> *We will all subscribe to a company-wide belief that our employees are entitled to expect:*
>
> — *clearly communicated goals and performance standards*
>
> — *an open constructive relationship with managers and supervisors*
>
> — *the training, information and authority needed to do a good job*
>
> — *fair recognition and reward based on performance*
>
> — *equality of opportunity based on merit*
>
> — *encouragement to learn and progress*
>
> — *respect and dignity at all times*

—   *encouragement to participate fully in the quest for continuous improvement.*

Such statements are not 'universally applicable to every company'. There are specific choices here which dictate what the company will and will not do.

Another healthcare example is that referred to earlier – Johnson and Johnson and their 'Credo'. Here is the people related extract from it:

EXTRACT FROM JOHNSON AND JOHNSON'S 'CREDO'

'We are responsible to our employees, the men and women who work with us throughout the world.

Everyone must be considered as an individual.

We must respect their dignity and recognise their merit.

They must have a sense of security in their jobs.

Compensation must be fair and adequate, and working conditions clean, orderly and safe.

We must be mindful of ways to help our employees fulfil their family responsibilities.

Employees must feel free to make suggestions and complaints.

There must be equal opportunity for employment, development and advancement for those qualified.

We must provide competent management, and their actions must be just and ethical.'

CHOICE OF PRINCIPLES

The way we manage people varies considerably, whether deliberately or by serendipity. What we want to avoid are bland, generic, universally accepted statements which do not provide a guide to action. We need 'second level' statements which are clearly a result of *choice*. They will be the core of our strategy.

Below we give some of the choices that might be made – either of which could be right, depending on the business. Each end of the scale will lead us to quite different HR policies and practice, although sometimes we might want to be in the centre. These 'options' can be combined into a series of scales and used as an exercise – see Table 6.6 on page 234.

> *We act mostly on the basis that people are costs rather than seeing people as investments.*

Of course people are both, but employees are quick to sense which is the prevailing mindset of their organisation. I have frequently asked groups of people to say: a) do their top management *say* 'people are our most important asset' (90–100 per cent say yes); and then b) do they feel that this is the prevailing mindset when people decisions are taken. It is unusual to get as many as 10 per cent saying yes to the latter. The test comes when a short- or medium-term financial hurdle has to be crossed. My own experience as an HR Director in situations where downsizing was needed was that a little patience and some dedicated redeployment effort, more often than not, took care of keeping the assets as well as saving the cash drain of redundancy. Alas, few HR managers are bonused on cash flow!

There are, however, some types of business where people are little more than 'labour', and therefore mainly, if not wholly, a cost. (See the analysis of 'people as assets' in Chapter 1.) If so, our people policies will probably be ones of keeping wages as low as we can, training only at the essential job level, and employee relations are likely to be collective and more about negotiation than consultation. Nevertheless, people can still expect to be treated with respect – engagement is still important. McDonald's is often perceived to be in this mould, with its derided 'McJobs', but employees who have worked there invariably speak well of the experience and training. The company has successfully created a highly working environment.

Most knowledge and service based businesses will have a majority of people that they want to grow, develop and keep. They will position their HR strategies accordingly.

We manage through hierarchy and control vs. we manage through teams and empowerment.

Management often says they want the second of these but their natural tendency is to the former, especially when under pressure. Again, different businesses have different requirements; strong control is sometimes optimal (in risk-based businesses, for example). Clearly the choice has major implications for structure – the second option having few layers, and this leading to different strategies to reward and promotion. There are also implications for job design, for training (especially of managers) and for communication strategies.

We only do training when essential vs. we believe in continuous development and learning as a way of life.

This does relate to the cost:investment scale, but it is deeper than that. The right hand option reflects a value given to learning – the desire to encourage in every way, to become a true 'learning organisation'. This has deep implications for the 'learning and development' part of the 'people strategy' – namely that we will not just provide lists of courses but will also invest in:

- helping individuals 'learn to learn';

- systematic on the job learning;

- coaching and mentoring;

- professional learning consultants, working with teams and individuals to help them make the best use of the learning opportunities around them;

- communities of practice for knowledge sharing;

- developing our people beyond what is necessary for the job they do today.

We base salaries on the current job vs. basing them on individual value.

Again this will depend on the nature of the business. Small companies tend to be to the right side; large bureaucracies to the left, where structure of perceived fairness is seen as essential. Others may have one approach for one group of employees (such as senior managers) and the other for more junior employees. If salary is a reflection of a person's cumulative and potential value to the organisation, there is no logic to base this only with the job they happen to be doing today. 'Broadbanding' is a common compromise which enables several levels of pay within one job depending on experience and contribution.

> *Managers are encouraged to use their own style vs. we seek a consistent supervisory experience for our employees aligned with our desired culture.*

Before we jump to the natural desirability of the right here, we must recognise how difficult it is to achieve. Companies with strong cultures will train all managers in 'Our Company Way', which is then reinforced through senior management (and employee) expectations. It requires a considerable, determined effort over a long time, and needs to be reconciled with other values such as 'empowerment'.

> *Our policies should be built on the assumption that people can generally be trusted vs. the opposite.*

It is amazing how many organisations talk about trust but then have policies which are built on the assumption that people will cheat them – whether in respect of customers or employees. This affects structure (jobs to check up on people) and culture (self protection, duplication) and is reflected in general HR (and Finance) policies. Trust is clouded by the legal context in which many countries operate today – more detailed procedures are required to protect from legal action.

> *Communication is based on the 'need to know only' vs. information about the organisation is fully open.*

This relates to the 'trust' issue, but it is more than that. It is a question of whether we want to make the effort to involve employees, listen to their opinions, and ensure they understand why we do what we do. Many public sector organisations are very much to the left here, which seems an anomaly. However, some types of business do lend themselves to the left stance.

> *We want to reward individuals for performance vs. we want performance rewards to be shared on a team or unit basis.*

This will depend on our value proposition (page 221) and the extent to which we subscribe to a value of 'teamwork'. Often this one will not be a case of 'either/or' but more of 'and', for example we want both to sit side by side.

> *Results matter most when it comes to promotion vs. behaviour and living the values matters most.*

The natural answer is to say 'both, of course'. If so, our reward and performance appraisal systems should reflect this, and often they do not in practice. This is one of those philosophies that are always tested under pressure.

> *Experimentation is discouraged vs. ideas and experimentation are both encouraged and rewarded.*

There are some organisations and jobs where the former is absolutely right – rigid procedures (as in flying an airplane) are essential. It will be more common to plump for the right hand option – but then the test comes when things go wrong. How do we treat such events? We can be certain that if it results in reprimand, it is a clear message of discouragement despite what might be publicly said.

> *Vacancies are filled by management decisions vs. vacancies are open for all to apply.*

The right hand side is far more common in Anglo-American cultures than in others. What is chosen needs to be consistent with our values, and again we may have separate rules for senior management. The two options require quite different processes to make them work. An associated dilemma is:

> *Managers should develop their people vs. people should be responsible for their own development.*

The latter is often heard as the desirable policy, but if so it places an onus on both managers and the HR function to facilitate individuals being able to take that responsibility. This choice affects the design of appraisal and training analysis processes, and personal responsibility for learning requires some guidance and 'learning how to learn'.

> *We believe in identifying and developing high potentials only vs. we believe that everyone has potential to develop.*

It is interesting how many modern organisations are almost obsessed with 'diversity', yet in a very narrow political sense, which often does not include the fact that people have different strengths and talents. Choosing the right hand side requires open and involving processes plus investments in counselling and coaching.

CHOOSING THE OPTIONS

What is for certain is that the options should *not* be chosen by the HR people. It is not just that they are natural idealists, but that these principles will never be reality unless owned mentally by senior management. HR may well facilitate the process of determining them, making sure all the options are considered, but not choosing them. One way to do this is to use the instrument in Table 6.5 as a starter for the team discussion; individuals plotting their own views, then collecting these and feeding back the summary – leading to a debate and final conclusion. If the senior team is reluctant to spend their time on such an exercise, the HR Director is entitled to plead that he or she needs to spend their time and money doing processes and initiatives that will have their full support.

We have argued elsewhere that there is a trade off between *relevance* and *effort*. Thus, it is simpler to have *one* set of principles for an entire organisation. However, we can see in a massive conglomerate, such as the UK's National Health Service, how impossible it is to create 'one size fits all'. So, there is a distinction to be made between 'universal principles' (such as in the example of Smith and Nephew), and perhaps supplementary sets for particular job families or subsidiaries.

Once we have our set of principles we need to consider how they should be publicised. Principles can often be expressed as policies, or at least summary policy statements.

On the next page are scales representing opposing beliefs in people management. Place an X for the *desired* position (what you feel would be best for your organisation) and an 'O' for the *actual* situation today. Join up the Xs and the Os. Where are the biggest gaps?

Table 6.5   Guiding principles of people management

We act mostly on the basis that people are costs	We act mostly on the basis that people are assets
We manage through hierarchy and control	We manage through teams and empowerment
We only do training when essential	We believe continuous learning is a way of life
We base salaries on the current job	We base salaries on individual value
Communications are based on 'the need to know' only	Communications are fully open
Managers act according to their own style	Managers operate to shared vision and values
Our policies assume people cannot be trusted	Our policies are built on assumed trust
Individual performance is what counts	Team performance is what counts
Results matter most	Behaviour matters most
Appraisal is a performance report	Appraisal is primarily about development
Experimentation is discouraged	Ideas and experimentation are actively rewarded
Managers decide what training is needed	We want all employees to take prime ownership for their development
Vacancies are filled by management decision	Vacancies are open for all to apply
Managers should develop their people	People should take personal responsibility for their development
We believe in identifying and developing high potentials only	We believe in identifying and developing the potential of all

6.6 Building the Strategies

What we have done in the last few pages is to prepare, or review, all the background we need to create, or revise, our strategies. We rarely start from a green field, so often it is a question of revisiting what we have currently and seeing if: a) we want to formalise it more systematically; or b) whether we should change anything. We have looked at:

- the business – its mission, vision and key long term strategies;

- its values and business philosophy;

- industry/sector changes;

- external factors to be taken into account;

- its strategic capabilities;

- its principles of people management.

All this comes under the step of 'analyse' in Figure 6.2. The next steps are evaluation, innovation and choice.

Evaluation is asking what are the implications of each factor for the structure and culture of the organisation, and for the five core HR areas.

Innovation is where we look at good practices elsewhere and seek ideas in addition to the obvious solutions, which will provide some paths ahead, dealing with the implications identified.

Choice is simply deciding what we will do and what we will not do. Each option has to be considered from the angles of effectiveness, feasibility and cost.

THE ORGANISATION AND CULTURAL STRATEGY

All our work so far should lead us to paint a vision of the type and structure of the organisation that will best serve all the factors we have analysed. On page 219 we listed four questions to be answered in this strategy – the optimum structure, the desired culture, the role of support functions, and the organisational processes that will make the organisation work effectively.

This is not the place to go into a treatise on organisational structural options. They will include, however:

- hierarchy or matrix?

- process or control driven?

- layers and spans of control?

- regional or product centric?

Often this is dictated by preferences of top management, or by advising consultants. The best rule is to decide by working from *customers* inwards and designing based on what organisation will provide the best service to them.

The desired culture will be led by the chosen values, but also should be considered from the point of view of customers and other stakeholders. In Section 5.10 on page 195 we described a methodology for creating a *cultural vision*.

The role and structure of support functions, such as IT, HR, Finance, and Legal also needs to be considered. How centralised or decentralised do we want them to be? How integrated with business units? Which policies will be global and which local? Do we want to fund them centrally or feed the costs into business unit bottom lines? How much authority would we give them, and what will be the dividing line between line and support accountability? To what extent do we want to outsource routine activities?

Our fourth question was about processes that make the organisation work successfully. They may or may not be owned by a support function. It is generally believed that *knowledge management processes* should be owned by a neutral 'chief information officer'. These need to be integrated in today's world with the use of *intranets* and *internal communication media*, often controlled by IT. The organisation's approach to *performance management* may be owned by Finance, but must be integrated with information systems and HR's ownership of individual and team performance reviews and evaluations. *Branding* needs to be considered – how many will we have? Public relations and image management need their own organisation wide policies. We might say that few of these have anything to do with HR, but that would be wrong. They are all included in making the organisation work effectively and how people work together to do that.

Our organisation and culture strategy will then consist of:

- principles of structural design for our business/organisation;

- the role and structure of support functions;

- characteristics of the culture that we want people to experience internally and externally;

- the processes which will make our organisation effective.

Followed by practical considerations such as:

- learning and change programmes that will achieve the desired organisation and culture;

- the resources required for these programmes and for ongoing maintenance;

- the measurement indicators for monitoring the strategy;

Some examples of how all this might be phrased are described in Table 6.6.

Table 6.6   Example of strategy statements for 'organisation and culture'

Policy statements:
We want an organisation that is agile and adaptable; therefore we will aim for a minimum number of layers between the front line and senior management
Wherever possible we will organise by process teams to maximise efficiency of flow to our customers, and minimise hierarchy
We want to build a culture that truly reflects our values, and all stakeholders will experience them. This culture will be clearly defined in terms of behaviours
It is essential for our business that new knowledge is rapidly shared. We will organise to minimise boundaries and make willing and skilful knowledge sharing a normal process. There will be small central coordinating team to stimulate and monitor this

Table 6.6   *Concluded*

Ongoing Processes: *We will have a steering committee on organisation design which will advise and approve all proposed changes in line with the policy statements* *We will set up a series of knowledge sharing processes, such as communities of practice, project reviews, expert seminars and virtual discussion groups*
Supportive Learning Programmes: *We will have a section of new employee induction that emphasises the cultural behaviours expected* *We will ensure all managers and employees understand the nature of empowerment* *We will have regular programmes to learn effective knowledge sharing techniques*
Resource Requirements to Implement this Ongoing Strategy: *The Organisation Steering Committee will consist of part time representatives from each main area of the business* *An 'Organisation Development' team of 2 people within HR will be needed to facilitate this ongoing strategy*
The Measurement Indicators for Monitoring this Strategy: *We will at least annually test our culture through perception surveys against the desired cultural template* *We will report regularly on the number of layers between employees at the bottom of each of division and their CEO; ratios of managers:staff by function and division; and the number of process teams* *We will monitor the number of knowledge sharing communities and the length of time they have been operational, and the number of virtual discussion groups* *We will conduct an audit annually to check for examples of waste and duplication caused by lack of knowledge sharing and will cost this*

Strategies often have just a series of intentions, such as the first box in Table 6.6. But it is the subsequent boxes that will make it all work. Proper resourcing, supporting processes, and regular monitoring are what will turn strategic intents into reality.

THE PEOPLE MANAGEMENT STRATEGY

On page 235 we listed six factors to take account of. For each we will ask the question – are there any implications in this for people management, dividing the answers into the areas of:

- resourcing

- learning and development

- rewards and benefits

- employee relations and communication

- general employment and compliance policies.

The most important of the factors is 'our principles of people management' and this can be organised from the start into the five areas which provide subheadings in the strategy.

We can create a tabular format which covers the following in each subheading:

- Principles and policies of people management;

- Implications of the other factors taken into account, and additional policies/directions arising from them;

- For each policy, the supporting processes needed to make it work;

- For each policy and/or process, the programmes and initiatives that are needed to support them;

- The resources required for implementation and maintenance;

- The measurement indicators for monitoring this strategy.

Above all, we cannot emphasise enough the importance of avoiding the bland and generic. Every process, programme and initiative that appears should have its provenance clearly in one of the factors of analysis.

A slightly different application of the tabular format is seen in Table 6.7, which is an extract from the People Strategy for a large FTSE 100 engineering company.

So far this has been about the 'umbrella' or 'continuing' strategy that is core to the organisation we want to become. It does not cover all that we are going to do in the people area in a given period. It describes the ongoing platform, on which we have to build the 'proactive' and 'reactive' activities described in Figure 6.4, appropriate for the period of planning.

Table 6.7   Extract from people strategy from large engineering company

Principle	Aims	Commentary	Objectives	Metrics
Opportunities to develop capability will be available to *all employees* but XX acknowledges that employees will follow different paths according to their potential. XX will therefore target resources on the companies' talent pools and in the competencies that it considers critical to achieving its goals	*All employees:* • access to training & development • high quality L&D initiatives • managers to use coaching style of leadership • annual training plans by business • employees to own personal development plans *Target resources:* • target resource at Talent or areas where capability is critical e.g. Project Management	90% of all training is devolved to the Business Units. The employee engagement questionnaire indicates lack of satisfaction in access to training by front-line employees. Training capability at local level is weak with one or two pockets of good practice. Top level executives receive a good standard of development from the Talent Management process. Their experience is different and of much higher quality.	To organise training and development as a central function delivery service to the business units. To develop and implement a Group Training & Development policy. To ensure that the Talent Management programmes are delivered across the business and that mid-level management Talent pools are identified. To review and refresh the Coaching programme. To ensure Organisation & Management Reviews (OMR), XX's succession planning programme extends across the business. To develop Capability Policy and programmes to embed core capabilities in the Group to attract and retain the best talent.	% of employees engaged in Talent Management process % of graduates who have received appraisals % of employees who feel that the business makes good use of their skills % of employees aware of their training and development needs % of employees who agree that their manager coaches them to be effective

6.7 Supporting Current Business Objectives

Now we want to address what we might actually consider as less strategic and more tactical, but no less value added – addressing: a) the current goals; and b) operational problems and issues in the organisation. We referred to these as the 'proactive' and 'reactive' strategies. Whereas the 'continuing strategy' is unlikely to be reviewed more than annually, we are now into frequent support, both systematically and pragmatically. For HR this is true partnership with business managers – how can we (HR) enable you (line manager) to achieve your objectives successfully?

As we well know, nothing is achieved without people. Every business objective needs 'the right people with the right skills at the right time in the right place' in order to succeed, and those people need to have the right level of motivation and engagement. This takes us right back to our value creating processes in Chapter 1. The essence of HR partnering with business managers is to ensure, together, that these conditions will be met.

A simple consultant methodology needs to be applied systematically. Most HR functions have resource limitations and it may be unrealistic to take this methodology through for every objective of every manager. But it can be done for, say, the three most critical that each manager has. The steps would be as follows:

For each objective:

- What is the objective and what are the current measurable time-based targets associated with it?

The latter are important so that progress can be checked – they are not always precisely defined:

- What factors are working *for* its achievement and what are working *against* it? How would they be weighted in terms of their likely influence?

Often these have not been analysed by the manager who has the objective. Here we mean the *business* factors, although 'people' may come up here in their own right. The weighting is important as it gives us guidance for future priority setting.

- *Who* (individuals or groups) are involved in these factors?

This is where we may find that success is dependent on other departments or groups in the organisation.

- What are the implications (if any) for the manager's unit as a whole, and each set of people so far identified in respect of: structure, culture, resourcing, capabilities (learning and development), employee relations, communication and engagement, rewards and benefits, and general HR administration?

In this stage we are asking relevant questions and coming up together with possible initiatives which would support the objective's success.

In this process we build a hierarchical tree of possibilities which will need prioritising. After doing this for each of the critical objectives one by one, we need to ask 'Which of all the actions and initiatives that we have noted would have the biggest impact on your goal achievement?' Some will be 'must-do', others will be chosen based on impact vs. feasibility/cost.

Table 6.8 shows a format that can be used, with an example filled in with some potentially 'relevant questions' – relevance being determined by the specific context of course. The answers provide the actions that could be taken. Sheets can be collected for each of the objectives.

Once they have been prioritised, the projects and initiatives that arise will need to be resourced and built into the overall activity plan for the period.

Table 6.8   Example of analysis of a business goal for a supermarket

Business goal	To reduce the level of customer complaints by 30% by year end		
Groups of employees/ managers involved	Implications for Organisation and People Management		
	Structure and culture	Resourcing	HR Policies
Cash and other store staff	Is the culture sufficiently customer-focused in the store? Are staff empowered to help the customer? Is the ratio of staff to supervision optimal?	Are there sufficient staff to meet queuing targets? Are absenteeism and holidays fully covered? Do people have to work excessive overtime?	Is there anything recently introduced or affecting this group particularly that might be demotivating them?
Store management	Is the culture customer-focused? Does the management empower staff to help customers?	Does the store manager have time to speak with customers and deal with difficulties?	Ditto
Area management	Do they emphasise the importance of customer satisfaction – could it be improved?	Is the Area management putting resourcing constraints in such a way that stores cannot meet customer service needs?	
Head office supply department	Does the HO:store structure cause problems? Is HO 'another' culture?		

Table 6.8   *Concluded*

Business goal	To reduce the level of customer complaints by 30% by year end		
Groups of employees/ managers involved	Implications for People and People Management		
	Learning and Development	Rewards and Motivation	Employee Relations (ER), Communication and Engagement
Cash and store staff	Have staff been trained in customer service management? Are there operational knowledge gaps?	Are there any incentives for good customer service?	Do they get to hear about all complaints from their store and work together to reduce them?
Store management	Have they been trained in total customer management? Have they been trained in staff motivation and empowerment?	What rewards/sanctions exist for minimal customer complaints? Does the motivation and reward environment focus too much on cost?	How and how often are they talking to the staff about this issue? Is there a problem with ER generally and staff attitudes?
Area management		What component of their reward is related to customer satisfaction?	
Head office supply department	What are the levels of professional capability – (how many complaints are due to lack of or wrong stock?)	Does the reward system encourage minimal stock levels and lowest cost suppliers?	Is there sufficient communication and feedback with stores to know what is happening on the ground?

6.8 Responding to Today's Problems

We have referred to being 'reactive' in the sense of responding to issues and problems. Plenty of people problems get referred to an HR department in the normal course of events, but here we are talking about *business* problems. Cause and effect analysis of any problem comes down quickly either to a people related cause or a systems/process cause, behind which may be a people issue anyway. The true HR Business Partner therefore keeps track of what is happening operationally.

Problems of absenteeism and turnover are naturally monitored through HR figures. How employees are feeling depends on the frequency of surveys. However, wherever targets are in trouble throughout the business, we are likely to have people problems. It may be due to internal conflicts, overlapping accountabilities, lack of necessary capabilities, weak or overbearing management, lack of morale, understaffing – all of which may be hidden, and often because the people concerned want it that way. So there is a proactive role, in order to be intelligently reactive.

A problem can be analysed using the same approach as in the last section. The questions become slightly different:

For each problem:

- What is the problem to be solved, and what are the current measurable gaps we want to close?

- What are the potential causes of this problem, and how are they weighted in importance?

- *Who* (individuals or groups) are involved in these factors?

- What are the implications (if any) for these people in respect of: structure, culture, resourcing, capabilities (learning and development), employee relations, communication and engagement, rewards and benefits, and general HR administration?

The worksheet format can be similar to that in Table 6.8 – in fact the example chosen could be taken either as a business objective or a problem to be solved. The best way to do this is a regular discussion with managers (say every three months), looking at their achievements and discussing issues. Other ways to keep in touch are:

- attendance at business reviews;

- studying the business status reports;

- reading customer reports;

- informal walking around.

Some sensitivity is required, but the credible business partner who clearly cares about managers achieving success will always be welcome. Sadly, HR may be perceived too often as preoccupied with its own agenda. Nevertheless there are many good case studies of Line/HR partnerships innovating together and leading to successful business achievement.

Initiatives that result from these discussions also need prioritising and will be added to those derived from the previous section.

6.9 A Strategy for the HR Function

It is always natural to have a primary focus on ourselves and our world. We have put this section last in this chapter to make the point that it is right to give the *business led* initiatives the greater priority – they determine *what* an HR function should be doing, over and above its normal administrative and daily support work. Now we need to address *how* it does all its activities as effectively as possible.

We can summarise the work of an HR function – and similarly any other support function, as being there to do the following:

- to carry out necessary administrative activities, in this case to do with people;

- to ensure compliance and integrity with relevant legislation and company policies;

- to represent the company externally on people issues as required;

- to design and manage, usually jointly with line management, people management processes;

- to apply professional knowledge to support the organisation and its managers in their goals, giving help and advice, and in achieving an organisation that is operationally effective;

- to provide data and information that enables management to manage effectively.

The HR function needs a strategy that will deliver all of these *efficiently* and *effectively*.

We have therefore to make choices about:

- organisation of the function, and the resources needed;

- capabilities of people in the function;

- process design, evaluation and review;

- 'tools' to support the processes;

- involvement and dialogue with others, internally and externally;

- professional knowledge sharing and knowledge management;

- measures and standards of performance;

- publicity and communication about what we do.

A few words now on each of these:

ORGANISATION AND RESOURCES

Dave Ulrich has had a significant influence on organisational models following on from his work on the roles of an HR function, as mentioned in Chapter 5. Indeed, the rather grand and often aspirational word 'transformation' is frequently used for what is basically a reorganisation of the administrative part of the function.

HR is a customer facing organisation – albeit internal customers – and any organisation design should be looked at through the customer's eyes to see how effective service delivery will be. However, designs of structure are often driven by ideology, by costs or by what the organisational leader wants to do. What would the expectations of managers be? We surmised this for some key players in Chapter 5, but we can summarise in a general way as follows:

- efficient accurate timely administration, involving me as a manager as little as possible;

- minimising bureaucracy and complex time consuming processes;

- easy and fast access to advice when needed;

- specific people related support for my business objectives;

- timely and useful information about my people;

- somebody I can talk to in confidence and trust.

So called 'transformation' has often gone wrong to the dismay of HR because it failed to involve or listen to its 'customers' in terms of what they wanted.

Having said that, efficiency, cost effectiveness, and technology usually dictate forms of shared, centralised, or outsourced administrative services. There is no reason, with good management, why these cannot deliver a level of service that meets expectations.

The more difficult question is the extent and distribution of 'business partners' (or 'advisers' as they are sometimes called), and the level of investment in internal 'centres of excellence' in specialist areas. The latter decision is one of cost, demand and also competitiveness. If we only need legal help from time to time it makes no sense to employ specialist employment lawyers, and most organisations do not. In general, however, unless we are too small to justify it, we would want at least one person taking the strategic overview of each of the key areas of HR professionalism. (One individual could take more than one area.) We mention 'competitiveness' because innovative approaches to our most precious assets are indeed sources of competitive advantage, and one would naturally want to keep that 'in-house'.

Where organisations have gone wrong is in re-titling HR people as 'business partners' and then giving them such a large remit that they cannot carry out that role because they have not got the time to work with managers in detail. Effectively they become no more than agents of the HR function, a very one-way partnership at best. As a general rule, to meet the suggestions for effective business partnership in this book, we recommend looking after no more than 25 managers, senior *and* middle level.

CAPABILITIES OF PEOPLE

It is one thing to reorganise and another to ensure people have the right knowledge and skills to take their roles. We discuss this in more detail in Chapter 8, since it is the key to a lot of the proposals for a more business orientated HR to become a reality. However, just to note here that our internal HR functional strategy must include the following:

- the strategic capabilities needed in HR;

- how they will be acquired and maintained;

- a career development path for HR professionals.

PROCESS DESIGN, EVALUATION AND REVIEW

HR is responsible for two types of processes. One group comprises those which others effectively implement. A good example is appraisal – designed by HR and carried out by managers. (I have heard HR people say 'managers are responsible for making this work, not us'. Well, I know who is called into the CEO's office if it is *not* working!) The second type of process is that which HR designs for its own professional activities.

Table 6.9 comprises a list of typical processes. The great majority are in the first category, and involve managers in the triangular partnership between HR, managers and employees. It is not essential to have every people process in the HR textbook, but we must have those which will support our 'continuing strategy' and our legal obligations.

Table 6.9   List of HR processes

RESOURCING	REMUNERATION
Job profiling	Job grading
Recruitment	Salary banding
Selection	Salary increases
Induction/orientation	Variable pay (bonus) systems
Vacancy management	Market benchmarking
Promotion	Recognition schemes
Succession planning	Performance management
Workforce planning	Flexible benefits
Outsource and agency management	Pension management
Exit management	

Table 6.9   *Concluded*

LEARNING AND DEVELOPMENT	GENERAL HR POLICIES
Personal development planning	Discipline
Training needs analysis	Grievance
Training design	Absence management
Training evaluation	Personal data management
Knowledge management	Health and wellbeing management
Further education	Home-working
Training authorisation	Safety management
Use of coaching and mentoring	
Career path mapping	
Potential assessment	
ER/COMMUNICATIONS AND ENGAGEMENT	**ORGANISATION AND CULTURE**
Information provision	Organisation design
Employee consultation	Organisation restructuring
Suggestion schemes	Culture analysis
Use of intranet	Accountability mapping
Upwards communication	
Opinion and engagement surveys	

At the time of reviewing the HR functional strategy, we have to ask:

- Do we have all the processes we need?

- Are they working efficiently and effectively?

- If not, should we do something about it?

Here are some criteria we might use to test whether a process is 'fit for purpose':

- its purpose is clear;

- it leads to the business being more effective – it adds value to one or more stakeholders;

- the cost and time of running the process is justified by the value it brings (as seen by line managers);

- the process is consistent with our values;

- the process has been recently examined for possible simplification.

Process engineering should be a core skill available in HR and we discuss this further in Chapter 8. Measures of process effectiveness are in the next chapter.

TOOLS TO SUPPORT THE PROCESSES

HR functions are bombarded daily with ideas and products, which we could describe as 'tools' and about which they have to make choices.

Perhaps the most important tool is technological – we need a Human Resources information system that will provide us with data and reports and keep track of our people. We need to decide how distributed it will be – what information managers and employees will have access to. We may use specialised software for particular processes also – such as performance management or talent management. The intranet provides us with many opportunities for communication, such as having policies and forms online. A whole part of our strategy will be how technology is deployed.

Then there are professional tools, which may or may not be automated. These instruments are either purchased, or specially designed internally, to help a process work more effectively. Table 6.10 gives some examples of tools that HR may deploy.

Table 6.10   A list of some tools used in HR

RESOURCING	REMUNERATION
Assessment centres	Job evaluation systems
Personality tests	Salary planning software
Ability tests	Flexible benefit models
Web based recruitment	
Structured panels	
Graphology (mainly in France)	
Biodata questionnaires	
Succession planning software	

Table 6.10   *Concluded*

LEARNING AND DEVELOPMENT	ORGANISATION AND CULTURE
E-learning programmes	Organisation design software
Development centres	Proprietary culture surveys
Competency frameworks	Questionnaires
RoI methodologies	Workforce planning models
Learning resource centres	OD tools and interventions
Talent management software	
Learning management systems	
360 degree assessments	
ER/COMMUNICATIONS AND ENGAGEMENT	
Web based tools	
Virtual discussion groups	
Conferencing tools	
Satellite broadcasting	
Pulse surveys	
Benchmarked engagement data	

Here are some criteria we might use to test whether a tool is 'fit for purpose':

- it makes a process more effective;

- it is consistent with our values;

- it *works* – it fulfils its promise;

- the cost of purchase, development and implementation is justified by the value it produces;

- it is easily understandable by non-HR people;

- it preferably can be used in several processes;

- it is appropriate for our culture.

It is normal for HR to want to introduce or modify one or more process or tool as part of their own strategy. This has to be set into the priorities of all the demands on resources.

INVOLVEMENT AND DIALOGUE WITH OTHERS, INTERNALLY AND EXTERNALLY

HR people are well known for their enjoyment of networking, and sometimes one suspects that some of them spend more time talking with fellow professionals than with their own managers. But one set of choices to make is a balanced view of what the function will get involved in.

Thus, the questions to be answered are:

- On what internal committees and review bodies should HR be represented?

- How often will we target to formally review the people implications of each operation?

- What will be the involvement of non-HR people in each of the processes for which we are responsible?

- On which of our activities would we benefit from a steering committee made up of non-HR people?

- What external benchmarking bodies will we belong to?

- What networking groups will we belong to?

- What kinds of surveys and research will we submit ourselves for?

PROFESSIONAL KNOWLEDGE SHARING AND KNOWLEDGE MANAGEMENT

There are some standard questions to be asked that would apply to any department, for example:

- How will we ensure that the special knowledge and experience of each member of the function is known about and is accessible?

- How will we ensure effective recording, storage and accessibility of 'case histories', project experiences (such as change and restructuring), and common data?

- How we will use the intranet for the benefit of employees, managers and ourselves?

- How will we ensure constant updating of each staff member?

- Should we have any special interest groups?

- What will be our policy on seminar and conference attendance?

- To what publications, on or offline, will we subscribe?

It is a good idea for one member of the function to be given the co-ordinating responsibility for this aspect of functional effectiveness.

MEASURES AND STANDARDS OF PERFORMANCE

This will comprise our approach to measurement and monitoring of the function and is covered in-depth in Chapter 7.

PUBLICITY AND COMMUNICATION ABOUT WHAT WE DO

There are many opportunities to tell the world of the great things the organisation is doing. The number of awards that can be entered seems to increase annually, as do surveys such as the 'Great Place to Work'. Numerous conference companies seek real life case studies from practitioners and provide plenty of platform opportunities. I recall one company I worked for, where the CEO instructed all functions to 'get the name of our company and the great things we do out there more than the competition does'. The danger is that a good story well delivered creates a demand for it to be retold and the platform can become a diversion.

Internally, we need to ensure that the 'people strategy' is well publicised and understood. The need to publish the internal HR functional strategy is far less.

6.10 Some Examples of People/HR Strategies

These examples do not follow necessarily the methodology suggested in this chapter. They are included to show how some organisations have chosen to tackle this area. It has to be noted that many HR or people strategies, in practice, pay no more than lip service to business imperatives and are largely a statement of the HR functional agenda.

BRITISH TELECOM (BT)

BT Group's iterative HR strategy process and rolling business planning model was developed during the early years of the new century and were designed to integrate five key elements that help to shape the company's goals and key activities:

- the BT Group's Strategic Imperatives;

- individual line of business operational drivers;

- implications of transformational and operational change on BT people;

- the BT HR strategic responses/interventions/deliverables;

- the functional and cost factors implicit in the BT HR business model, including the outsourcing of all transactional and shared service activities and the continuous professionalisation of members of the BT HR team.

In 2004/5 there were eight 'Strategic Imperatives'. These were worked through, very much on the lines of the approach of this chapter, into their people implications, with 'strategic change levers' and strategic programmes' to support each imperative. A separate BT HR model was developed for members of the function to deliver these programmes together with optimal operational efficiency.

SKANSKA

Skanska is a global construction company based in Sweden with some 76,000 employees. In 2006, the HR and L&D strategy for the UK division covered the following headings:

- key business issues, followed by HR and learning implications for each;

- the actions to be taken in respect of the implications;

- the resources and support needed;

- project/programme plans and dates;

- who is responsible;

- relevant comments;

- how it will be evaluated.

EALING COUNCIL

A very thorough people strategy was put together for Ealing in 2006, which involved some 33 pages long. It consisted of the following sections:

1. Introduction – building blocks and constituent drivers.

2. Background and Context – Council objectives and other relevant drivers such as demographics and government directives.

3. Implications for Ealing's Workforce by 2011 – the People Strategy Vision for 2011, strategic objectives, and detailed components of these with performance indicators; gap analysis between the vision and the current state.

4. Implications for 2008/9 – activities and milestones.

5. Conclusions.

LARGE RETAIL BANK

This HR strategy started with an introduction that restated the company's 'people strategy objectives' for three years ahead. The second 'chapter' was entitled 'goals and objectives', with one overriding goal as '*Investment in learning for all our people and our business to enable them to grow and prosper together*'. Nine objectives followed; a mixture of longer term cultural goals and specific programmes to be delivered. This was followed by a third section which lists nine priorities within these main objectives. This was then backed up by a detailed 'implementation plan', and finally a list of 'roles and responsibilities'.

The document then lists three-year objectives, followed by detailed deliverables on each. Appendices comprehensively summarised the roles of key players in HR, including managers.

6.11 Summary

A business strategy is not complete without a people strategy, since nothing can be delivered without people. The emphasis is unquestionably on the people strategy and initiatives that the business *needs* – and that means that we do not start with what HR would like to do.

We looked at the key elements of the business strategy planning process and how it should be integrated with functional strategies. A matrix was then drawn up with three different timescales – the continuing approach to organisation and people management, on which we add specific initiatives which are built to: a) support current business objectives; and b) to deal with current operational problems. Each of these is considered for their implications for a strategy for organisation and culture, and one for people management and development. The factors to be taken into consideration were discussed and examples of methodologies, worksheets and templates given. Particular attention was paid to defining 'principles and policies' in dealing with people. We showed how this all integrates into workable strategy documents.

The factors to be examined for an HR functional strategy were debated, particularly in the choice of processes and tools. Finally, we looked at some examples of case study strategies.

6.12 Challenges for Action

- Are the senior people in the HR function trained in strategic thinking and comfortable with the basic models of strategic analysis?

- Has the top team created an organisational and cultural vision that will support the business strategies, in a way that defines clearly the kind of processes and behaviours that will be visible?

- Has the top team defined a set of people management principles, appropriate for the business and aligned with the organisational values? Do they provide sufficient guidance on what we will *not* do as well as what we will do?

- Has the organisation clearly identified its 'strategic capabilities' and built a plan to acquire, retain and grow them?

- Are there regular and systematic conversations between HR and the business managers to be able to identify and act on any people implications of both business objectives and operational problems?

- Has HR itself got a clear strategy for its own organisation and operation that maximises effectiveness and efficiency of delivery?

6.13 References and Further Reading

Ansoff, I.H. (1986). *Corporate Strategy*. New York: McGraw Hill.

Boxall, P., and Purcell, J. (2003). *Strategy and Human Resource Management*. Palgrave MacMillan.

CIPD. (2005). *HR Strategy: Creating the Framework for Effective People Management*. CIPD Professional Tool, 2005.

CIPD. (2005). *Performance Management*. London: CIPD.

Davies, R. (1993). *Making Strategy Happen. European Management Journal*. Volume 11(2), 201–213.

Gratton, L. (2000). *Living Strategy*. FT Prentice Hall.

IRS Employment Review. (2006). *HR Believes Line Managers Hold Key to Improvements in Performance*. August 2006.

Johnson, G., and Scholes, K. (1997). *Exploring Corporate Strategy*. 4th ed. Prentice-Hall.

Kearns, P. (2003). *HR Strategy: Business Focused Individually Centred.* Oxford: Butterworth-Heinemann.

Lundy, O., and Cowling, A. (1996). *Strategic Human Resource Management.* Routledge.

Mayo, A.J. (2004). *Creating a Learning and Development Strategy.* London: CIPD.

Porras, J.I., and Collins, J.C. (1994). *Built to Last.* New York: Harper Business.

Shuler, R.S. (1992). *Linking the People with the Strategic Needs of the Business.* American Management Association.

Syrett, M. (2004). *Redefining Strategic HR. Business Intelligence.*

Ulrich, D. (1997). *Human Resource Champions.* Harvard Business Press.

Ulrich, D., and Brocklebank, W. (2005). *The HR Value Proposition.* Harvard Business School Press.

www.dilbert.com

www.jnj.com

7

A Scorecard for the HR Function

We have explored in Part 1 the types of measures one might use for 'human capital'. The term 'HR metrics' is often used to embrace a confusion of loosely people related measures. In the Introduction, we quoted Tom Stewart, 'The question remains – can you prove that the company would not be better off without you?' We must, therefore, ask how would we judge that an HR function adds more value than it costs? In this chapter we want to look at those measures which relate to the professional contribution of HR as a function. Having looked at the strategic contribution of HR, this chapter naturally follows – how can the function measure and monitor its effectiveness.

7.1 The Need and Framework for an 'HR Scorecard'

The *effectiveness* of any unit is defined by its outputs. Its *efficiency* is about what it takes to deliver those outputs. Support departments, such as HR, IT, Marketing, Quality and Finance have two different sets of activities – as follows:

- There is the day to day *operational* function of providing and delivering services to managers and employees.

- There are '*strategic*' programmes and initiatives which may only occur once, and each has separate and unique objectives.

The quantitative measurement of these activities – by all functions, not only HR, has often been somewhat casual. Securing a budget to spend has been the name of the game – and ensuring this increases year by year if at all possible. Departments made their judgements about priorities and submitted them for approval. There has often been little demand by others for rigorous justification, and sets of objectives are often written as a series of *activities*, rather than aimed at any particular defined benefits. For example in HR we might find:

- 'to introduce a revised competency framework';

- 'to introduce a high potential development programme by Q3';

- 'to run five development centres for call centre managers'.

All of these beg the question 'why?' What dimensions of organisational improvement are these aimed at? Or are they just good ideas, areas of interest for the professionals concerned? There is considerable pressure to change this rather soft approach. Both business and public sectors are getting more numerate, more demanding, more target and ratio driven. There are too many stories of large projects that seem to have achieved very little.

The professional HR practitioner needs, therefore, some essential tools. She/he needs to be able to:

- understand and articulate the meaning of 'value' and 'value added' from the perspective of a support function;

- be able to quantify, with the necessary business knowledge, both costs and returns in relation to people and organisation management;

- be confident and competent in justifying investments that relate to people.

This is a demanding requirement, not so much because of the 'technical' nature of the tools needed, but because our 'people capital' is not subject to the same rules as 'financial capital'. Judgements and assumptions have to be made, and many of the returns from initiatives, though real enough, cannot be expressed in financial terms.

BECKER, HUSELID AND ULRICH

These three authors produced a book in 2001, entitled The HR Scorecard, which deserves mention before we propose our own approach. They were influenced by Kaplan and Norton's Strategy Maps.

When they refer to 'HR', however, they mix together 'people' measures and functional indicators, which we have recommended separating. They have four components as follows:

- Identifying HR Deliverables: these are outcomes from HR activities – either as a result of processes or projects – turnover, or competence levels, for example.

- Use of High Performance Work Systems: this is essentially about process measures.

- HR System alignment: these are measures which relate specifically to elements of the business strategy.

- HR Efficiency: cost and productivity measures.

It is not particularly easy to categorise measures between these four. The book has many helpful parts but the model for an HR scorecard does not seem to be in widespread use by HR functions.

THE PWC-SARATOGA HUMAN CAPITAL PROFILE

The Saratoga Institute, led by Jac Fitz-enz, we have featured before as a pioneer in the people measurement arena. In the UK their business was bought by PwC, the consultants, and they have a model as illustrated in Figure 7.1.

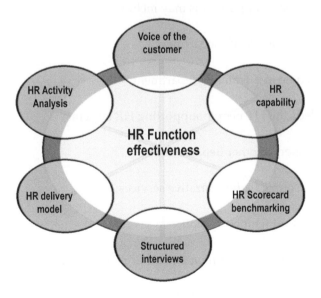

Figure 7.1   PWC-Saratoga 'Human Capital Business Model'

Their HR scorecard is the main vehicle for the sector-based benchmarking service they offer, and includes top level ratios such as revenue and profit/ FTE and their 'human investment ratio' (See Section 1.6 for a discussion and summary of their key ratios.)

This model is a mixture of HR functional measures and high level financial ratios, and was developed in the US.

7.2 Return on Investment for the HR Function?

It is not particularly helpful to try and answer the question 'What is the Return on Investment for the HR function?' An organisation, at the very least, has to administer its people. It may choose to do this in-house or by outsourcing, but one way or another it has to pay for doing so. There is a baseline of cost that has to be paid for; and we may want to keep that cost as low as we can, but this is a cost of being in business. Beyond that is the 'discretionary spend' and this is what needs to be justified project by project.

HR functions vary enormously in scope and activity, and in the range of resources they use. If we think of HR as the 'people support activity', rather than a discrete headcount group or department, we might well be interested in all aspects of people support. This may include:

- people in an HR department;

- people in a Training department;

- dedicated IT people supporting HR systems;

- trainers in other departments;

- outsourced administrative services;

- relevant temporary staff;

- subcontracted training and other professional services;

- consultants doing projects.

In practice, as organisations work with budgets defined by the organisation chart, it would be rare for this total data to be collected. What is seriously misleading, however, is to make judgements based on 'headcount'. Many games are played in resourcing and numbers of people on the payroll distort the true costs. This is why great care must be taken in benchmarks such as 'ratio of HR people to total headcount'. It is easy to show a good ratio with creative flexible resourcing.

So if we want to understand whether we are getting 'value for money' from HR, we need to first make a judgement as how the total cost and quality of delivering the 'people' service stacks up against best practice. Secondly, we need to have a rigorous methodology for assessment of the costs and benefits of specific activities. Figure 7.2 shows the different areas that would form part of an 'HR scorecard':

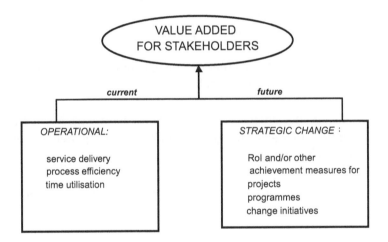

Figure 7.2   The components of an HR functional scorecard

OPERATIONAL:

- HR provides services – in administration, advice, policies and procedures, counselling, compliance, data provision and monitoring, and problem solving.

- HR manages continuing processes – recruitment assignments, communications, appraisals, pay and bonus schemes, and so on.

- HR may provide operational training, meeting compliance needs or ensuring a necessary standard of knowledge or skill.

The *effectiveness* of HR in this category will be measured by the levels of value added to its stakeholders. The *efficiency* with which it delivers has three components:

- the cost of service delivery;

- the efficiency of process management;

- productivity and the way time is utilised.

MANAGING CHANGE:

- HR initiates and manages HR projects, bringing in new methodologies, systems or processes.

- HR diagnoses what is happening with human capital, at individual, group and organisational levels.

- HR initiates, manages or supports organisational change (such as culture, mergers, structuring and restructuring, new systems, and new markets).

- HR provides learning and development programmes supporting individual and organisational change.

This leads us to two connected types of assessment of 'return', which we will use to judge whether we are spending money and time to best advantage:

- the 'future value added' for stakeholders;

- the 'return on investment' from specific projects and programmes.

7.3 How an HR Function Adds (or Subtracts) Value

The starting point for measuring effectiveness must be to identify the nature of the value that is added to different stakeholders, to decide on a quantitative measure for each area, and to set standards or targets to meet.

As we mentioned in Section 5.2, the term 'adding value' requires the preposition 'to' – that is, to whom? And a support function can as easily subtract as add value. There is also a role in 'maintaining value', that is, ensuring it is not lost through negligence or bad practice. HR is involved in many areas here such as

- the way it deals with employees and potential employees;

- accurate and timely administration;

- compliance with the law and other government requirements;

- avoiding negative reputational issues such as inappropriate adverts, unwanted court cases, bad external audits, and/or poor industrial relations;

- providing correct advice and guidance to managers.

Figure 5.1 summarised the potential 'stakeholder map' for an HR function, and Table 7.1 shows how HR activities can influence value.

Table 7.1   Added value from HR activities

HR Stakeholders and the nature of value added	Examples of practical contribution from HR and L&D initiatives	Examples of value measures
Owners/shareholders • Financial • Reputational	• Productivity gains, cost of service delivery, costs of benefits • Employment brand	Cost ratios League tables, contests, external research, awards
Parent company • Financial • Reputational • Synergistic • Strategic	• Cost of the function • Employment brand; handling of legal issues • Support for corporate HR initiatives and policies • Achieving employee alignment with vision and values	Cost ratios League tables, awards, contests, external research, court case statistics Internal audits, corporately defined targets Employee surveys, appraisal statistics
Senior management • Financial • Reputational • Strategic • Continuity • Organisational effectiveness	• Cost and service levels of the function • Employment brand; handling of legal issues • Creating HR strategies and policies that support business strategy • Achieving employee alignment with company goals • Describing and achieving a cultural vision supporting the business goals • Talent and continuity management • Organisational design; communication frameworks; people related processes	Cost ratios, service targets League tables, awards, contests, external research, court case statistics People strategy audit, feedback surveys Employee surveys, appraisal statistics Cultural template and periodic evaluation against it Talent, succession and continuity measures Process measures, change project evaluations, targeted surveys

Table 7.1   *Concluded*

Operational management		Feedback surveys,
• Strategic	• Creating initiatives which support departmental goals	Feedback surveys, project by project evaluations
• Advisory	• Problem based consultancy	Feedback surveys
• Employee engagement and performance	• Recognition programmes; people related measures; performance management	Increases in value of people and teams, productivity, engagement, process measures, capability profiles, absenteeism and turnover
Employees		
• Financial	• Salary, bonus and benefit structures	Opinion surveys, labour turnover statistics
• Motivational	• HR policies and programmes	Opinion surveys, diversity statistics
• Developmental	• Learning and development; career planning	Opinion surveys, reasons for leaving statistics, capability profiles, promotion statistics, training investment ratios
Trade unions		
• Employee benefits	• Successful negotiations	Balance of give and take, costs conceded
• Communication and respect	• Consultation, information provision	Feedback
Communities		
• Support	• Financial and human support for local projects	£ and man hours donated
Suppliers		
• Financial	• Amount of business	Volume of business and repeat business
• Reputational	• Prestige, endorsement, recommendation	Recommendations given

If an HR initiative is aimed at increasing value added and includes non-financial elements, we cannot set good objectives unless we can quantify those elements.

The three principal direct stakeholders of HR are senior management, operational managers, and employees. In setting up a scorecard we would start with selected measures of the value we add to each.

This will involve surveys of different kinds, and we mentioned 'issues of design' in Section 1.2. The three primary surveys HR would be involved in are:

- opinion surveys

- engagement surveys

- service feedback surveys.

TOpinion surveys may otherwise be known as climate surveys, the employee voice, or employee satisfaction. We discussed in Chapter 3 the notion that 'satisfaction' is important but not enough – it is engagement we are after. The latter is mostly due to the environment on the ground and to line management actions or lack of them, and HR would help with the design and analysis of such surveys. However, satisfaction is still important. The annual opinion survey has its role in getting feedback on what employees think about policies and practices, communication, salaries, culture and so on – much of which is managed and owned by HR.

The service feedback survey is more of a customer survey, and might have different versions for each stakeholder group. It can be administered online and would be done every 4–6 months. It would cover degrees of satisfaction with items such as:

- ease of doing business with HR

- availability

- attitude of HR staff

- administrative responsiveness

- administrative accuracy

- use of technology

- user friendliness of technology

- perceived value of processes and tools such as appraisal or competence frameworks

- quality of advice given

- support given for business goals.

The study below is an example of a perception study of a training department. It is more focused on attitude than operational performance – both are important in a survey.

HOW IS A TRAINING DEPARTMENT JUDGED IN PRACTICE?

In a study conducted by Ian Rose of Canada, he found that the principal measure used to gauge the value of training is *management's perception of the training department and its services.*

Some of the things that are looked for are as follows:

Business Focus:
- A thorough understanding of the business, listening to where the business wants to go, and determining what needs to be in place on the human side.
- Works forward from the strategy of the organisation rather than backwards from the department's own agenda.
- Sees training as a lever of change and puts a lot of effort into 'organisational learning'.
- Is seen by the business as a prime resource providing essential services.
- Is always looking ahead to ensure the people are prepared for what is coming down the road.

Culture Change:
- Plays a key role in supporting, and at times even shaping, the culture of the organization.
- Provides a common core curriculum for mission-critical skills, including active and continued support for vision and values.

Customer Focus:
- Develops training strategies in partnership with customers.
- Has regular contact with customers and a thorough understanding of their business needs, and how to tailor internal training to meet them.

Focus on Performance:
- Sees its mission as way beyond the design and delivery of training interventions, but rather to help organisational units and individuals achieve performance improvement goals through provision of effective learning opportunities.
- Is an integrator with other functions within and beyond HR.
- Invests resource in the understanding of effective learning at all levels.
- Acts on a consulting basis to help reduce the need for training by encouraging (and helping with) alternative learning methods.

7.4. Operational Efficiency – Service Delivery

For many years it has been customary to centralise – and often outsource – payroll management. The trend over the last decade had been to extend this to 'people administration' – all the documentation relating to employment with the organisation, and to 'FAQs' about policies, procedures, legal requirements, and common situational dilemmas. The most popular model today is a combination of outsourced routine activities and centralised intranet and 'shared service' personal support – with unit based HR 'business partners' left to work on added value activities. This is at least is the theory. In practice, it seems managers often like to use the 'live and accessible' support as a bridge to the background services, which causes some frustration and confusion.

If the service is provided externally it will be the subject of a contracted 'service level agreement'. A typical external agreement covers the following:

- purpose;

- services to be delivered;

- performance, tracking and reporting;

- problem management;

- fees and expenses;

- client duties and responsibilities;

- warranties, legal issues, dispute resolution, security and termination.

If provided internally, we may be less formal and even have no standards of delivery published. However, there is much to be said for laying out the levels of service that departments can expect from HR, and regularly checking that these are being achieved. It can also be worthwhile to define the costs of particular services: for example, 'it costs £5,500 per graduate recruited'. This helps managers to think before requesting a service, but can also have an undesired effect in a 'market-driven' culture – in the sense that managers may feel they could get a better deal elsewhere. This then leaves the HR resources under-utilised – the unit doing the external subcontracting makes its own P&L

(profit and loss) look better, but overall the organisation is incurring greater costs. This does need to be controlled.

Efficiency is the balance between the level of service provided and the cost of its provision. Targets can be set based on benchmarking, or simply continuous improvement. The following tables illustrate some of the factors to be considered in building an efficiency measurement framework:

Table 7.2   Payroll and administrative management; advisory services

• Service standards	• Costs	• Measures
• Accuracy • Timeliness • Responsiveness • Turn round times • Complaints • Helpfulness • Competence	• System costs • People costs • Materials costs • Premises costs • (these will be bundled in a commercial contract with an outside supplier, which will include the supplier's profit margin)	• Cost per employee • Cost per transaction • % achievement of service levels in the agreement • Internal customer satisfaction (see above) • Complaints per month • Average time to respond to queries

Examples of defined service levels in an external contract might be:

- 100 per cent of people will be paid on the due date.

- Administrative queries will be turned round in two hours.

- Call centre waiting will not be more than 90 seconds.

- Satisfaction with responsiveness will be greater than 8/10.

- Complaints about lack of knowledge of any question asked will be less than 3 per month.

7.5 Operational Efficiency – HR Owned Processes and Their Effectiveness

Every function should monitor how well it carries out the processes that it owns. In Table 6.9 we listed processes for which HR is normally accountable.

For every process there are:

- Outcomes – the end purpose of the process, ideally measured by value added to the beneficiary.

- Outputs – the visible results from the process.

- Inputs – usually in the form of activities.

- Process measures – indicating the efficiency of all or part of the process.

Here are some measures and how they fit into this classification:

- Participation in a process (such as percentage of people having individual development plans, or participation in employee surveys) – *input*.

- A cost ratio (such as cost per candidate per development centre) – *process measure*.

- An improvement ratio (such as percentage annual change in average performance rating, or change in percentage of involuntary resignations) – *outcome*.

- A delivery ratio (such as training days per employee) – *input*.

- A productivity ratio (such as successful recruits/recruitment officer, or training days delivered per trainer) – *process measure*.

- Employee perceptions of the process (such as helpfulness, manager involvement) – *output, or sometimes an outcome*.

Let us illustrate this once more for a particular process – that of recruitment. The outcome of the recruitment process is not that a candidate is selected, offered and accepts – this is an output. The outcome is that a vacancy is filled to the standard required and is performing well after the anticipated learning period. This might require six months, post start date, to assess.

Examples of input measures might be the quality of job/person specifications (against some preset criteria), employee brand data, or the quality of induction provided. There might be a number of process measures – cost per offer made, percentage offers accepted, average time taken from start to acceptance, or candidate perceptions of the process.

How do we know if an indicator is good or bad? Benchmarking is possible on some – but must be used with caution. Individual organisations vary so much in their demands, their values and their circumstances. We can at least track whether an indicator is improving or not and set some targets.

At the end of the day it will be management judgement. For example, let us suppose that the appraisal process consumes X management and HR hours in a year, and yet participation is low and the perceived benefit is low. Management must make a judgement as to whether to carry on, to abandon the process, or to 're-engineer' it to make it more effective.

We could end up with a very large number of measures here – too many to manage if we are not careful. Those that are strategically important in their impact, or are very costly, would deserve priority. This will almost certainly include recruitment and talent management.

USING SOME STANDARD COSTS

It will help us in measuring efficiency, and in estimating the Return on Investment (RoI) of special projects, to have some standard *formulae* to work to in estimating the costs of common activities.

For example, we can create a template for the cost of external recruitment as follows:

- time of recruiter (salaries + benefits – hours x hourly rate);

- time of management selectors (salaries + benefits – hours × hourly rate);

- assessment centre costs (if applicable);

- sundry purchased services (advertising, tests, and so on);

- subcontractors (recruitment consultancy fees and expenses);

- travel and accommodation (interview expenses);

- relocation costs (if applicable);

- salaries + benefits of new employee for induction, training and on the job learning;

- 'Golden hellos' (if applicable).

If this recruitment is a result of unwanted attrition, we may add additional costs – not all of which will be found in the accounts:

- excess costs of covering the post by temporary or interim staff, or by overtime;

- lost added value through lack of a person in position;

- lost productivity during learning curve.

As discussed in on page 127, experience may lead us to use a 'rule of thumb average cost' based on a multiple of salary. Thus, we may conclude that the cost of recruiting a senior manager to replace one that was lost is – on average – 1.5 × salary; and for a call centre operator 0.3 × salary: such 'shortcuts' need to be revalidated at least annually.

Other candidates for this approach of 'standard activity costs' in HR would include (*inter alia*):

- internal job selection

- conducting employee surveys

- 360 degree feedback

- providing external coaching

- 'standard' internal or subcontracted training events

- basic induction

- salary surveys

- assessment/development centres

- internal communications

- appraisal process

- routine administration procedures

- absenteeism.

There is an advantage for benchmarking in using industry accepted *formulae*: one such for absenteeism is the 'Bradford Factor' discussed in Chapter 3.

A comprehensive guide to calculating many standard process measures can be found in Bucknall and Zei's *Magic Numbers for Human Resource Management* (2006).

7.6 Operational Efficiency – Productivity and Time Utilisation

This is a much neglected area, which we discussed in Section 1.7, thinking of people generally. We will consider it here in the context of HR specifically. The nature of HR is so varied that it is particularly difficult to measure productivity in any sense of activities per hour or per person. Productivity is defined as output over inputs, and we can certainly look at some of the value added measures discussed above and relate them to HR staff costs, total costs, time spent, and so on. The way time is spent is certainly a useful tool in assessing our efficiency. Few organisations have a system for analysing what the time of people is used for – unless of course they are acutely conscious that time is money, such as the major professional firms. And nowhere is time recording welcomed as an activity by employees.

Support departments such as HR have to spend time on 'internal maintenance', without any clear contribution to a stakeholder. A major aid in effectiveness is to have a clear understanding of what is and what is not 'added value' work. This is not what feels useful, but is what is *directly* related to adding value to stakeholders.

In Ulrich's 1997 book *Human Resource Champions*, where he outlined the four key roles of HR, he included a questionnaire about how time was spent. 'How much time, effort and intellectual energy does your department spend on the following?' was asked regarding a description of each of the four roles. One hundred points are allocated between the four. This remains a useful approach to analysing HR activity.

Not everyone will agree with Table 7.3, but it suggests a division between 'value adding' work and 'non-value adding' work for an HR department. We prefer this terminology to the distinction between 'strategic' and 'transactional'.

Table 7.3   Table of value adding activities in HR

Maintenance	Non-Value adding	Value adding (to)
• Employee administration	• Internal meetings	• Training (employees)
• Salary administration	• Travel time	• Counselling (employees, managers)
• Job evaluation	• Problem and grievance resolution	• Recruiting (managers)
• Policy writing	• Absence management	• Workforce planning (managers, senior managers)
• Policy administration	• Procedure writing	• Talent management (all)
• Survey analysis	• Benchmarking	• Assessment (all)
• HRIS maintenance	• Reporting	• People strategy formulation (all)
	• Government form filling	• OD projects (senior management)
	• Regulatory compliance	• Incentive and recognition system design (managers, employees)
	• Routine consultation	• Coaching managers (managers)
	• Internal negotiation and cross charging	• Process re-engineering (managers)
	• Review meetings	• Exit interviewing (managers)
	• Budgeting	• Post – survey action planning • (employees, managers)

Table 7.3   *Concluded*

		• Succession planning • (senior managers)
		• Career and Development planning • (employees)
		• Engagement action planning • (managers, employees)
		• Absence management • (managers)

We can see from this table that the number of opportunities for adding value is very great – so the question is how much time from the function is devoted to it? Inundated as functions often are with the demands of the other two columns, the question is how we can make a shift.

We come back to the options for increasing productivity. It is popular in some quarters to try and shift non-value adding work to the line. Of course the line should take responsibility for managing their people in the sense of relationships, motivation and development. But HR cannot forget that actually the line does do more important jobs than they do – their job is to support the line. Process engineering is a key – how can we eliminate steps in the processes we use? And how can we better use technology to achieve more effective results – always remembering that we are dealing with humans, and technology never has all the answers.

7.7 The Return on Investment of HR Programmes and Initiatives

The return on investments made in people related programmes, such as HR projects and training programmes, is notoriously difficult to assess. Whereas investment in IT or quality can normally be targeted at cost savings or measurable customer benefits, the objectives of many HR programmes are more diverse. Some, indeed, are undertaken more as 'an act of faith', an intuitive belief that the programme will benefit the business either short- or long–term, but with the assumption that it cannot be directly proved. However, there is no doubt that many programmes and initiatives are undertaken in organisations where even a simple evaluation would show there was no significant measurable benefit. Or if there is, it is not proportionate to the investment.

Coaching programmes are a good example. A survey by Personnel Today in 2007 showed that only 13 per cent of HR people having such programmes took any trouble to assess RoI. It may not be easy, but that is largely because there is often no clarity about what the specific goals are.

The heart of these acts of faith is a belief in a chain of cause and effect that will eventually lead to a bottom line benefit. The famous eighteenth century Scottish philosopher, David Hume, described three conditions that must occur to scientifically prove 'cause and effect':

- the cause and the effect must be adjacent to each other;

- the cause must always come before the effect;

- there is a constant relationship between them in that the cause must always be present whenever the effect is obtained.

This provides good advice in understanding whether an HR or training intervention has any effect on business measures. Being able to draw up valid cause and effect links is a basic skill that is needed in our context, simply because the *direct* effects of many initiatives on 'bottom lines' will be hard to show.

If there is only one link in the chain, the task is relatively easy. However, in the HR area this is rarely the case. The immediate objectives are often not financial. Each link in a chain brings contaminating factors, that is, other influences which dilute the effect of the original intervention and the directness of the link diminishes. To evaluate any return that is at least credible financially, we not only have to establish realistic links but also to be skilled at assessing the financial impact or otherwise of non-financial benefits along the way.

MUST WE SEE ROI AS PURELY A FINANCIAL CALCULATION?

This might seem like a strange question. But we know that value can be both financial and non-financial. As an individual I spend money on, for example, a holiday to receive a number of different non-financial returns – time with my family, experiences, relaxation, and so on, and at the end of the holiday I intuitively make an assessment as to whether what I got from it was worth what I spent. Even in business we spend money for non-financial gain – prestige, reputation, building political positions, for example. Sure, we believe they are in the long-term interest of the bottom line but we would not attempt to prove it pound for pound. It is a matter of judgement whether the gain – expected or realised – is worth the investment, and there will probably be different opinions about that.

In the fields of training, organisational change, and HR initiatives we are more likely to be aiming for non-financial benefits, in the first place at least, than for a targeted bottom line gain. Where projects have direct goals such as reducing labour turnover, or absenteeism, or increasing productivity or safety – then the benefits can be translated fairly easily into financial gain. We need to be careful not to claim savings which are not actual cash – the classic error is to accumulate time savings and assume it is real money. (In theory it may release time to be spent on other, more value adding, things – but this would be very difficult to estimate.) If we are investing in culture change, diversity awareness, strategic understanding, team building or even leadership development, financial gain will be much more difficult to assess. One government department spent a million pounds with a prestigious business school and the stated aim was to enable the top 100 managers to manage major change effectively. This was almost impossible to evaluate, other than the perceived benefits by the participants.

Figure 7.3 illustrates some typical cause and effect chains.

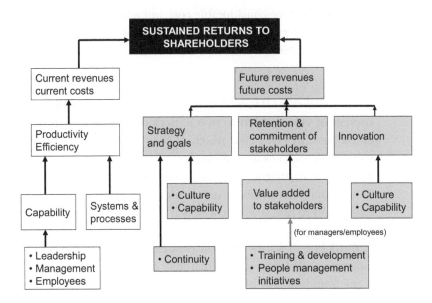

Figure 7.3   Cause and effect chains of HR initiatives

The left hand chain is about greater revenues or less costs – through improved performance of people, or better ways of doing things. It is focused on *operational* improvement. Typical HR interventions aimed at this chain are about enhancing the *capability* of leaders, managers or employees, or by introducing new *policies, processes and systems*.

On the other side of the value chain we have 'building for the longer term', requiring *strategic* interventions. In the diagram the influences on future success have been divided into three, which constitute 'desirable bottom lines' in their own right. They are:

- *The internal strength of the organisation*: this concerns the organisational strategy, its vision, values, long-term goals and culture. There will be many HR initiatives taken here which will have such a long-term effect that it will be impossible to measure financially. For example, we may:

  - conduct communication and awareness programmes;
  - invest in culture change;
  - embed values;
  - build a succession planning process;
  - initiate a knowledge management programme.

Some of these initiatives have considerable cost, but are, nevertheless, deemed important for the longer term health of the organisation. Success is sometimes elusive, and certainly will be so without a system for measuring and monitoring progress.

- *Adding value to stakeholders per se*: in the Appendix, we list sources of value added to two important groups – customers and employees. In HR's case much of their work is aimed at adding value to employees and managers. It is done through training and development programmes, and other HR initiatives that benefit them. What we need here is to understand the nature of the value added and to find a way to assess it.

- A third line of value creation is suggested under the heading of '*innovation*'. This is treated separately because it is so important – it is the foundation of building *future* added value. We can measure success in terms of sales based indicators of new products and services as the prime output – but may want to measure inputs also in terms of culture, behaviours, processes and participation in idea generation.

The chain can be adapted for public sector organisations.

WHY THIS IS NOT DONE VERY OFTEN

The most prominent writer in this area is an American called Jack J. Philips, who has numerous books in this niche field. He identifies a number of barriers that make most HR and Training people shy away from doing full RoI assessments.

Costs and Time – it takes time to do RoI studies, especially post-project evaluation. Phillips reckons it may add 3–5 per cent to the costs. Certainly this prevents a lot of RoI work, although one would not hesitate to do the necessary work before embarking on a 'tangible assets' project.

Lack of skills and interest from HR professionals – not only do many HR people struggle with the technical part of costing (the author has used a simple RoI exercise for a HR strategy training programme and no participant has yet got it right), but they have difficulty in seeing the business cause and effect chains referred to earlier. Because most programmes focus on 'soft objectives' they have difficulty in seeing how to apply RoI.

Fear – related to the above, but an anxiousness that 'I might not get the answer I want', and also of having to justify their calculations and arguments in front of business people.

Discipline and planning – if a project is to be evaluated pre-commencement and post- completion it requires a pretty disciplined process. Without it, the study may fall over and not get completed because – for example – necessary data is not collected.

Cultural factors – the organisation may not have a culture of measurement and accepts that 'initiatives that sound right should be supported'. If this is so, there will be very little pressure on HR to justify what it does and thus very little incentive for evaluation.

The lack of available data is also a real problem – the better the regular metrics for both human capital and the HR function, the easier it is to assess RoI.

Apart from the difficulties, perhaps the most common reason for the lack of RoI assessments is the lack of pressure from senior management. Most HR and training professionals will express interest and concern that they should be better at it and do more of it, but few organisations demand it of them in any rigorous way. There are exceptions, particularly some very measurement orientated American companies, but it seems that most organisations, private and public, are more concerned to agree a budget for support functions and let them spend it in the way they feel is best. In practice, as in IT and Marketing, a lot of money can be spent for little gain.

THE IMPORTANCE OF CLEAR MEASURABLE GOALS

Donald Kirkpatrick did his PhD thesis in 1959, and little did he know that he and his methodology would be a household name even 50 years later as the classic methodology for 'levels of evaluation' of training programmes. He identified four levels:

Level 1 – general satisfaction with the experience of the initiative or programme.

Level 2 – change in skills, knowledge or attitudes; evidence of learning.

Level 3 – application and implementation – evidence of behaviour change or the initiative working as planned.

Level 4 – measurable business impact.

As we have shown earlier, Level 4 is not necessarily financial.

Jack Phillips added RoI as 'Level 5'. However, there is a level we might call 'Level 0' which is fundamental, and that is the setting of the objectives of the programme. The specification of what we are trying to achieve – clearly and measurably – will, in itself, determine the nature of the benefits we will assess. If we are 'investing' in team building, for example, it may be that our objective is that the team will make better decisions as a result. But we will never know that for sure. We will probably have an objective that team members felt good about the event and it 'increased morale'. That might be much easier to assess, as well as be the real goal anyway. Objectives, therefore, may be at any of the 'levels' – whichever one it is that dictates the level of cost/benefit balancing.

We have argued that *everything* can be measured in some way: morale, understanding, competence, commitment, culture change, and reputation – however intangible. We need some carefully designed rulers but they can be created, and we listed the different types in Chapter 1. Often our objective may be phrased as *a percentage change* in a chosen measure. If we have clear, measurable objectives, it is but a short step to assessing whether they were achieved. The problem is that in many HR related initiatives we do not have these. They are often phrased as vague generalised, aspirational hopes. This is nearly always true of one of today's major expenditure areas, namely 'leadership development'. What exactly are the visible results we seek from our investment? The perceptions of leaders by their 'followers'? Improved morale and productivity? Better decisions? How do we measure these and what percentage change from the current status do we seek? When such programmes are evaluated one usually finds that the individual participant feels very positive about the experience. They have gained personal insight and feedback, and many will talk of their intentions to lead/manage in a different way. However, the realisation of that in any tangible measure is much more difficult. The fact is that they go back into the culture and organisational system they left and the intention to change is often subject to slow erosion. Some such programmes are justified by 'group projects' – by giving participants a task to solve or an area to innovate in. There is plenty of evidence that groups do come up with ideas that benefit the bottom line during such development programmes. The programme has provided the platform, although one could argue that the provision of time and incentive could have been done without it.

Table 7.4 shows a number of typical HR initiatives, firstly of an operational nature, and then those that are more strategic, together with the generally appropriate level of evaluation, the kind of objectives that might be set, and appropriate measures. It is always preferable to choose measures that are readily available than to design new measurement systems from scratch.

Table 7.4   Typical HR initiatives, objectives, levels of evaluation and measures to be used

a) Operational

Driver of the intervention 'why we are doing it'	Level of evaluation	Specification of objective 'to what end?'	Measurement 'how will we know we succeeded?'
Business Performance			
Revenue increase or cost saving	Four	Actual amount of £ or a % improvement within a timescale	Accounting measures
Other business management target – service, quality, productivity	Four	Target level to be achieved or % improvement	Standard business measures
Resolution of an operational problem	Three/Four	Target level to be achieved or % improvement	Standard business measures
Team performance	Three/Four	Target level to be achieved or % improvement	Standard business measures; peer perception of team cohesion/support
Individual performance	Three	Target level to be achieved or % improvement	Standard business measures; measures of personal commitment; management and personal observation
Rewards and recognition as incentives	Four	Business results	Results achieved/cost of scheme
Process efficiency			
Process or system knowledge	Two	Ability to use the process Degree of participation	Tests % of relevant populations
Process efficiency	Three/Four	Speed of process per transaction Costs per transaction	Improvements in end goals of the process Improvements in time taken and cost per transaction
Job 'Enablement'			
Regulatory or conformance requirements	Two	Attendance within a timescale	Attendance and/ or knowledge demonstration
Job induction	Two	Speed of learning curve	Knowledge and skills demonstration
Maintenance or enhancement of core capability	Two	Depth and breadth of expertise	Capability levels % at a certain level
Essential knowledge/skills training	Two	Defined capability levels	Knowledge and skills demonstration

Table 7.4   Continued

Resourcing			
New ways of working	Three/Four	Productivity	Appropriate ratios
Recruitment projects	Three	To specification within a timescale	Achievement of objectives Cost per recruit
Downsizing/rightsizing	Three/Four	Headcount goals	Headcount measures 'Loss of human capital value' Cost per head

b) Strategic

Strategic alignment			
New business strategy	Four	Level of understanding required; alignment	Feedback instruments
Consolidation of company values	Three	Behaviours	Feedback instruments
Organisational change – structure, culture, new systems, M&A	Four	Desired behaviours; achievement of change objectives	Feedback instruments; process efficiency measures; achievement of milestones
Potential and succession planning	Three	Process effectiveness; retention of talent; internal appointments; continuity	% internal appointments % of designated talent pools leaving use of the process and plans
Adding Value to Stakeholders			
A motivational and enjoyable experience, or change that is positively received by employees	One	Employee motivation	Evaluation sheets; surveys; ratings
Specifically targeted programmes	Three/Four	Stakeholder benefits	Value added measures; stakeholder retention
Investing in People			
Leadership development	Two/Four	Improved competencies, productivity and business decisions Increased loyalty	Productivity Business growth 360 perceptions Succession ratios Retention of talent

Table 7.4   *Concluded*

Individual employee development	Two/Three	Realisation of potential Increased loyalty Achieving future capability needs	Retention of talent Fulfilment of development and career plans Capability levels Increase in 'human capital' value
New reward, recognition and motivational programmes; new HR policies	Three/Four	Retention Motivation, engagement and commitment	Retention and absenteeism Employee perceptions Productivity ratios
Young entrant recruitment	Three	Numbers and quality	Cost per recruit Acceptance ratio Retention ratios Increase in 'human capital value'
Innovation			
Cultural change	Four	Desired behaviours	Employee perceptions Volume of suggestions, ideas Cost savings through innovation % of sales due to new products/ services
Creative and innovation techniques	Two	Competency levels	Competency demonstration Plus business benefits described above

Source: This table is taken from the author's *Understanding HR Return on Investment,* a 'One Stop Guide' from Personnel Today Management Resources.

SOME EXAMPLES OF GOOD OBJECTIVE SETTING:

'This training programme is aimed at increasing the level of 80% of participants in continuous improvement techniques to knowledge and skill level 'C', with a view to improving the number of genuine cost saving suggestions to X per person p.a. to achieve annual cost savings of y% per year in departmental operating costs'.

'To develop leadership capability in order to:

Provide a shared understanding of company strategy

To achieve a 75 per cent level of confidence by staff in their leadership

To increase Financial Added Value/employee by 10 per cent in a two year period'

'To introduce a stress management programme for dept X in order to reduce stress related absence by one third over the following 12 months and improve retention in this group by 25 per cent over the same period'

In deciding at what levels we will define the expected benefits of a programme or initiative we need to be clear where it fits in the value chain, and decide:

- If we achieve these benefits are they part of a chain which clearly leads to a benefit higher up?

- If so, at what levels will we conduct the measurement?

7.8 Justification and Evaluation

There are two processes required; one an extension of the other:

- preparing a case to justify an initiative;

- evaluating whether the initiative met its anticipated returns.

Investing in balance sheet assets follows a well defined discipline. The costs of a project are assessed. There are always traps in under costing, especially not allowing for hidden costs. Then the financial returns are evaluated over the life of the project. They are always best estimates and no manager usually gets away with a proposal where his or her assumptions are not challenged. A hurdle of return must be reached for the capital to be authorised. The real work is in the thorough analysis of the costs and potential benefits that will stand up to scrutiny.

Such disciplines are rarely demanded of 'soft' or 'intangible' projects, and yet the rationale for doing so is clear. This arises partly from the anachronistic distinction between 'capital' and 'revenue' expenditures in today's knowledge based world, and of course from the often non-financially quantifiable benefits. True, a 'business case' may need to be made for an initiative, but it is the rigour of analysis that is often missing. If the effort were made to justify and scrutinise projects before they started we would rarely want to go to the difficult job of trying to assess the return on investment afterwards.

Nevertheless, just as capital expenditure over a certain limit will require a full appraisal, so we can define some criteria which would guide us on whether a full post project evaluation is likely to be worthwhile. Clearly the amount of expenditure would be one factor – the threshold would vary with the size of the organisation, and might be set at a certain percentage of the department's budget. A second criterion might be that the outcome of the project is strategically important and we really do need to know if it was successful. A third, particularly in the public sector, might be that there is a need to prove to other parties that money was well spent.

THE STEPS REQUIRED IN AN ROI JUSTIFICATION

In 'making the case', we have four steps to go through:

- define the objectives of the initiative;

- calculate the estimated costs of the project;

- estimate the returns derived from the initiative;

- balance the two and conclude that the initiative is or is not a worthwhile use of resources.

THE STEPS REQUIRED IN A PLANNED ROI EVALUATION

If we want to assess the impact of an initiative it requires considerable additional planning. There are many more steps – 11 are suggested below. Practitioners often start the process of evaluation after a programme or initiative has taken place. This is difficult to do because: a) the initial objectives may have been imprecise; and b) the data we need has not been collected. The steps are as below:

- defining the objectives of the initiative;

- making a data collection and evaluation plan;

- collecting data before the initiative if before/after comparisons need to be made;

- collect data during the initiative as needed;

- collect data after implementation;

- calculate all costs involved at each stage;

- isolate the effects of the programme;

- calculate financial impact of the data;

- compare with the costs;

- present together with the non-financial benefits;

- judge whether RoI was satisfactory.

ESTIMATING THE COSTS – JUSTIFICATION AND EVALUATION

The costs of an HR project can be split into different phases as follows:

- needs analysis (Steps 1, 6 in a planned evaluation);

- planning and design (Steps 2, 3, 6);

- implementation (Steps 4, 6);

- ongoing operation (Steps 5, 6);

- evaluation (if to be conducted) (Steps 6, 7, 8, 9, 10, 11).

Table 7.5 provides a checklist to work to, as a reminder of all the *possible* costs. This checklist should be applied to each of the phases above as shown below.

Table 7.5   Cost recording

Area of cost	Needs analysis	Design and planning	Implementation of project	Ongoing operation p.a.	Evaluation
Salaries and benefits of those involved in leading the project – hourly equivalent x hours required management professionals support staff					
Travel					
Accommodation and meals					
Consultant fees					
Additional IT costs					
Space costs					
Purchased materials					
Printing					
Equipment hire or purchase					
Additional purchased services					
Time spent by managers and employees in discussion and/or learning (see note below)					
Time spent by managers and employees in implementation (see note below)					
Time spent by managers and employees in ongoing operation (see note below)					
Other					

Strictly speaking, the time spent by the 'beneficiaries' of the project or programme is not an extra cost. We would be paying for their salaries anyway. By using their time on the project we prevent them from doing something else, and the real cost is the lost added value that they would otherwise be contributing. Since – in the nature of knowledge workers – a good proportion of that lost added value will probably be made up one way or another, it is very hard to define a cost for their time.

Thus for a training event, for example, it is recommended that the cost of the trainers and their support staff is included, but the time of the participants is not. Other HR projects and initiatives should be treated on their merits, using logical common sense.

Arguments will rage whether 'overheads' should be included or not. Financial purists argue that they should be. The author would recommend that it unnecessarily complicates the issue. The overheads exist anyway. What we want to find out is whether by spending an *additional* amount of X, it will be justified.

COSTS – THINGS TO WATCH FOR

Once a project is approved, there is a need to be disciplined in actually *recording* what was spent. Clearly the system for doing so must be set up in advance if we anticipate evaluating.

Change projects often produce *'hidden costs'* that will not appear directly in the accounts or cost summaries. This is particularly important to comprehend when it comes to 'honest' evaluation.

These fall into the following categories:

- The effects of uncertainty or change in loss of motivation, and hence in productivity.

- The unanticipated 'knock on' effects on people's time, leading to extra non- added value work by people not on the costing plan.

- Achieving the benefits requires sacrificing value added elsewhere.

  (Of course there may be unanticipated 'hidden *benefits*' also.)

The evaluator will need to make estimates in these areas, usually as a percentage of an overall cost. Thus, we could say that such and such a restructuring change is expected to lead to a loss of productivity of 10 per cent over the implementation period, which has a financial effect on cost per unit of 10 per cent, which will affect margins on products sold and, therefore, profits by 10 per cent.

Often a project takes *more than one year* to implement, or the returns are expected over several years. In this case we need to estimate the costs over each year of the project's life, and discount appropriately using 'net present value' analysis. Applying this technique may require specialist help, but is not particularly complicated and it takes account of the fact that the value of money changes with time and looks at the value of future costs and benefits as at a particular point in time. Shell, for example, spend a lot of money recruiting 5,000 graduates a year but amortise the costs over an expected length of service of 10 years for the average graduate.

Sunk costs are the total costs and effort invested in a project to date. We are often very reluctant to abandon projects when considerable money has been spent even though it is clear that the returns will not materialise. At any given point in a project two things matter – what amount of time and resource will be needed to complete the project and the *present value* (see last point) of the returns that it will generate. This may sometimes lead to 'enough is enough'.

WHERE THE JUSTIFICATION IS COST AVOIDANCE – AN EXAMPLE OF NEEDS ANALYSIS

There will be initiatives that are designed specifically to reduce costs. In this case some research will be needed to estimate the scale of the unnecessary cost. An example of a research questionnaire on knowledge management was given in Chapter 5, Section 5.9.

This kind of analysis has several benefits:

- It unearths 'hidden costs' that do not stare out from any lines on the accounts.

- It brings an awareness of 'a problem to be solved'.

- It makes management aware of the 'cost of doing nothing' – which is always an alternative.

ESTIMATING THE RETURNS – JUSTIFICATION

At the justification stage, we will decide on the expected benefits. Benefits may not all happen at once – we need a timeline which will tell us the rate at which they will be realised. The overall time it takes to get the benefits will be a major factor in the justification. Plus, an essential analysis tool will be the logic of cause and effect links.

LEVEL ONE

It will be rare that our objectives will be confined to this level. However, some programmes may be aimed solely at motivation or reward. It can be argued that the motivational effect will be seen in retention and productivity – whereas this may well be so, it will be very hard to prove. For example:

- We may send an executive to a prestigious business school course. He or she will certainly learn, and *may* make some significantly different decisions as a result, but the main objective was to provide the person with some personal benefit – perhaps a good CV addition, help them extend their network, show some appreciation for work done.

- Some courses offered for personal development are just that: *personal*. Efforts to convince others that they have real business benefit are tenuous. For sure, there *may* be some far off potential business benefit but the prime reason for making the course available is as a benefit to the employee.

- It is not unknown for a course to be chosen just to give *some* opportunity to go on training. Real learning is not the actual goal, despite how much it may be dressed up.

- Many team building events are essentially motivational, rather than aimed at causing change in the business. They often also strengthen individual relationships and provide personal challenges that are long remembered. But assessing how people felt about the event – was it well run and was it personally beneficial – is probably as far as we can go.

- Some HR initiatives such as the provision of information (for example, a new form of benefits summary), or a new house magazine, are aimed at employee appreciation – and this is the level for measurement.

The programme objective (and subsequent evaluation) will be set at achieving a preset level of satisfaction with both the conduct of the event and the perceived personal benefit.

At this level, the *timeline for realising the benefits* is immediate – at the end of the programme.

LEVEL TWO

This level is about changes in knowledge, skills, attitudes, or other aspects of capability. This applies particularly to learning initiatives, and also may be a sufficient level in itself if the goal is confined to this. However, this would be a fallback position, only when it is deemed unrealistic to measure at Levels Three or Four.

Confinement to this level may apply to a learning programme where the learning itself is the goal, without any particular anticipated changes in the workplace attributable to the learning. This would apply to some regulatory training, where attendance and subsequent certification is the only goal. It would also apply to some knowledge learning programmes, such as induction and background learning.

The objectives and subsequent evaluation will be set in terms of an acquired level of expertise – typically a test or examination for knowledge programmes, or an observation for skills programmes.

Another aspect of capability is *experience* itself. HR programmes may be aimed at providing people with specific experiences as part of their development, or as contributing to a strategic goal. Here the objective and the achievement is the experience itself happening and being in line with its purpose. Some examples:

- a programme to second graduates to a different country for six months, and during this secondment to have experience of X,Y and Z;

- to provide N children of employees with a work shadowing experience;

- to spend x months working in a specific department in order to experience A, B or C.

'Experience' programmes will often have a higher level objective as well – such as building succession or changing behaviour.

The *timeline* here is also immediate when the programme has completed.

LEVEL THREE

This is the level of behaviour change and HR programme implementation. The justification will state what will be different as a result of the initiative. For example, goals might be described as:

- 'there will be no cases of sexual harassment attributable to ignorance of what constitutes harassment';

- 'the appraisal system will be operated according to the prescribed process';

- 'the flexi-time system works satisfactorily as planned'.

A justification which ends at this level is unlikely to be satisfactory on its own, and we should expect it to be combined with some Level Four indicators.

The *timeline* of Level Three will depend on the implementation phases of the programme. If it is behavioural change we are looking for we would expect to see this achieved within say six months of the programme completion.

LEVEL FOUR

HR and Training professionals frequently say how hard it is to evaluate their programmes at Level Four. This is often because it was never clear from the objectives whether there were any Level Four goals – or there was no systematic justification of the initiative in the first place.

We have identified several Level Four objectives, and they fall into three categories:

those with direct financial impact

These include direct cost reductions, direct revenue increases, or the avoidance of costs that might otherwise be incurred in the future.

We have mentioned earlier the trap of misusing the saving of *time*. If we save 10 minutes per supervisor per week, we have given the supervisor the opportunity to do other things, but we are still paying his or her salary. If no *cash* is saved we have not saved anything on the bottom line. Should the time saving result in less overtime being paid, or an actual reduction in staff, or less hours from temporary helpers – then these are real savings. Just saving time itself may not be.

This does not mean the saving of time *per se* is undesirable of course, but care is needed to work out the bottom line effect. (An example is given below where a real bottom line effect can be argued.)

Another area to watch is where revenue growth is anticipated. We must always remember the maxim 'a pound saved is a pound profit on the bottom line, but a pound of new revenue only gives a fraction, maybe 10p, of profit': so, 'operating margins on sales' needs to be understood. We must keep our eyes all the time on *cash* – the net of what goes out and what comes in.

those with a financial impact that can be reasonably estimated

Here we have such areas as productivity and efficiency improvements; reductions in attrition of and absenteeism; better customer retention; increased internal resourcing/less external recruitment, and improvements in innovation leading to more new product sales.

Some calculations giving examples in these areas may be helpful.

CASE A

A stress reduction programme is expected to reduce stress related absenteeism (currently running at 4.3 per cent) in a factory of 2000 people by an average of 2 per cent p.a. Currently, half the absenteeism is covered by overtime at 1.5 x normal rate; the rest is absorbed by the existing people. The average basic salary for the factory workers is £25,000 p.a. Workers are paid fully for sickness absence up to three months; thereafter there is a sliding scale. Almost all stress related sickness is less than three months in a year.

The anticipated savings are therefore:

$$2000 \times 0.02 \times 0.5 \times 1.5 \times 25,000 = £750,000$$

CASE B

A leadership development programme is planned to increase the quality of leadership to achieve, *inter alia*, higher productivity of people, reduced attrition, reduced absenteeism, and a higher ratio of internal promotion.

The attrition rate is hoped to reduce overall from 8.5 per cent p.a. to 7 per cent for the 10,000 staff, and from 4.6 per cent to 3 per cent for the 100 senior leaders who will go through the programme. For staff, the weighted cost of replacing unwanted attrition is 0.6 x the average salary of £32,000 p.a.; for senior managers it is 1.3 x an average salary of £95,000 per annum.

Thus, the anticipated savings from lower attrition will be:

$$10,000 \times 0.015 \times 0.6 \times 32,000 + 100 \times 0.016 \times 1.3 \times 95,000$$

$$= £\,2,880,000 + 197,600$$

$$= £\,3,077,600$$

NB. It is sometimes useful to work out the average cost per beneficiary, particularly if some financial return is expected attributable solely to an individual and we can make individual RoI comparisons. For example, if the cost per participant of a course in 'Management Excellence' was £5000, can individuals show (on average) increased effectiveness or specific decisions resulting from the course which can be valued?

those where a financial impact cannot be reasonably assessed

This category will include areas such as:

- strategic and cultural understanding and alignment

- creating 'feel good' factors

- relationship building

- growing capability

- image building

- behaviour change

- knowledge sharing

- mentoring.

The lack of a financial impact does not mean we should avoid quantifiable objectives. Stating them in 'wannabe' terms, as is often done, will never facilitate evaluation. Table 7.4 gave many examples. Here are some more:

- To achieve a level of strategic understanding amongst all staff at grade X and above, such that they can personally articulate the strategies and their own business plans are fully aligned to them.

- To achieve a diversity-conscious culture; which demonstrates 80 per cent plus in a 'mostly or always observed' survey, based on the set of behaviours defined in our 'diversity check'.

- To be in the top five of 'the best companies to work for' league table in our sector.

- To achieve at least 12 favourable local stories in the media regarding our employment and community support practices.

- To achieve an 80 per cent positive response in the employment survey in questions related to the encouragement for innovation, and management's response to ideas.

The timelines to fully realise the benefits at Level Four may be up to a year. However, if the justification extends too long other factors are bound to dilute the influence of the programme.

Managerial judgement about a good or bad RoI here may be the subject of debate. If we spent £1,000,000 to build up our employment image and this resulted in winning some 'best employer' awards and rising up league tables, was this money well spent? We expect the return in better quality of recruits, but that will take time and the contaminating factors are many.

Again, if we spent a similar amount of money to ensure all employees understand the corporate values and could apply them in their daily work –

and at the end of the project 85 per cent of employees could recite the values, and customer evidence was that there had been a 10 per cent increase in the reality of those values as they saw them – was that money well spent?

In these cases an amount of money is estimated and voted and is generally then regarded as 'sunk'. But clarity of objectives and a deliberate plan to measure achievement will, at the very least, teach lessons about effective and ineffective ways to achieve change.

THE STAKEHOLDER APPROACH TO BENEFITS

The focus of many evaluations will be on the primary beneficiaries and what happens to them as a result of the intervention. However, in reality there may be a variety of stakeholders who have an interest in the intervention and its success, not least the implementers themselves. All of these may gain in some way.

We can thus draw up a diagram of *all the beneficiaries* and the expected added value to them as a result of the intervention – both in terms of '£ benefit' and 'non-£ benefit'.

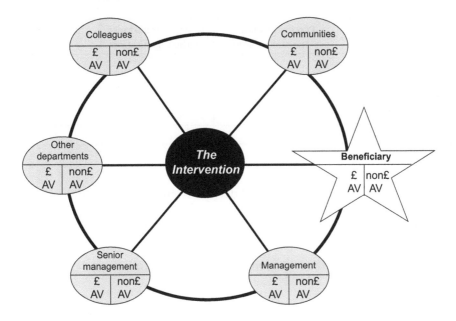

Figure 7.4   Beneficiaries in an HR intervention

Suppose we introduce a change management programme for team leaders. Most of the benefits will not be financially quantifiable. But we expect the participants to have new levels of capability (knowledge and skills) in planning and implementing change; we expect the team members to report in due course that they felt better led through change and suffered reduced productivity loss at times of change; the team leaders' supervisors will spend less time supporting them; senior management will see change initiatives happening faster; and the trainers will have learnt practical re-usable examples and ideas from the trainees. We can evaluate the overall effect using some simple scales:

- Overall perceived value added to the stakeholder on a scale of 1–10, where 10 is a substantial increase in the relevant capabilities or factors.

- Strategic importance to the organisation of this particular value contribution to this particular stakeholder on scale of 1–10.

- The *Value Factor* – the product of the two.

Table 7.6   Example of value added in the eyes of stakeholders

Stakeholder	Perceived value to the stakeholder	Strategic importance to the organisation	Value factor
Prime beneficiaries – team leaders	9	8	72
Team members	6	9	54
Supervisors	6	7	24
Senior management	6	8	48
Trainers	5	4	20

Summary indices can be defined and derived from this kind of analysis.

COMING TO CONCLUSIONS ABOUT THE JUSTIFICATION

The standard formula for return on investment is the following:

$$\text{Return on Investment} = \frac{\text{Benefits} - \text{Costs}}{\text{Costs}} \times 100$$

Thus, if we take example C – the leadership programme outlined above – the estimated returns from improvements to attrition alone were £3,077,600. Let us say the costs of the programme were £800,000.

Then:

$$RoI = 3,077,600 - 800,000/800,000 \times 100 = 285\%$$

The other benefits can be costed also, but if the one we are most sure about shows a clear return we need not go further.

It would be normal to take the returns in the first year. Future returns may also exist and can be discounted (using discounted cash flow techniques) to give a total expected return. However, if the first year will be sufficient to give a good return, this is not necessary.

Another ratio that can be used is the 'benefit-cost ratio', which is simply the benefits divided by the costs. A ratio of 1.0 means that the costs were recovered but no actual financial gain was achieved.

What will be an acceptable ratio? An RoI of 100 per cent is to break even. But we should expect it to be higher than for fixed tangible investments because of the uncertainties involved in estimations and the general nature of human unpredictability. Leaving aside the intangible benefits and any political drivers for an initiative, our starting point would be to aim for an RoI in excess of 200 per cent.

There are other techniques, but HR people are unlikely to use them and, if needed, can get specialist advice. They include internal rate of return, discounted cash flow, payback periods, and utility analysis.

ADDING IN THE INTANGIBLE BENEFITS

If the purely financial ratio is satisfactory on its own, then we may regard the non-financial benefits as a bonus. Wherever possible, and where a clear cause-effect link exists, we should try and make financial calculations arising from intangible benefits. Some writers insist that this must be done using whatever assumptions and estimates are necessary. But this will not always be credibly possible, and as we have seen some projects do not have financial goals at all.

The total benefit is the combination. So, we will add the change in intangible factors to the financial RoI (if we have one). Together we can then use a judgement as to whether the initiative is/was worthwhile.

Thus:

TOTAL Benefit/Cost Ratio = (Financial + Non Financial Benefits)/Costs

Where the benefits are all 'intangible', management must make a judgement whether the costs of achieving them add up to a sensible business decision. There are four possible outcomes from this assessment:

- management believes the benefits are well worth the costs;

- management are sceptical about the balance, but believe they have no choice;

- management believes the costs are too high for the benefits and request a lower cost solution;

- management believes the costs are too high, the benefits too low, and opts for the *status quo*.

PLANNING A FULL EVALUATION IN ADVANCE

So far we have looked primarily at making a case for an initiative up front. If it is intended to monitor and evaluate the initiative all the way through to completion, additional planning must be done, as in the eleven steps outlined on page 289.

There are three main areas to be considered:

- planning the data to be collected;

- using control groups;

- isolating the effects of the HR initiative from other influences.

PLANNING THE DATA TO BE COLLECTED

Steps 2–5 are relevant to this and were:

- making a data collection and evaluation plan;

- collecting data before the initiative if before/after comparisons need to be made;

- collect data during the initiative as needed;

- collect data after implementation.

We shall be collecting *costs*, as well as benefits. There are nearly always unforeseen costs, and the costs of data collection itself must be included.

There may be several *sources* of data. If our objectives are quantified business measures, we need to be sure the accounting and performance measurement systems have the right measures. Then there will be several groups of people whose observations we want to collate. There are, first, the primary beneficiaries of the programme itself. Then there are all the other stakeholders – their managers, team members, maybe subordinates, internal customers and, in some cases, external customers or other external stakeholders. Where possible each group should be involved in defining the measurement instrument to be used.

A time plan needs to be made, which will depend on the nature of the initiative, for before, during, and after implementation. The time when the full effects of implementation are expected should be defined and this period may need more than one data collection as time progresses.

USING CONTROL GROUPS

Ideally, to understand the effects of an HR intervention we would want one group to benefit from it and an *exactly similar* group not to go through the experience. Both groups should be subject otherwise to the same conditions and influences.

For example, suppose we designed a new 'people scorecard' for a retail organisation with roughly similar geographical branches, which linked training and environmental factors to performance. We could see how the use of such a scorecard for people management decisions in one branch made a difference as compared to another branch where the scorecard was not used. Or we could put one branch through a customer loyalty programme and compare the effects with a branch that did not go through it.

In practice this is not as simple as it sounds. It is very rare for two groups to go through identical conditions, although we may need to isolate differences in some key areas that happened in the experimental period. Another problem is *contamination* – accidentally, the control group gets exposed to some of the initiative. Finally, the truth is that most business people do not have the patience for detailed research, and prefer to 'just get on with it'. The logic behind the approach remains sound nevertheless.

ISOLATING THE EFFECTS OF THE HR INITIATIVE FROM OTHER INFLUENCES

What makes HR evaluation difficult is that, at the higher levels particularly, a number of other factors may influence the outcome that we are trying to measure.

Jack Philips offers some advice on possible approaches here:

- Use control groups whenever possible.

- Use trend lines of a measure, and see what changes occur after the intervention, assuming it was the only one at a point in time.

- Using forecasting methods which take account of the trends of other variables using mathematical equations.

- Participant estimates – what percentage of any change do they attribute to the HR intervention?

- Manager estimates – similar questions.

- Customer or subordinate input, where appropriate.

- Using external experts to asses the effect.

- Calculating the impact of other factors, where significant.

If the effect of the initiative is to be quickly seen, it helps considerably. However, for many HR initiatives this is not the case and the Level Four effect may be impossible to isolate.

ELIMINATING 'CONTAMINATION' FACTORS

The longer and more complex the cause and effect chain, the more we will have 'contamination factors' – or 'additional influences' on the end benefit. Philips goes to some lengths in discussing how these can be isolated. The clearest option is a control group. Thus, we could compare two similar groups of leaders, one group going through a development programme and the other not. Burt and Ronch (2007) reported on such a study carried out in the Chicago Graduate School of Business in relation to their Business Leadership Programme. They concluded that 'program graduates are 36 per cent to 42 per cent more likely to receive top performance evaluations, 43 per cent to 72 per cent more likely to be promoted, and 42 per cent to 74 per cent more likely to be retained by the Company'. They also said, however, that statistically the level of significance of these results was low.

Other methods for isolating causes are to use trends and forecasts and to see how they vary from what would have been expected without an intervention; manager and participant perceptions of the effects, or using an external expert study. All of these approaches take time and money and are not to be undertaken lightly.

7.9 Summary

Any department or function needs to have a scorecard to monitor its effectiveness and its efficiency – the first being about the quality of its outputs and the second about the resources needed to achieve them. We distinguished between two types of functional measures – day to day operational, and investments in projects and initiatives. The ways in which HR adds value to its stakeholders were listed and discussed.

Operational efficiency comes in terms of service delivery, process measures and time utilisation. Productivity is particular difficult to measure in HR, but analysis of how time is spent is a good indicator. Activities can be divided into value adding, non-value adding, and maintenance.

Understanding the return on HR initiatives and programmes has always been a difficult area. We suggest that initial clarity about measurable objectives is the key and will not only assist the justification process but guide subsequent evaluation, if it is deemed necessary or worthwhile.

As always we have to make choices about exactly how many measures we will choose to monitor. Our first choice should be those that will support our strategies or will help to monitor change programmes. We would then pick any others that are not difficult to do and which could have a potential impact on performance. Figure 7.5 shows a model format which would embrace all we have talked about. It would be used for setting targets, monitoring actuals, and identifying variances.

Some organisations have used a version of the balanced scorecard for the HR function. For example, the State of South Carolina uses the four quadrants of finance (cost based metrics), process effectiveness, workforce capacity and customer satisfaction.

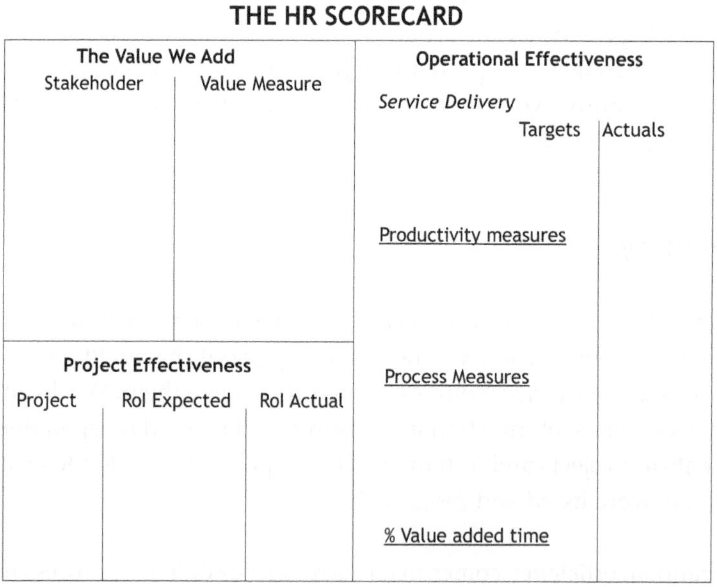

THE HR SCORECARD

The Value We Add		Operational Effectiveness	
Stakeholder	Value Measure	Service Delivery	
		Targets	Actuals
		Productivity measures	
Project Effectiveness		Process Measures	
Project	RoI Expected RoI Actual		
		% Value added time	

Figure 7.5   A model for an HR scorecard

7.10 Challenges for Action

- To what extent does the HR function have clarity about the value it adds and to whom? Does it have defined and agreed indicators of value for each stakeholder?

- Does HR have clear standards of performance for its service delivery, and seek feedback on this at regular intervals?

- Has HR assigned clear ownership for the processes it manages, and defined process outputs which are regularly monitored?

- Does HR do time utilisation analysis from time to time, based on added value and non-added value tasks? Can we see positive progress over time?

- Do we have a clear methodology for justifying and evaluating projects, initiatives and programmes in HR? Do we have at least some skilled people in applying this?

- Is the whole HR function aligned behind a consistent HR scorecard that assists in building better performance in the function?

7.11 References and Further Reading

Beaton, L., and Richards, S. (1997). *Making Training Pay – A Toolkit*. IPD.

Becker, B.E., Huselid, M.A., and Ulrich, D. (2001). *The HR Scorecard: Linking People, Strategy, and Performance*. Boston: Harvard Business School Press.

Bedingham, K. (1999). *The Measurement of Organisational Culture. Journal of Human Resource Management*. January 1999.

Boudreau, J.W., and Ramsted, P.M. (2007). *Beyond HR*. Boston: Harvard Business School Press.

Bucknall, H., and Zheng, W. (2006). *Magic Numbers for Human Resource Management*. Singapore: John Wiley.

Burt, R.S., and Ronch, D. (2007). *Teaching Executives to See Social Capital: Results from a Field Experiment. Social Science Research*. 2007.

Conner, M.L. (2002). *How Do I Measure Return on Investment (ROI) for My Learning Program?* Training & Learning FAQs [Online]. Available at: http://www.learnativity.com

Granoff, T. (2001). *'A White Paper' on the Procourse Method of Measuring Success.* ProCourse Scientific Advisory Board.

Haffenden, M., and Lambert, A. (2004). *Effective HR. Evaluation Careers Research Forum Research Report.* London, November 2004.

Kearns, P. (2000). *Maximising the RoI from Training – Measure the Value Added by Employee Development.* FT-Prentice Hall.

Kearns, P. (2005). *Evaluating the ROI from Learning – How to Develop Value Based Training.* London: CIPD.

Kirkpatrick, D.L. (1975). *Techniques for Evaluating Training Programs.* Evaluating Training Programs, Alexandria, VA: 1975. American Society for Training and Development, pp. 1–17.

Mayo, A.J. (2004). *Understanding HR Return on Investment.* One Stop Guide Series. Personnel Today Management Resources.

Phillips, J.J. (1997). *Return on Investment in Training and Performance Improvement Programs.* Houston, TX: Gulf Publishing Company.

Phillips, J.J., Stone, R.D., and Phillips, P.P. (2001). *The Human Resources Scorecard – Measuring the Return on Investment.* Butterworth-Heinemann.

Yeung, A.K., and Berman, B. (1997). *Adding Value Through Human Resources: Reorientating Resource Measurement to Drive Business Performance. Human Resource Management*, Fall 1997, Volume 36(03), pp. 321–335.

www.procourse.com (including 23 minute video presentation on Training Evaluation)

www.e-validates.com

www.pwcservices.com (now embracing the Saratoga Institute)

www.franklincovey.com/jackphillips (website of Jack Philips Centre)

www.service-level-agreement.net

www.groups.yahoo.com/group/roinet (long standing ASTD discussion group on RoI of Training)

http://www.astd.org/communities/networks/ROI/

8

Building Human Capital Management Skills

In this final chapter we acknowledge that there are areas of knowledge, skill and attitudes that are essential for human capital management to work, both with managers and people professionals. We analyse the capabilities needed and propose some routes to their development.

8.1 An Attitude of Mind

This book assumes an underlying belief that everybody with authority and influence in the organisation believes in the asset value of people. This is not the same thing as mouthing the platitudes. Can I listen to the CFO tell me about the potential of people in the value adding process? Will the HR Director expound to me the way she/he is making the business more successful through their HR projects? Or will I be lectured by the former on the 'number one cost that we have' and by the second on their 'departmental transformation?

HR as a function frequently feels unappreciated and misunderstood (they are not alone – IT people often feel the same). There are three dimensions to this problem.

Firstly, senior management's perception of HR may be that it is an unfortunately a necessary overhead cost that should be minimised as much as possible. There are many examples of enlightened CEOs who see a far greater role and contribution – but it is not so common in smaller companies and in the developing world.

Then secondly, managers may see HR as a time consuming, bureaucratic, policing function to be kept at a distance except when absolutely needed. Those with a truly value adding HR business partner will not feel this way – but there are probably not too many of those.

Thirdly may be the attitude problem of HR itself. Despite its honourable desires to be a serious partner, it is often consumed with its own agenda and administration. Despite the public positioning, the truth may be that there is both a lack of interest in and knowledge of business matters with many of the HR people.

One's observation is that people, at the top – whether line or HR – often do see the critical importance of the issues in this book to organisational success. But they are let down by the next levels.

CHANGING ATTITUDES

The best way I know to change attitudes is to put people into the shoes of others. It seems very rare today for HR graduate schemes to include any secondments to operational roles; or for mature professionals within HR to have had such experience. So we have legions of well intended HR people wanting to be credible partners with the business but with very little practical knowledge of it. There are exceptions – it is normal in the pharma industry, for example, for all trainers to have come from sales roles – and often in smaller companies HR roles are taken as a way of broadening experience. The well-known people orientated company, John Lewis, at the time of writing has a CEO who spent some years as HR Director as part of his development.

It is not so difficult to achieve. It can be built into graduate schemes that a six month operational role is mandatory, and some roles can be identified where a level of real accountability can be taken for a short period. Secondments to projects or line support roles which immerse individuals in the daily business are not difficult to organise if the will is there. HR functions are often so busy that they feel precious resource cannot be spared. But this is like the would-be delegator who says 'Alas, I don't have time to delegate'. It becomes self-defeating in the end.

Although I personally started in production management and came into HR roles after some years of line experience, I mentioned earlier my personal experience of moving back to a line position after several years in HR. I very quickly had a whole new sense of priorities and interests. But I learnt so much too –about inter departmental politics, about negotiation, calculating margins, the software business – and the business of my major clients too. And about how to fend off annoying support departments.

8.2 Models and Frameworks of HR Competency

There are, of course, as many variations of competency models for HR as there are for organisations generally. Our concern is to focus on those which are needed specifically for effective human capital management and partnership between HR and line managers.

The World Federation of Personnel Management Associations (WFPMA) published a set of HR competencies researched for them by the Centre for European Human Resource Management at Cranfield.

This is a very thorough set, focused on personal and functional capabilities but with less emphasis on business, process and change. We reproduce it here as it is a useful checklist.

Table 8.1   WFPMA set of HR competencies

I. Personal	
I.1 Communication	Communicate and influence Interpersonal effectiveness Written, oral and other communications media Sensitivity to others Persuasion skills Negotiation skills Listening skills Presentation skills Ability to initiate/conduct/promote/facilitate interactions
I.2 Decision making and problem solving	Cognitive complexity and agility Analysis Problem solving Decision making Access to decision makers
I.3 Business acumen	Business acumen Strategic planning Results orientation
I.4 Credibility and professionalism	Personal credibility Achievement directed assertiveness Partnership development Define own role in organisation Develop and maintain a professional image Continuous learning Technological competence

Table 8.1   *Continued*

I.5 Leadership	Visionary Proactive Influence Inspire Guide Provide clear direction Resilience to opposition
I.6 Relationship management	Understand group processes Team commitment Ability to work with others Relationship orientation Skilled manager of relationships Manage expectations
I.7 Adaptability	Creativity Tolerance for stress/ambiguity/change

II. Organisational	
II.1 Knowledge of the external environment	The social/economic/political environment, including product and labour markets, legislative and regulatory frameworks, and so on
II.2 Knowledge of the industry/sector	Stakeholder perspectives Sector/industry standards
II.3 Knowledge of the organisation	Market position, vision, mission, management style Organisation structure and culture Organisation development and change Cross-functional flexibility Who the stakeholders are
II.4 Impact assessment	Awareness of the environment Ability to assess the impact of the external environment on the organisation Strategic business perspective How to achieve strategic contribution to organisation success Understand and contribute to the organisation as a whole Alignment with organisation needs and goals
II.5 The HR department as a part of the organisation	Manage the personnel function: vision and fit, staffing, physical resources, financial resources Provide organisational consultancy Plan, model and forecast trends Develop and implement strategies, policies, practices Measure results Understand the contribution/role of the department to/in the organisation as a whole – manage the interface Empower line management and employees

Table 8.1   *Continued*

III. Managerial	
III.1 Management of self	Performance management Time management Career management
III.2 Management of people	Lead/guide/give feedback Identify development needs Evaluate performance Able to gain trust and respect Concern for others (individuals and groups) Effective working relationships Fair and ethical Corporate loyalty and responsibility Strategic management
III.3 Management of resources/assets	Plan, budget, control and evaluate Human Financial Technical Systems
III.4 Management of operations, including outsourcing	Manage projects and products Plan, implement, maintain Quality orientation Customer value creation Auditing Use of outsourcing
III.5 Management of information	Identify, gather, manipulate, interpret and report information Manage information systems Statistical and financial skills Deal with qualitative and quantitative data
III.6 Change management	Change management Innovation, creativity Reorganisation Process change – goal clarification, problem identification Culture change – sharing knowledge across boundaries, employee behaviour

IV. Functional	
IV.1 HR planning and staffing	HR planning, staffing, resourcing Gather information, identify trends, analyse, forecast, plan, take action and monitor Develop/implement/monitor recruitment, selection, appointment, deployment and placement processes and activities (including the use of assessment tools, interviewing, advertisements, contract preparation, and so on) Job analysis, job description, job specification Work organisation (flexibility, and so on) Promotion Succession planning Employee absence (maternity, sickness, holiday)

Table 8.1   *Continued*

	Knowledge of legal framework of employment rights Equal employment opportunities Termination – organisational exit International HRM: culture, legislation, expatriation and repatriation, multinational corporations
IV.2 Performance management and development	Key principles/techniques of learning Knowledge management and the value of intellectual capital Managing learning processes Organisational learning/learning organisation Funding and cost/benefit analysis Training needs analysis and employee performance monitoring Total performance management Training interventions: plan, design, develop, recommend, deliver, implement, measure, monitor, evaluate Induction Performance development Career planning/management Developing groups and individuals Long-term development Management development Technology-based learning Total quality management Appraisal: goal setting, results measurement/assessment process, feedback processes, evaluation Appraisal criteria, standards, documentation and methods Managing poor performance
IV.3 Employee and labour relations	Recommend/implement/monitor industrial relations and employee relations strategies (staff consultation and participation) Knowledge of and compliance with legislation employee counselling, support and welfare Awareness of organisational culture and management style Ethical approach Deal with union representation and collective bargaining Produce and enforce terms and conditions of employment Produce and enforce disciplinary and grievance procedures Dispute/conflict resolution and corrective action Design, implementation and evaluation of communication programmes Employee involvement: teamworking, suggestion schemes, participative management, employee attitude/opinion/satisfaction surveys International employee relations

Table 8.1   *Concluded*

IV.4 Compensation and benefits	Total compensation: reward, benefits, recognition and remuneration Develop/implement/administer strategies and programmes Job pricing and job evaluation, pay structures Budgeting and cost control Fixed and variable pay schemes Non-money benefits Pensions Payroll systems management (including taxation) Develop equitable (legally compliant and externally competitive) policies and systems – to encourage people to join, contribute, remain with the organisation Awareness of needs of special groups – executives, expatriates Team/individual reward Equality management
IV.5 Health, safety, welfare and security	Understanding of issues and legislation Management and evaluation of policies and programmes Occupational health and hygiene Employee assistance programmes Employee wellness programmes Stress management Ergonomics Behavioural science Compensation for torts
IV.6 Systems and information management	Determine requirements (integration of information) Develop/maintain information systems: manual and computerised Formulate/implement/manage systems, programmes, practices Information technology capabilities (computerised human resource information systems) Research, analyse, report, disseminate Awareness of confidentiality/sensitivity issues Internal communication processes
IV.7 Organisational design and development	Organisation structure and design Organisation development Organisation performance *vis-à-vis* HR effectiveness Strategic HRM Change management: causes/diagnosis, process, implications

ULRICH AND COLLEAGUES

In his book *Human Champions* Dave Ulrich summarised well four areas of knowledge and skill that were needed to meet his model of the roles of HR.

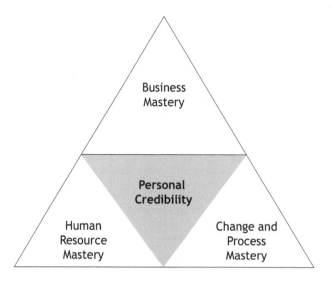

Figure 8.1   Ulrich's HR competency model

Source: By permission of Harvard Business School Press. From *Human Resource Champions* by Dave Ulrich, Boston, MA, Figure 8-5, p. 253. Copyright © 1997 by the Harvard Business School Publishing Corporation, all rights reserved.

This sums up the essentials in a very concise way. 'Human Resource' mastery refers to expertise in all the commonly understood aspects of HR work. He then chose 'change and process' mastery – often underestimated in importance by HR functions: the systematic management of change processes and the ability to engineer effective processes. Ulrich uses the term 'business mastery'. In practice, in many businesses if one has not been trained in the operational side it is unreasonable to ask for 'mastery' as some are not easy to understand. However, there are some generic areas of knowledge that should be mastered by the business minded professional:

- understanding the basics of financial management, costing and cash flow;

- understanding the business model of the organisation – how and where money is made or spent;

- numeracy and statistics;

- measurement, estimating and return on investment – including non–financials;

- ethics and governance.

Becker, Huselid and Ulrich in *The HR Scorecard* described an ongoing study of 5,000 HR professionals in the 1990s and this led to five domains of capability:

- knowledge of the business;

- delivery of HR practices;

- management of change;

- management of culture;

- personal credibility.

In their chapter on 'competencies for HR professionals' they added *strategic HR performance management* as an addition to the above five groups. It is not the best title because the terms can mean many things, but it is built around measurement, the subject of their book. They divided it into four dimensions:

- critical causal thinking;

- understanding principles of good measurement;

- estimating causal relationships;

- communicating results to line managers.

These are all very relevant to the themes of this book, and are fundamental skills that are core to effective human capital management. It is the expertise needed to see how people related measures link to, and drive, performance, to be able to measure appropriately and then have a productive dialogue about the results.

One more example from Ulrich's stable comes from the Human Resources Competency Study regularly undertaken by consultancy RBL and the Ross School of Business in the University of Michigan. Their 2007 study gave these six core competencies for HR professionals:

1.   *Credible Activist* – high performing HR professionals are credible (respected, admired, listened to) and proactive (have a point of view, are willing to challenge assumptions, make things happen).

2.   *Operational Executors* – high performers effectively and efficiently administer the day to day work of managing people inside an organisation.

3.   *Business Allies* – high performers understand both the business and external and industry factors that influence success.

4.   *Talent Manager/Organisation Designers* – the HR professional masters theory, research, and practice in both talent management and organisation design. Talent management focuses on strategic competencies, assessment, how individuals enter and move up, across, or out of the organisation. Organisation design is the expertise of embedding capability (for example, collaboration) into the structure, processes, and policies that shape how an organisation works.

5.   *Culture and Change Stewards* – high performers understand, respect, and evolve the organisation through improvements in HR systems and practices.

6.   *Strategy Architects* – high performers are effective business partners in building winning strategies by linking people and organisation practices to competitive requirements.

This is a powerful set and a demand indeed on HR professionals.

THE CIPD'S HR PROFESSIONAL MAP

Launched in 2009, the CIPD's HR Professional Map is described as 'a comprehensive view of how HR adds the greatest sustained value to the organisations it operates in, now and in the future. It combines the highest standards of professional competence with the closest alignment to your organisational goals, to deliver sustained performance.

According to the CIPD, 'It captures what HR people do and deliver across every aspect and specialism of the profession and it looks at the underpinning skills, behaviour and knowledge that they need to be most successful. It also creates a clear and flexible framework for career progression, recognising both that HR roles and career progression vary.'

It consists of:

- Ten 'professional areas' which are described at four levels of experience and hierarchy.

- Eight 'behaviours' also described at the four levels.

- 'Bands and transitions' – the four levels (called 'bands') and how they relate to relationships, activities, how time is spent, service delivery and measuring success.

Figure 8.2 shows the 10 professional areas and Figure 8.3 the behaviours.

This new map was extensively researched (within the HR community) and is designed to cover the whole of HR's activities. See www.cipd.co.uk/hr-profession-map for full details.

Figure 8.2   The CIPD professional map – professional areas
Reproduced with permission.

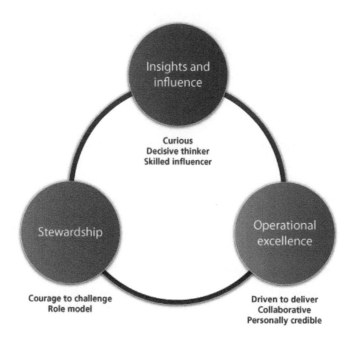

Figure 8.3   The CIPD professional map – behaviours
Reproduced with permission.

In a search for references to people related measures, these are to be found under 'Leading and Managing the HR Function'. Most are confined to Level 2, the Level of 'adviser'. At Level 4 (leadership colleague, client confidante and coach) we find only 'knows how to use an appropriate performance management tool such as the balanced scorecard to manage, measure and monitor human resources delivery against objectives'. It seems strange that people measures are not seen as more 'strategic'.

In Table 8.2 we start from a clean sheet and list the knowledge and skills that this book would like to see in business minded HR professionals, especially at the senior level.

8.3 Being Effective at Human Capital Management

In Chapter 9 of their book *Human Capital Management* (2007) Baron and Armstrong consider the capabilities needed in HR professionals to meet the challenges of an HCM programme. They list the following:

- understanding the business – its strategies and drivers;

- appreciating how HR strategy interacts with the business strategy;

- knowledge of the data;

- understanding what information managers need;

- knowledge of how to collect and analyse data;

- presenting data and reporting on the outcomes of analysis;

- working as part of a management team;

- working with the finance function.

They note that HCM also requires line managers to have their own changes in attitudes and skills.

In Table 8.2 we have summarised the knowledge and skill that would enable both HR professionals and line managers to apply effectively the principles and ideas of the chapters of this book. They do overlap a little – the skill is, of course, being able to put the knowledge into practice.

Table 8.2   **A summary of the knowledge and skills needed for human capital management and partnering with the business**

	Knowledge	Skills
Chapter 1 Value Creation	• The nature and processes of value creation • The nature of productivity • The drivers of productivity • The measurement of innovation	• Measurement techniques and choices • Survey design and analysis • Identifying value added to stakeholders • Defining and measuring productivity • Work and time analysis
Chapter 2 The Value of People	• Intangible assets • Valuing intellectual and human capital	• Assessing and managing capabilities • Linking human capital to performance
Chapter 3 Engagement and Performance	• The nature and drivers of motivation and engagement	• Engagement research • Survey design • Measuring engagement and linking to performance • Working with managers on engagement action plans
Chapter 4 Integrating and Reporting	• Workforce analytics and links to strategy • Service profit chain • Balanced scorecard • Human capital Monitor	• Choosing and presenting appropriate measures • Interpreting and communication • Using statistics
Chapter 5 HR Professionals and Business Contribution	• Stakeholders of HR and how value is added to them • The nature of business partnership • The organisation's business model and strategy • Investment decisions • Organisational effectiveness • Mergers and acquisitions management • Leadership development • Culture • Corporate governance	• Creating value-exchanging business partnerships • Making senior teams more effective • Decision making • Estimating Return on Investment • Changing culture • Managing OD interventions • Defining objectives and programmes for leadership development • Influencing others • Communicating externally
Chapter 6 People and organisational strategies	• Mission, vision and values • Business strategy and the strategic planning process • Strategic analysis tools	• Deriving HR initiatives from business goals and strategies • Prioritising • Planning and project management
Chapter 7 HR Scorecard	• Understanding value added to HR's stakeholders • Return on investment, especially non-financial benefits • Process effectiveness • Process efficiency	• Designing an HR scorecard • Cause and effect analysis • Process engineering • Estimating Return on Investment • Performance management
Chapter 8 Capabilities	• Competency models • Defining capabilities • Career development	• Assessing and developing capabilities • HR career planning

8.4 Core Personal Skills

Several works on business partnership written for HR professionals concentrate almost entirely on personal skills and behaviours and say very little about the knowledge areas described in Table 8.2.

Kenton and Yarnall wrote *HR – the Business Partner*, published in 2005 and based on their work at Roffey Park. This is totally about the personal skills needed, and takes a consultant view of the role, covering consultant skills, networking, influencing, leading change, and self-understanding. It has many self-assessment tools included.

In similar vein, Dalziel, Strange and Walters put together a toolkit on HR business partnering for the CIPD in 2006. This is a little more comprehensive, including something on process engineering and strategy development. Neither mentions coaching of line managers in people management skills, which does seem rather important.

When we think of other kinds of partnerships and what makes them successful, we will list a number of personality characteristics such as trust, integrity, reliability, listening, counselling and supporting. The CIPD set of eight behaviours in Figure 8.3 includes 'personal credibility'. This is seen in five dimensions – delivering on commitments, taking responsibility and accountability where needed, standing up for knowledge and beliefs, self-awareness and receiving feedback positively, and giving sound advice.

The theme of this second part of the book is the link between HR and business, and it is thinking and acting as part of the business that is the thread that runs through all that we have covered. The world we seek is one where HR professionals use their knowledge and skills to make managers more successful in *their operations*– not just better people managers. A key element of 'personal credibility' will be the genuineness of their interest in what is happening in the business. We will see behaviours such as:

- enjoying discussions about business challenges with managers, both formally and informally;

- keeping up to date with progress, problems and opportunities;

- attending business reviews;

- volunteering for task groups and committees;

- reading relevant material about the organisation and its sector;

- providing business ideas;

- making the effort to understand what people do operationally.

I always recommend to people seeking career advice in HR to join an organisation where they can get excited about the mission and products/services of that organisation. Then the behaviours listed above will come naturally.

8.5 Developing Business Minded HR Professional Careers

Practices vary between countries in the development of HR professionals. Some are built on disciplines such as psychology and law. In the UK there are even bachelor's degrees in HRM, and a large number of both generalist and specialist Masters' degrees. These tend to be the starting point for HR people, combined with the CIPD accreditation. This, in future, will be based on the professional map referred to earlier.

However, knowledge and skill are built up through work experience and it may be many years before a person gets involved with the material in this book. When careers follow the HR silo, and people change from sector to sector with ever increasing frequency, the building of business knowledge can be very deficient. Professor Ulrich's message in 2009, 12 years after his introduction of the concept of the strategic business partner, was that HR had become obsessed with its own 'transformation' and yet still did not have the level of business links that he originally was advocating.

My contention would be that the role of Business Partner should be a special one, and not just a title handed out to advisors and generalists in a renaming exercise. The Director or VP of HR should be the role model. The title should be confined to senior people who have been specifically trained to represent the function in the themes of this book. Such individuals would have spent time in the business, even if only a three month secondment. They are allied with one business team, maybe two, but that is enough for them to play the full role needed.

8.6 Summary

In this brief chapter we have looked at the importance of a business mindset, an attitude of interest and support for making the business successful through its people. We have mentioned various models of HR professionalism and skills but it is hoped the summary of what is needed chapter by chapter (Table 8.2) to apply the themes of the book will be useful.

Developing these capabilities is a key issue and our suggestion is that there should be a specific road to the senior 'partner' which builds them in through experience and targeted learning – and is not for everybody. Not all HR people have the desire or capability to take such a role, and it helps nobody to hide under a title that has no substance.

8.7 Challenges for Action

- To what extent has the HR function identified clearly the skills and capabilities needed to be an effective partner with the business?

- If so, did it consult with line managers as to what they saw as important?

- Does the HR function have a specific development plan for individuals destined to be 'business partners'?

- Have positions or secondments been identified where HR people could gain some operating experience?

- Is there someone at least in the function who has a high level of numeracy and is expert at the art and science of measurement?

8.8 References and Further Reading

Baron, A., and Armstrong, M. (2007). *Human Capital Management*. London: Kogan Page.

Brewster, C., Farndale, E., and van Ommeren, J. (2000). *HR Competencies and Professional Standards*. Cranfield: Centre for European Human Resource Management.

Dalziel, S., Strange, J., and Walters, M. (2006). *HR Business Partnering – How to Diagnose Gaps, Develop Capabilities and Become a Business Partner*. London: CIPD.

Kenton, B., and Yarnall, J.(2005). *HR – The Business Partner*. Elsevier.

Ulrich, D. (2007). *Talking to Anat Arkin: In the Hot Seat. People Management*. 28 June 2007.

Ulrich, D., Brockbank, W., and Johnson, D. (2008). *HR Competencies: Mastery at the Intersection of People and Business*. SHRM.

http://www.cipd.co.uk/hr-profession-map

http://rbl.net/index.php/research/detail/HRCS/

Appendix:
Examples of Non-financial Added Value to Stakeholders

Reproduced with permission from *The Human Value of the Enterprise* (Andrew Mayo, 2001, London: Nicholas Brealey)

Non-financial Value Added to Stakeholders – *Shareholders*		
Nature of the Value	**Contributors**	**Measurement Examples**
• Alliances and mergers managed to achieve business goals and maximise retention of intellectual capital	• Chief Executives • Acquisition managers • HR managers	• Achievement against business goals • Unplanned loss of acquired staff • Increase in enhanced human capital value • Increases in strategic capability levels
• Investor confidence generated through communications	• Investor relations • Public relations	• % favourable press references of total • Share price relative to sector trend • Brand credibility assessments

Non-financial Value Added to Stakeholders – *Parent Companies*

Nature of the Value	Contributors	Measurement Examples
• Living the 'corporate values'	• Chief Executives and senior managers • All employees • HR managers	• Employee and leadership surveys • Outcome measures of values such as customer satisfaction and community reputation
• Reputation of the parent enhanced	• Marketing managers • PR staff	• Image surveys
• Parent's fulfilment of its strategies	• Chief executives and senior managers	• Progress indicators that relate to strategy achievement
• People and knowledge transfer	• HR managers • Knowledge managers • IT managers	• Transfers in/out of sister companies and HQ as % of all job moves • Participation in cross-organisation 'communities of practice'

Non-financial Value Added to Stakeholders – *Customers*

Nature of the Value	Contributors	Measurement Examples
• New products/services • generated	• Product development • Market research • New product introduction	• % of sales from products/ services introduced in last 2 years
• Reputation/ image enhancement	• Marketing promotion • Public relations	• % new business coming from referrals • Image perception surveys
• Quality of service delivery	• Call centre staff • Customer service representative • Trainers	• Customer surveys • Alignment to service delivery agreements • Achievement of set targets
• Reliability of product delivery	• Logistics managers • Installation staff • Accounting staff • Quality inspectors	• % deliveries on time • % deliveries fully complete • % accuracy of invoices
• Brand definition and recognition	• Marketeers	• Brand perception surveys

Satisfaction and *loyalty* created	• Sales staff • Customer service staff • Call centre staff • Technical help staff	• % repeat customers • Customer satisfaction measures
• 'Added value' services	• Service sales staff • Service delivery staff	• Proportion of revenue coming from defined 'added value' services
• Inter-transfer of information, knowledge and skill	• Sales staff • Marketing staff • Product development staff • Efficiency engineers • HR staff	• Perception that it happens and examples of it happening

Non-financial Value Added to Stakeholders – *Employees*

Nature of the Value	Contributors	Measurement Examples
• Challenging and interesting work	• Managers	• % of +ve opinion survey responses re work
• Potential discovered	• L&D staff • Managers	• % of people with agreed potential development plan
• New competencies developed and potential grown	• HR/L&D managers • Trainers	• % of populations with desired potential categories • Increases in competency profiles for selected groups
• Provision of feedback on performance	• Managers • HR managers • Trainers	• % of people undergoing feedback process • % of people finding positive value from? process
• Training towards better performance	• HR/L&D managers • Trainers	• Days training per person • Increases in job related capabilities
• Feeling motivated, committed and recognised	• Managers • HR managers • Trainers	• % of people surveyed indicating high levels of commitment, satisfaction and recognition • Absenteeism rates • Attrition rates
• Enjoyment of the working environment	• Buildings managers • HR managers • Managers	• % of people surveyed reporting satisfaction with different aspects of culture and environment • Health and safety statistics
(Potential Employees) • Desirability of the company as an employer	• HR Managers • Communications	• Employer league tables • Applications per advert

Non-financial Value Added to Stakeholders – *Suppliers*

Nature of the Value	Contributors	Measurement Examples	Target
• Enhancement of their reputation/ image	• Purchasing managers • Public relations staff	• Number of mentions in favourable publicity • % new business coming from referrals • Image perception surveys % of sales from products/services introduced in last 2 years	
• Onwards references	• Purchasing managers	• % new business for supplier from our recommendation	
• Ideas for innovation	• Knowledge managers • Quality managers • Purchasing managers • Product design staff • Field service staff	• Volume and value of ideas for product change • Volume and value of ideas for forecasting or delivery efficiency • Quality of delivery	

Non-financial Value Added to Stakeholders – *The Public*

Nature of the Value	Contributors	Measurement Examples	Target
• Service levels	• Department managers	• Achievement against service level targets	
• Responsiveness	• Department managers	• Satisfaction levels with responsiveness to queries • Time to respond	
• Accessibility	• Public relations	• Availability of 'one-stop' information sources • Satisfaction levels with accessibility	
• Consultation about change	• Public relations	• % public consulted on major issues	

Non-financial Value Added to Stakeholders – *Government*

Nature of the Value	Contributors	Measurement Examples	Target
• Support for government programmes	• Public Affairs • HR managers • Relevant technical staff	• Number of government programmes being actively supported	
• Ideas for change provided	• Public affairs • Part time role of various employees	• Number of government bodies on which represented	
• Resources seconded/ exchanged	• Public affairs • Various managers	• Weeks of exchange time provided in both directions • Number of secondees either way	
• Provision of education and knowledge of private sector activity	• Public relations • Various support functional managers	• Number of responses to requests	
• Provision of information	• Public affairs • HR, Finance, Legal managers	• Degree of compliance with requirements • Hours spent providing voluntary information, completing questionnaires, and so on.	

Non-financial Value Added to Stakeholders – *Community/Environment*

Nature of the Value	Contributors	Measurement Examples	Target
• Development of young people – providing work experience	• HR and L&D managers • Managers	• Number of young people given work experience or equivalent • Number of managers involved in development of young people externally	
• Resource seconded/ • exchanged	• Public affairs • Various managers	• Weeks of exchange time provided in both directions • Number of secondees either way	
• Support of ecological balance; enhancement of the visual and aural environment	• Public affairs • Site managers • Environmental managers	• Investment level in improving the environment • External Image perception surveys	
• Provision of resource for local programmes and committees	• All levels of staff	• Number of staff involved in local programmes and committees	

Index